Introducing American Religion

Introducing American Religion provides a lively and concise overview of the historical development of religion in the USA. Charles H. Lippy traces the history of American religion from Europe, Native American and African life, through to the age of independence, and on to the late twentieth century up to the present day.

The narrative lays particular stress on the development of diversity and pluralism in American religious life. It explores the African American experience through slavery, Roman Catholic and Jewish immigration, political and economic factors, the impact of Latino culture, and the growth of Hinduism and Buddhism, as well as the concept of American civil religion.

Introducing American Religion is ideal reading for students wishing to develop a broad understanding of American religious history. Illustrated throughout and featuring quotations from original sources, it includes text boxes, summary charts, study questions, a glossary and lists of further reading and web links to aid students with revision. The accompanying website for this book can be found at www.routledge.com/textbooks/9780415448598.

Charles H. Lippy is the LeRoy A. Martin Distinguished Professor of Religious Studies Emeritus at the University of Tennessee at Chattanooga, USA.

World Religions series

Edited by Damien Keown and Charles S. Prebish

This exciting series introduces students to the major world religious traditions. Each religion is explored in a lively and clear fashion by experienced teachers and leading scholars in the field of world religions. Up-to-date scholarship is presented in a student-friendly fashion, covering history, core beliefs, sacred texts, key figures, religious practice and culture, and key contemporary issues. To aid learning and revision, each text includes illustrations, summaries, explanations of key terms, and further reading.

Introducing American Religion
Charles H. Lippy

Introducing Buddhism
Damien Keown and Charles S. Prebish

Introducing Chinese Religions
Mario Poceski

Introducing Christianity
James R. Adair

Introducing Daoism
Livia Kohn

Introducing Hinduism
Hillary Rodrigues

Introducing Islam
William Shepard

Introducing Japanese Religions
Robert Ellwood

Introducing Judaism
Eliezer Segal

Forthcoming:

Introducing New Religious Movements
Introducing Tibetan Buddhism

Introducing American Religion

Charles H. Lippy

Routledge
Taylor & Francis Group
LONDON AND NEW YORK

First published 2009
by Routledge
2 Park Square, Milton Park, Abingdon, Oxon OX14 4RN

Simultaneously published in the USA and Canada
by Routledge
270 Madison Ave., New York, NY 10016

Routledge is an imprint of the Taylor & Francis Group, an informa business

© 2009 Charles H. Lippy

Typeset in Jenson and Tahoma by
Bookcraft Ltd, Stroud, Gloucestershire
Printed and bound in Great Britain by
CPI Antony Rowe, Chippenham, Wiltshire

All rights reserved. No part of this book may be reprinted or reproduced or utilised in any form or by any electronic, mechanical, or other means, now known or hereafter invented, including photocopying and recording, or in any information storage or retrieval system, without permission in writing from the publishers.

British Library Cataloguing in Publication Data
A catalogue record for this book is available from the British Library

Library of Congress Cataloging in Publication Data
A catalog record for this book has been requested

ISBN10: 0–415–44858–1 (hbk)
ISBN10: 0–415–44859–X (pbk)

ISBN13: 978–0–415–44858–1 (hbk)
ISBN13: 978–0–415–44859–8 (pbk)

Contents

List of illustrations viii
Acknowledgments x
Preface xii

1 **Religious diversity in the age of colonial conquest** 1
   Native American understanding of religion 1
   Key elements in African tribal religions 6
   Diversity within European Christianity 9
   European Christian misunderstanding of tribal religious expression 12
   Judaism and Islam in the age of colonial conquest 13

2 **European settlers increase religious diversity** 17
   The Spanish and French bring Catholicism to North America 17
   Varieties of Protestantism in the first English colonies 21
   The religious mosaic of early New England 25

3 **The expanding religious culture of English colonial America** 30
   The importance of the middle colonies 30
   William Penn's experiment in religious diversity 32
   Maryland and the Carolinas cradle more religious options 35
   The impact of the Evangelical surge and the Enlightenment 37

4 **Religion in an age of revolution** 45
   Religious challenges in the late colonial period 45
   The impact of the American Revolution on religious life 48
   Legal moves in the era of independence 52
   The denominations and the explosion of diversity 55

5 Native Americans and African Americans challenge religious life 61
Early English colonists, Native Americans, and African slaves 61
Evangelical missionary efforts among African Americans and Native Americans 65
Revolution and revitalization 68

6 Evangelical America 75
Evangelicalism's harvest time: the frontier camp meeting 75
Revivalism cements the evangelical style on American Protestantism 79
Evangelical Protestants and the erosion of Calvinism 81
The evangelical vision of a moral society 85

7 Religious experimentation brings more diversity 91
Recapturing original Christianity 91
Bringing heaven to earth 95
The adventist impulse 98
Exploring new religious worlds 102

8 Catholic and Jewish growth stretch diversity 108
Catholics in the new American nation 108
Immigration spurs rapid Catholic expansion 110
Catholic doubts about America amid nativist backlash 113
Jews find a home in America 117
Ethnicity's impact on American religion 120

9 The impact of Civil War and regionalism 123
Debates about slavery spur regional religious consciousness 123
The Civil War as a moral and religious event 127
Region's impact in larger perspective 130
Other facets of religion and region 134

10 Immigrants, industries, and cities 137
The United States becomes an urban, industrial nation 137
Immigrants and in-migrants reshape traditions 139
Diverse Protestant responses to an urbanizing nation 146
Ethnicity, gender, and reform in urban America 150

11 Other dimensions of urbanizing America 154
American religions encounter world religions 154
Gender issues add new dimensions to American religion 159
New currents among Native American tribal religions 164
Bible conferences and summer retreats offer relief from urban life 167

12 Modernity brings more change — 172
New intellectual approaches challenge traditional thought 173
Fundamentalism's impact on American Protestantism 176
Other intellectual currents bring more variety in belief 179
Pentecostal stirrings enrich religious life 182

13 Reaction and retreat — 187
Prohibition as social reform and as a reaction to diversity 188
Growing intolerance reflects fears of a pluralistic culture 190
The vision of a reborn Klan 193
Communications media move in new directions 196

14 Quests for unity amid diversity — 201
Depression and another world war complicate religious life 201
A righteous nation confronts "godless" communism 205
Other efforts to promote common identity 207
Cracks start to erode the veneer of unity 211

15 The "new pluralism" of the later twentieth century — 217
New religious movements spark interest and fear 218
The new immigration and growing religious pluralism 220
The courts wrestle with pluralism 226
Pluralism's impact on spirituality and worship 228

16 The many faces of pluralism in postmodern America — 233
Postmodernism brings other dimensions of pluralism 234
A resurgent evangelicalism brings more diversity 236
Public issues reveal moral differences 241
The many, changing faces of religious pluralism 244

Glossary — 249
Resources — 257
Index — 259

Illustrations

The following were reproduced with kind permission. Every effort has been made to trace copyright holders and obtain permission. Any omissions brought to our attention will be remedied in future editions.

1.1	Cherokee Green Corn Dance	3
1.2	Lakota sweat lodge	5
2.1	Puritan meetinghouse in Massachusetts	24
3.1	A colonial Quaker meetinghouse	33
3.2	George Whitefield	38
4.1	Reverse of the Great Seal of the United States	51
4.2	Shaker Marching Dance	57
5.1	Mothel Bethel AME church	72
6.1	Cane Ridge meetinghouse	76
6.2	Certificate of temperance	88
7.1	Mormons reaching Utah	95
7.2	Pastor Russell	101
7.3	Mary Baker Eddy	103
7.4	Mother Church of Christ Scientist, Boston	104
8.1	Ursuline convent	116
9.1	Abraham Lincoln	128
9.2	Appalachian serpent handling	132
10.1	Jewish Theological Seminary (front entrance)	144
10.2	Dwight Moody	147
10.3	Billy Sunday	147
10.4	Evangeline Booth	148
11.1	John R. Mott	155
11.2	Seneca Falls convention	160
11.3	Maria Woodworth Etter	162
11.4	Masonic symbol	163

11.5	Ghost Dance of the Sioux Indians	167
12.1	Charles Darwin	174
13.1	Ku Klux Klan Klansmen marching in 1925	194
14.1	Buddhist Church of America	204
14.2	Billy Graham crusade	210
15.1	Contemporary mosque in the USA	222

Acknowledgments

More than a decade before writing this text, I began to think seriously about the impact of religious diversity and pluralism on life in America. The initial result of that reflection appeared as *Pluralism Comes of Age: American Religious Culture in the Twentieth Century* (Armonk, NY: M.E. Sharpe, 2001), a study that focused on the recent past.

Opportunities to press further came as a result of several invitations. First, James A. Banks and Cherry A. McGee Banks kindly asked me to write an essay on the character of American religious life for the fifth edition of the textbook they edited, *Multicultural Education: Issues and Perspectives* (Hoboken, NJ: Wiley, 2004). My "Christian Nation or Pluralistic Culture: Religion in American Life" has undergone two revisions, as the seventh edition of that book is now in press.

Then, in April 2005, David Engstrom and Lissette M. Piedra asked me to speak at a symposium sponsored by the University of Chicago's School of Social Service Administration to honor the retirement of Dr. Pastora San Juan Cafferty. My contribution, "Religious Pluralism and the Transformation of American Culture," appeared in the collection they edited, *Our Diverse Society: Race and Ethnicity—Implications for 21st Century American Society* (Washington: NASW Press, 2006).

Two years later, Profs. Charles Cohen and Ronald Numbers organized a conference that looked exclusively at the impact of religious diversity, held at the University of Wisconsin. It was my privilege to speak on "From Consensus to Struggle: Pluralism and the Body Politic in Contemporary America." The presentations from that conference will soon appear from Oxford University Press.

To all of those individuals who nudged me to think more carefully and more systematically about matters related to diversity and pluralism I am grateful. While working on these endeavors I received one more invitation, this one from Charles Prebish and Damien Keown, who were overseeing a series of textbooks on various religious traditions and religious life in different cultures. When they asked me to prepare a proposal for a textbook on religion in American life, it seemed only natural that the theme of diversity should become the organizing principle. I value their ongoing support for this endeavor.

Along the way Routledge editor Lesley Riddle, whose counsel was most helpful, circulated the proposal and then clusters of chapter drafts—in some cases the manuscript of the entire book—to a host of scholars whose comments were transmitted to me anonymously. The final work benefits greatly from their observations and suggestions. I wish only that I could have taken every suggestion, but had I done so, the final result would have been a multi-volume work rather than a textbook designed for a one-semester introductory course. A few students in my Religion in American Life class at the University of Tennessee at Chattanooga also read bits and pieces of selected chapters, offering comments from the perspective of those for whom the book was intended.

Finally, I cannot express the extent of my gratitude to Routledge editorial assistant Amy Grant, who has gone more than the extra mile to help ready the book for publication. She tracked down images, got permission to use them, coached me through the preparation of some of the apparatus that accompanies the book, and patiently responded to all questions and queries. Thank you, Amy.

Preface

"Why do they keep rewriting history?" asked a student many years ago when I was teaching the American history survey course at Clemson University. "I mean, the past is the past, isn't it?" she observed. "So how come you keep changing it?" For a historian, the past is never just the past, as if it were contained in a museum display case for the ages. Rather, the past is alive here and now. From our own lived experience, we are always asking fresh questions of the past. As the world evolves around us, we seek to understand what forces have given shape to our world here and now. The past, really, is always present.

Scores of textbooks already look at the religious culture of the United States. Yet, like the past that is always changing as our questions shift and our angle of vision moves, this one tries to explore the story from a fresh perspective. Decades ago, when I first began to study American religious history, the primary focus was on what were called mainline white Protestant denominations and the dominant theme was the ways in which the Puritan culture of colonial New England had directly or indirectly influenced everything since. There was scant attention paid to the rich story of African American religion and almost nothing at all said about Native American religious cultures. The major players were all men, and organized institutions the major centers of action. Little, if anything, pointed to the ways ordinary men and women made sense out of life, how they went about the business of being religious. What became known first as "popular religion" and then as "lived religion" remained on the margins.

As we approach the second decade of the twenty-first century, much has changed. White Protestants in the United States are poised to become a minority of the total population. An African American heads the executive branch of the government. A woman serves as presiding bishop of the Episcopal Church. Mormons, adherents of what in the nineteenth century seemed an exotic new religion born on American soil, outnumber Presbyterians, once one of the larger bodies, by a few million. Immigration means that Islam, Buddhism in its many manifestations, and Hinduism are among the more rapidly growing religious traditions in the nation.

Even among American Christians, things no longer look the same as they once did. Some still light candles and burn incense; others might handle serpents as an act of worship and devotion. Some sing grand hymns accompanied by mighty organs; others belt out snappy songs accompanied by rock bands. Even in the public sector, Americans add moral and religious dimensions to a host of issues, from debates over abortion and homosexuality, to protecting the environment and scientific inquiry involving stem cell research.

In other words, American religion is incredibly diverse. The aim of this textbook is to demonstrate how and why that diversity came to be, how the United States became what analysts call a religiously pluralistic nation. The story is not always a happy one, for along the way there was often much conflict—some of it violent—as the American peoples struggled to juggle a variety of religious approaches. Even legal provisions for religious freedom, the so-called separation of church and state, have had hotly contested meanings. Yet almost inexorably, the nation moved ever more in the direction of increasing diversity, towards a genuine pluralism, even as it struggled to provide its people with some kind of shared framework of meaning for their common life.

So the pages that follow do not tell the story of individual denominations or the thoughts of great theologians, though both are present. Rather, the effort is to explore the roots of diversity, for they are there even among the Native American cultures that flourished long before Europeans saw the American continents as places for imperial expansion and colonization. If the narrative is broadly historical in its organization, the interpretation emerges from the conviction that religious developments transpire in a larger social, cultural, and intellectual setting and cannot be separated from that broader context. At the same time, the understanding of religion implicit throughout draws on methods associated with what analysts call the "history of religions" or a comparative approach that tries to appreciate all religious phenomena as having an integrity of their own.

Looking at American religious life from these many vantage points will, I hope, enable students to have a sense not only of the world in which we now live, but of the myriad forces whose interaction helped bring us to the point where diversity and pluralism have become the norm.

1 Religious diversity in the age of colonial conquest

In this chapter

This chapter identifies selected themes and ideas from Native American, European, and African religious life that were current in the age of colonial conquest. It will also show how European ideas of religion were different from those found in tribal societies in both the Americas and Africa.

Main topics covered

- The way religion cut through every aspect of Native American tribal cultures
- Key elements of African tribal religions
- The increasing diversity within Christianity in Europe after the Reformation
- How Europeans understood or misunderstood the religious expression within Native American and African tribal cultures
- The interplay between Christianity and both Judaism and Islam at the time Europeans came to the Americas

Native American understanding of religion

Today, most of us think of religion as one dimension of life, perhaps ideas and activities associated with what we hold as sacred. It's concerned with our values and our understanding of the meaning behind what happens in our lives. Since what we call the Age of the Enlightenment of the seventeenth and eighteenth centuries, religious belief and practice have become compartmentalized. We're used to buildings used just for religious purposes—churches, synagogues, temples. We tend to divide all aspects of life into neat categories. So we talk about politics, economics, education, recreation, and a host of other parts of daily life as if they were separate and distinct from each other and also from religion. That's not how life worked in the hundreds of tribal societies that flourished in North America before Christopher Columbus in 1492 "discovered" what was to Europeans a new world.

Like tribal societies virtually everywhere, Native Americans did not carve their existence into separate spheres, each with its own label. Rather, everything was seen to exist in relationship to everything else. A holistic understanding of life characterized Native American tribal cultures. There was no sharp distinction between what we today call the sacred and the secular. Both were part of a single whole. Historians and anthropologists have identified hundreds of different tribal cultures that were all thriving in North America at the dawn of the sixteenth century. None in North America, at least, had a written language. Because only spoken languages existed, we sometimes call these societies "oral" cultures. Even so, unlike European languages, no known Native American language had a separate word for religion. That does not mean that these millions of people were not religious in any sense of the word. But it does mean that their tribal focus gave them a different way of understanding the world. It meant that religion permeated every aspect of tribal life, from how food was procured to how people dealt with birth and death and to how they understood their relationship to the space—the very land—around them. Most oral cultures have had similar ideas.

Central to virtually all Native American cultures was some idea of what we call myth. By myth, we do not mean fairy tales or even legends that may have some basis in history. Rather, a myth is a story that tries to communicate a basic truth about human life, passed on from generation to generation. It really makes little difference whether a myth is grounded in actual fact; that dimension is the least important feature of a myth. The most important is what the story tells us about who we are and why we do things the way we do them. Because of what myths tell us, they take on a sacred quality that makes them different from other stories. To be sure, there is a dimension of entertainment involved because stories are almost always entertaining. The way myth worked in Native American cultures is somewhat like the way the stories work that families tell when they come together for family reunions. In hearing and telling the stories, members cement their bonds with each other and affirm their identity as part of the family. Other families tell different stories; they have different identities as groups. So it was with the indigenous societies whose presence in the Americas long antedated the arrival of Europeans.

For example, among the Cherokee, stories were told about the unusual power attributed to certain phenomena in the natural world, especially things that did not seem to fit easily into standard categories. Among them were creatures that had four feet and thus should walk on the ground, but could also fly—a skill not usually associated with having feet for walking. One Cherokee myth talked about how hawks and eagles had given wings to some squirrels and bats so they could fly and play a game akin to lacrosse. As a result, attaching a bat's wing to a lacrosse stick allowed human players to tap into this unusual power; it also had the effect of enhancing the thrust of the lacrosse stick in actual play. Telling the story not only accounted for something in the natural world, it also explained why a game was played with

Figure 1.1 Cherokee Green Corn Dance. Southeastern tribes, like the Cherokee, cultivated crops before the arrival of the Europeans and joined agricultural and religious pursuits in rituals such as the Green Corn Dance (Green Corn Dance, Santa Domingo, N.M. (w/c on paper) by Frank Applegate (1882–1931). Fred Jones Jr. Museum of Art, University of Oklahoma, USA/The Bridgeman Art Library. Nationality and copyright status: American, out of copyright.)

special equipment. Other Cherokee stories or myths described differences between the moon and the sun and how they seemed to move across the skies.

To be sure, not all Native American tribal societies did things alike. In what later became the southeastern part of the United States, for example, tribes had begun to develop a particular bond to the land, in part because the climate allowed them over time to cultivate crops for food. In order to raise crops, people had to stay in one place to plant seeds, take care of the crops, and then harvest them. Among both the Cherokee and Creeks in this area celebrations that marked the agricultural cycle culminated in festivals that were clearly as religious as they were concerned with having food for the coming year. In what later came to be called the Great Plains, where agricultural pursuits were more challenging, tribes often instead hunted for animals whose meat provided food and whose skins could be used for everything from making clothing to providing shelter. These tribes, such as the Lakota Sioux, realized that their survival depended on having herds they could hunt. When the animal supply began to dwindle because so many had been used for food and other purposes, the tribe might move to a different location nearby, where herds were more plentiful and survival was thus easier. These groups had celebrations when they prepared to go on a hunt in order to assure success, and again when they returned as they set about using every part of a slaughtered animal they could to benefit tribal life. In some cases, hunters offered an apology to the animal before the kill since it, too, was a living being. Some might even treat the slain animal as a welcome guest in the festive celebration that followed.

> **Characteristics of Native American religions**
> - Religion was part of a holistic understanding of life
> - Myths or sacred stories and rites expressed religious understanding
> - This understanding linked everyday life to a realm of supernatural power
> - Special rites called vision quests helped individuals find their way and seek supernatural power
> - Specialists called shamans assisted tribal cultures in relating to the supernatural

If none of these groups had a word in their language for religion, we can see even in this brief description that there was a strong sensitivity to a realm of sacred power—whether that power assured a large crop at harvest time or success in hunting—and an understanding that human life was intertwined with sacred forces that could not be seen, but that could act for either the benefit or the detriment of the group. These same forces might be called upon at times of childbirth, when there was obvious danger to both the mother and the newborn, or at times when individuals dealt with sickness. Without a scientific understanding of disease and its causes, Native Americans usually attributed what went wrong—whether getting sick or having a bad crop—to supernatural forces working against them. It was far better to try to harness those supernatural forces to work on behalf of the people.

Those who have studied Native American cultures point out that the interplay between the realm of the supernatural and everyday life was central to how tribal society worked. Having the ability to connect to that realm of sacred power was vital. Hence vision quests, or organized rites in which tribal members might glimpse this sacred world and feel its power, were important features of many tribal cultures. Often the transition from childhood to adulthood was marked by rites, sometimes rather arduous, that introduced one to a world of power. In some groups, there were rites like this for both women and men. The Lakota sweat lodges provided other opportunities for tribal members to maintain contact with the realm of sacred power. So called because the heat inside would cause persons to sweat, thus ridding them of both literal and symbolic dirt, the lodges and the rites associated with them allowed those who were purified to enter a spiritual space where the gap between the sacred and the ordinary collapsed.

Among many tribal societies, although the content of the stories varied, some of the most important myths were the stories told of common ancestors who emerged from the earth and thus gave birth to a tribe. This sense of origin, of a common creation, allowed Native Americans to have a profound awareness of the ties that bound members of a tribe not just to each other, but also to the place—the land—where the tribe carried out its daily life. Indeed, the land belonged to the tribe, not to individuals. In fact, most Native Americans, at the time they first encountered Europeans, had no idea of what we

Figure 1.2 Lakota sweat lodge. Several Plains tribes, such as the Lakota Sioux, had initiation and purification ceremonies that involved spending time in a sweat lodge (All rights reserved. Bailey Archive, Denver Museum of Nature and Science.)

call private property. Since everything belonged to the tribe, the destiny of one was tied to the destiny of all.

Of course, different members of the tribe had different skills, and sometimes individuals would be recognized as having unusual ability to summon supernatural powers to act on behalf of the tribe or its members. Sometimes called shamans and later dubbed medicine men by Europeans (since the expertise of these gifted persons was often especially needed when someone was sick or facing other health issues), these persons were basically religious functionaries, even if they were not called by a religious label, because they helped mediate between the realm of ordinary life and the realm of sacred or supernatural power. Some tribes recognized women as having shamanic power. In one sense, all shamans were engaged in healing, for their incantations and dances and other ritual activity healed the breach between the spiritual realm and that of ordinary life. They could heal differences that emerged among tribal members. They could also bring healing to sick bodies.

As we shall see, when Europeans encountered Native American cultures, they rarely understood them. No longer part of oral cultures themselves, Europeans were perplexed by the lack of written languages. And moving into a stage of development that tended to compartmentalize and label different aspects of life and see them as operating almost independently of each other, they could not appreciate the holistic richness that permeated Native American life. Christopher Columbus (1451–1506), when writing about his voyages and describing the people he called "los Indios," observed that they had no religion at all and therefore might readily be converted to Christianity. Europeans were no more adept at understanding what they saw in African tribal societies.

Key elements in African tribal religions

Europeans began to interact with Africans even before they turned their attention to the Americas, but sustained engagement with African peoples from areas south of the Sahara pretty much paralleled the early intrigue with life in the New World. About seventy-five years before Columbus arrived in the Caribbean, the Portuguese began to sail along the western shores of Africa, and in 1486 Bartholomew Diaz (c.1450–1500) commanded the Portuguese ships that first sailed around the southern tip of Africa, today called the Cape of Good Hope. Just over a decade later, other Portuguese ships, led by Vasco da Gama (1460–1524), continued past the cape and sailed to Asia. Even so, the Portuguese and those who followed them had little sense of the integrity of African tribal life. Nor did they realize the extent to which Islam had made its way into Africa and Asia.

Looking back, what stands out is how unprepared Europeans were to deal with some of the differences they found between the world that they had known and what they encountered in Africa. Particularly significant when they began to establish trading centers along the western coast of Africa south of the Sahara was a visual difference. Europeans simply did not know what to make of darker-skinned Africans. So striking was the difference between "white" Europeans and "black" Africans that the knee-jerk reaction of most Europeans was to see their own appearance as the norm and to assume that everything else was somehow inferior. That meant that they had little predisposition to look at African peoples, organized into hundreds of tribal societies as were the Native Americans, as having civilizations that matched their own in terms of internal integrity and dynamics. Today it is easy to see that this way of thinking was seriously flawed and mistaken. It was not so easy in the later fifteenth century.

Like the oral cultures of the Native Americans, however, the African tribal societies exhibited an abiding sense of the interconnectedness between a world that could not be seen, a world of sacred power, and the world of daily life. Among many of the West African tribes that provided the initial contacts for Europeans and later became the source of the first slaves brought to the Americas, myths of origins also abounded, as they did among Native Americans. For example, among the Yoruba, a people who provided a major source for those later brought to North America as slaves, a High God called Olurun assigned creation of the world first to Obatala, his oldest son, and then to a younger son. But neither was able to complete the task, so, working through spiritual beings known as *orishas*, Olurun had to finish creation himself. In turn, the *orishas* became intermediaries that various Yoruba villagers could summon, although Olurun remained rather aloof and uninterested in ordinary human affairs.

For some African tribal cultures, these myths of origins centered on supernatural beings and a sense in which there was a world where divinities existed that paralleled the world of the tribe. There was thus a correspondence between how African tribal societies worked and the mythic realm of the gods. As in many other oral cultures, here too, one could glimpse that other realm through ritual song and dance. Among West African tribes, a conviction that divine power could enter the bodies of ordinary men and women and for a time take control of the body meant that what we call spirit possession was an important part of the tribal heritage. Possession in this sense is something good that is to be cultivated, for it lifts the one whose body is joined for a time with spiritual forces to another world.

Often this conjoining of the spiritual world and the empirical world in spirit possession came through ritual song and dance. If Europeans regarded song and dance as recreation in the sense of enjoyable leisure-time activity, for many African tribal peoples such activity quite literally brought about a re-creation of the world on a moral and symbolic level, for it infused the ordinary with sacred power and meaning. Among African tribes, such dance often involved circular motion, with the music accompanying it having a striking, syncopated rhythmic pattern.

These rites, like those of Native American peoples, served important functions in giving a tribe a sense of social solidarity and corporate identity. But this identity was not limited simply to the present time. After all, what was done and how it was done had been passed down from generation to generation. So whenever ritual song and dance occurred, those participating were linked not only to each other but also to those of the tribe of preceding generations who had also accessed a domain of supernatural power through the very same rites. Among West African tribes, burial practices were also significant, for one was interring not only the physical remains of a family member. Rather, one was also dealing with the supernatural world with which that body, that physical being, had been intertwined. All this endowed African tribal spirituality with what Europeans mistook for ancestor worship, or at least reverence for ancestors. In reality, it was a highly organic notion of the unity of past and present, sacred and secular at work, not a pre-scientific, mindless devotion to generations long past.

African tribal peoples also developed other ritual activities designed to assure that these supernatural powers and the residual power still identified with earlier generations would work for the good of the people now. Sometimes animal sacrifice allowed them to make a symbolic offering or gift, particularly if times had been difficult or there was conflict with another tribal people. On some such occasions, once the blood of the animal sacrificed had been poured on the earth, the meat might be cooked, with some offered to the gods and the rest eaten by the tribal members. Because the supernatural powers were symbolically eating the same flesh as the tribe, the two again could become one. As the saying puts it, you are what you eat.

As with other tribal cultures, most African societies also marked transitions in life with ceremonial activity. Childbirth provided one such occasion. For example, the Ashanti, who later became one of the early sources of slaves, celebrated new life with a naming ceremony about a week or so after birth. Given the high rate of infant mortality, waiting for a week was a sign that life itself had actually taken hold. So, too, African rites of passage signaled the transition from boyhood to manhood, girlhood to womanhood. African peoples also recognized

African tribal religions and the encounter with Europeans

- Africans also had a holistic view of life in which a sacred realm corresponded to the world of daily life
- Vibrant song and dance were part of tribal religious expression
- Spirit possession was one way in which people came into contact with sacred power
- Europeans dismissed African tribal peoples and their religions because of the difference in skin color

that there were persons especially adept at accessing supernatural power, those whose bodies the spirits and the ancestors were more likely to possess. Although not priests in any traditional understanding, these shamanic figures, like their counterparts in Native American cultures, often acted on behalf of others or of the entire tribe to bring healing and wholeness and a firmer connection between the unseen sacred realm and the world of daily life.

The stunning integrity behind African tribal cultures, with a sense of spirituality that infused all of life, escaped Europeans as they first encountered Africa south of the Sahara, just as did the richness of Native American tribal life. For most Europeans, anything that was other than the Christianity that they knew, or perhaps the Judaism that they had marginalized, was subject to dismissal as heathen superstition.

Diversity within European Christianity

Even the Christianity that dominated European civilization when Columbus's voyages sparked interest in the Americas was becoming increasingly diverse. Christianity, despite the pronouncements of church councils and the increasing power of bishops and popes over the centuries, had never been as monolithic as officials liked to think. There was then, as there is now, sometimes a significant difference between the doctrine and practice promoted by the institutional church and the lived religion of ordinary people. For example, the more we come to understand about the writings popularly called the Gnostic gospels—probably Coptic translations of documents going back as early as the second and third centuries—the more we realize that there was extraordinary diversity within Christianity in its formative centuries. Standard histories acknowledge the growing differences between the strand of Christianity oriented towards the old imperial capital of Rome and that which aligned itself with the eastern capital of Constantinople. That difference became cemented in 1054, when the leaders of each tradition declared the other (along with all his followers) to be excommunicated or no longer members of the "true" Christian church. Their major disagreements were concerned with the authority of the pope, the use of icons or images in worship, and the precise wording of ancient creeds. Most of the Europeans who later looked to establish colonial empires in the Americas traced their allegiance to the Roman strand, today commonly called the Roman Catholic Church, although missionary monks identified with the Orthodox Church, the broad name for the eastern strand, were ministering in what is now Alaska at least by the 1790s.

Twenty-five years to the month after Columbus's crew landed in the West Indies, the Roman Catholic tradition experienced a major rift. In October 1517 a German monk named Martin Luther (1483–1546) proposed to debate several points of traditional doctrine and practice. Although he did not intend such, the result was the Protestant Reformation, a split in western Christianity. Luther's movement centered on the idea that one was justified or restored to a right relationship with God only by grace through faith, not through any human action. He also insisted that scripture was the ultimate authority, not popes, bishops, or even councils. The Protestant movement spread quickly through Germany and other nearby areas. Its rapid growth resulted in part from the recent invention of movable type and the printing press, which revolutionized communication in that age, much as the Internet did at the end of the twentieth century.

Within a generation of Luther's challenge to church authority, several other forms of Protestantism began to appear, with each new teacher claiming to have the last word. French-born John Calvin (1509–1564), for example, brought a sharp, legally trained mind to an effort to refine Protestant belief and practice after he settled in Geneva, Switzerland. Thus, soon, alongside Lutheran Protestants there were Calvinist Protestants. In Zurich, Switzerland, Huldreich Zwingli (1484–1531) offered yet another alternative. Elsewhere, some challenged all traditional teaching and formed what has been called a "left wing" of the Reformation. Many of those associated with this cluster are also known as Anabaptists because they insisted that their believers who had been baptized as Catholics be rebaptized, since the initial baptism had been authorized by a body now seen as corrupt and unfaithful to authentic Christianity.

When Luther first proposed his topics for debate, the Christian church in England was firmly identified with Rome. The English king, Henry VIII (1491–1547), even wrote a tract attacking Luther's views and consequently was honored by the pope, who bestowed on him the title "defender of the faith." But there was growing resentment in England about sending church offerings to distant Rome and also a dispute brewing between the king and the pope that had both political and religious dimensions. Not long before Henry VIII became king, there had been civil war in England to determine who would rule. In that War of the Roses, as it was called, Henry's father triumphed and became the first monarch of the Tudor dynasty. His son wished to avoid any question about succession to the throne, fearful that unless he had a male heir there would be another civil war. We cannot recount here all the details and intrigue surrounding Henry's efforts to have a legitimate son to succeed him and the well-known tales surrounding his six wives. Suffice it to say that Henry's dynastic concern combined with growing English nationalism so that, in 1534, the English parliament decreed that the king, not the pope, was the head of the church in England. Thus was born yet another alternative strand of Christianity, the Church of England.

The formation of the Church of England did not end the religious intrigue. Many in England still identified with the old Roman tradition. Some, aware of what was happening on the Continent, believed that the English Reformation was piecemeal and had not removed all corrupt practices from the church. In the mid-sixteenth century, when Henry's older daughter, Mary (1516–1558), became queen following the death of her younger half-brother, she sought to restore Catholic practice, and many who refused to submit to this restoration of Catholic ways fled to the European mainland, where they quickly absorbed, especially, the views associated with the developing Calvinist heritage within Protestantism. When they returned from exile after Elizabeth I (1533–1603) succeeded Mary, they launched what was at first an underground movement to purify the Church of England; hence they became known as Puritans. Soon the Puritan movement became much more open and controversial. But here is more evidence of the diversity that was causing turmoil within Christian circles in Europe.

On the mainland of Europe, the turmoil often resulted in armed confrontation, leading to an age of religious wars. Even in England, the situation was more complicated than just having an official Church of England, a minority who continued to practice Catholicism in private, and a growing Puritan movement that sought more radical change. The Puritan movement itself was not of a single mind. Some believed that they had to leave the established church and start a separate one in order to remove themselves from spiritual pollution. Others thought that although the Church of England might not be perfect, they could continue the work of reformation best by remaining within. Soon there were those, such as the Quakers, who felt that neither of these approaches was adequate.

The religious wars and undercurrents of conflict convinced many political leaders that religious uniformity—having only one religion in an area controlled by one government—was necessary for political stability. This conviction also had a religious basis: If religion concerned absolute truth, then there could not be any variation. If there were, then truth would be relative and not really be truth at all. This idea was also part of the European Christian anxiety about the presence of Judaism and Islam in the larger religious world. If either Judaism or Islam contained truth, then Christianity must not be absolutely true.

Of course, some areas of western Europe remained staunchly Catholic, at least in name. Spain was one of those areas. The age of the Reformation saw Spanish influence within Roman Catholic circles increase significantly as Spanish monarchs began to think that they had a duty to protect the Catholic Church as the only authentic Christian body. Close behind in terms of trying to insist that the traditional Catholic

> **Diversity in European Christianity**
> - A major division in European Christianity in 1054 resulted in the (western) Roman Catholic Church and the Eastern Orthodox Churches
> - The Reformation of the sixteenth century split the Roman Catholic Church, with several forms of Protestantism resulting
> - The Church of England also soon broke away from the Roman Catholic Church, but also had a lot of internal diversity, with groups pushing for greater change
> - The "left wing" of the Reformation produced many smaller, more radical Protestant groups that were part of European life and culture

way was the only legitimate form of Christianity were the French, although from the sixteenth century on there had been a decidedly Calvinist subculture within French Christianity. The most well-known French Calvinists are the Huguenots, who for a time were granted the right to practice what they believed in a restricted area within France. Mention of the Spanish and the French, along with the earlier discussion of English developments and the Lutheran push in Germany, adds another dimension to the diversity that was transforming western European Christianity, for there was also a growing tie between national identity and ethnicity and a particular style of Christianity that complicated the diversity that was growing in terms of formal belief and practice.

Hence, by the time Europeans were consumed by interest in colonizing and conquering the Americas, Christianity had already become rather diverse. There was no one expression of Christianity to which all people called Christian gave support. That diversity would have signal influence in shaping North American religious life.

European Christian misunderstanding of tribal religious expression

When Europeans began to explore the Americas and establish settlements there, they exhibited what in retrospect seems stunning misunderstanding when they encountered other forms of religious expression. The simplest reason for this lack of appreciation for tribal religious life is also the most obvious: It was different from what Europeans were accustomed to seeing as religion. It was "other" than the style of religious belief and practice with which they were familiar. They simply classified what was "other" as inferior and therefore not a real approach to being religious at all. This lack of understanding helps explain why Columbus insisted that the indigenous people he encountered had no religion.

For example, since Native Americans often talked about a realm of spirits with perhaps some Great Spirit having a special relationship to a particular people, Europeans misconstrued this as a crass polytheism, or certainly not belief in the one God affirmed by Christians, regardless of what strand of Christianity they accepted. Because they did not have structures that were the equivalent of church buildings, Europeans almost always missed the sense in which Native Americans regarded all land as sacred, but especially the land associated with the tribal heritage. Then, too, Europeans looked askance at the ritual celebrations of Native Americans, with their song and dance, seeing them as recreational activity at best and as sacrilegious at worst. In other words, Europeans readily dismissed Native Americans as pagans who were ignorant of the one true God, who was identified exclusively with the God in whom Christians claimed to believe. Anything else was just plain wrong. In a few cases, Native American custom seemed to Europeans to be immoral and therefore dangerous. Then, too, when Europeans arrived in the Americas, they tended to view the indigenous peoples as rivals for control of the land and its resources. Seeing themselves as superior, they failed in almost every case to see themselves as intruders. Hostile relations often resulted, even though European settlers themselves benefited greatly from the knowledge of the land, of what could be cultivated on it, and the like, knowledge that was virtually intuitive wisdom among the tribal peoples but unknown to Europeans.

This inability to appreciate the richness of Native American life also in time contributed to some ambivalence about just how to relate to the tribal peoples whose presence in the Americas long antedated the arrival of Europeans. Should they be converted? Spanish and French Catholic priests and missionaries were propelled by a conviction that Native Americans were people to whom the Christian gospel should be proclaimed, but, as we shall see, their intentions often conflicted with those who were primarily interested in conquest or economic opportunities. The English, when they established enduring settlements, also in theory thought they had a religious duty to try to bring the tribal peoples into the Christian fold, but they were sometimes thwarted by the lack of a written language among the native tribes, as well as by a shortage of ministers and missionaries, especially in the southern colonies.

All these complications became magnified when it came to how Europeans related to African tribal peoples. The visual difference further compounded the problem. Like the Native American tribal peoples, Africans were regarded as pagan polytheists at best, people who engaged in frenzied song and dance and other strange activities rather than in the more staid worship of a jealous Christian deity. Europeans became so blinded by the contrast in skin color, for example, that many even concluded that Africans were not really human at all. As we shall see, some even doubted that Africans had souls. If African tribal peoples lacked souls, then Europeans could rationalize not only coercing them into slavery, but also only half-heartedly sharing with them the Christian gospel, however skewed that gospel was in order to sanction slavery.

That same smug superiority also marked European relations with two other religious traditions that were nevertheless intertwined with European culture at the dawn of the age of colonial conquest. If Europeans failed utterly to grasp the religious integrity of Native American and African tribal societies, they did at least recognize

> ### European views of tribal religions
> - Europeans mistakenly saw Native Americans and Africans as pagan polytheists
> - Europeans did not understand how song and dance, along with things like spirit possession, could actually be religious
> - Europeans thought tribal cultures were inferior because they had no written language or word for religion
> - Christians were ambivalent about whether they should try to convert Native Americans and Africans to Christianity

both Judaism and Islam as part of the religious world of the day. But they were willing to take extraordinary efforts to try to keep both of those traditions and their adherents marginalized, if not subdued.

Judaism and Islam in the age of colonial conquest

From its origins, the Christianity that dominated European life, whatever its particular form took, had an intimate, if sometimes awkward, relationship with Judaism. After all, the pivotal figure in the Christian tradition, Jesus of Nazareth, was himself a Jew and the very first followers of Jesus were drawn from the ranks of Palestinian Judaism. But after Christianity began to emerge as a distinct religious tradition, the ties to its Hebraic or Jewish roots became more complicated. Christians began to see themselves as the fulfillment of Judaism, not as a child of that tradition. Once Christianity became the only legal religion in the old Roman Empire, its leaders all too frequently forgot what they owed to Judaism and instead repudiated their ties, claiming that Jews had been responsible for the death of Jesus.

By the time Columbus set sail from Spain in 1492, Europeans had a long history of restricting where Jews could live and excluding them from full participation in society. Indeed, that same year, Columbus's patrons, the Spanish monarchs Ferdinand (1452–1516) and Isabella (1451–1504), decreed that all Jews who lived in the area they controlled had either to convert to Christianity—a strict Roman Catholic Christianity—or be expelled from the land. Neighboring Portugal followed suit a few years later. Elsewhere in Europe, Jews were often confined to ghettos, scorned by those who wielded either political or religious power. Yet some evidence suggests that there were Jews among Columbus's crews, and once the Spanish and Portuguese began to conquer lands in what is now South America, many Jews relocated there rather than suffer persecution or forced conversion at home. Efforts to require conversion or even to force Jews into the ghetto did not eliminate a Jewish presence in European life. That presence is

> **Religions on the margins**
> - For centuries, Judaism had flourished in Europe, although Jews were frequently persecuted and subject to legal constraints
> - Almost as soon as it was founded, Islam began to grow rapidly in the Near East and Africa and for a time had several strongholds in Europe
> - European Christians were hostile to both Jews and Muslims, organizing Crusades to defeat them and sometimes banishing them unless they converted
> - Jews and Muslims were among the first Europeans and Africans to come to the New World

another sign of the religious diversity that was part of the world that shaped those Europeans who initially came to the Americas.

If anything, relations between Christians and Muslims were even more strained. Islam's beginnings on the Arabian Peninsula in the seventh century reveal that it, too, had foundational ties to Judaism. Muhammad, whose teachings form the basis of Islam, most likely had extensive contacts with Jewish traders and merchants. Islam's emergence as both a religious and a political force came at a time when the old Roman Empire had pretty well disintegrated and European life lacked the stability that Roman rule had once provided. Consequently, Islam was able to expand rapidly across northern Africa and penetrate into Europe, controlling for a time what later became Spain. Muslim movement into what for both Christians and Jews was the Holy Land in the Near East helped spur the crusades from the eleventh century on. The crusades led not only to the slaughter of thousands of Muslims and Jews in the area around Jerusalem, but entrenched a mutual hostility and suspicion between most Christians and Muslims that endures to the present. Like many Christians who saw their religion as the only true one, followers of Muhammad believed that the Muslim religious way represented the only true religion, and Islam remained aggressive in seeking converts and in trying to expand its influence. By 1453, Constantinople (Istanbul), once the Eastern capital of a presumably Christian Roman Empire, came under Muslim control. As a result, Moscow in Russia became the center of Eastern Orthodox Christianity. Tensions between Muslim empires and European nation-states remained an important undercurrent of life even as Europeans began to stake their future on colonies in the New World. As late as 1683, for example, the Ottoman Empire of the Muslim Turks was pressing close to Vienna, Austria, then one of the centers of the Hapsburg domain, and the Hapsburgs were staunchly Catholic. Earlier, in places like Spain where Christians had managed to eliminate Muslim political power, Muslims were subject to some of the same marginalization as Jews, forced to abandon Muslim allegiance and convert or else to leave the land altogether. As with Jews, these efforts were never entirely successful, and many Muslims, like Jews, kept their faith almost as part of an underground movement.

Islam is vital to the religious world of America in the age of conquest for another reason. Even as Islam in the centuries after its founding was expanding rapidly in the Mediterranean world, it was also moving into parts of Africa then virtually unknown to most Europeans. Muslims made inroads into African tribal cultures long before European Christians began to regard these societies as a convenient source of slave labor. Often overlooked but no longer able to be ignored is the devotion to Islam of some of those Africans who were forced to come to the Americas as slaves. If European Christians could readily dismiss African tribal religiosity as being less than authentic, they could not do so with Islam, for Islam had long been seen as a "real" religion, albeit one that was often in conflict with Christianity.

Hence, when Christopher Columbus laid the groundwork for a continuing European interest in the Americas, the religious world of both Europe and the Americas exhibited remarkable diversity. With scores of Native American tribal religious expressions, a variety of strands of Christianity, many African tribal cultures exhibiting their own religious styles, and with Judaism and Islam long a substratum of European life, the western religious world at the time of European exploration and conquest was amazingly diverse. It would continue to become ever more diverse.

Key points you need to know

- Native American and African tribal societies had a holistic idea of religion very different from that of the Europeans.
- European Christianity was already becoming diverse at the time colonial conquest in the New World got underway.
- Europeans tended to regard their way of life, including their own form of Christianity, as superior to everything else.
- Europeans generally regarded what was unfamiliar to them as inferior and without value.
- Judaism and Islam were important to European religious life, even though Europeans tried to marginalize them.

Discussion questions

1. How did Native American and African tribal societies understand religion? How were their religious approaches similar?

2. How was the European understanding of religion different? Why did Europeans believe their way was better?
3. What role did myth and ritual play in tribal religious understanding? Why did European Christians misunderstand that role?
4. In what ways was European Christianity becoming increasingly diverse at the time colonial exploration and conquest began?
5. How did Judaism and Islam affect the religious world of Europeans when they first began to settle in the New World?

Further reading

Crawford, Suzanne J. *Native American Religious Traditions*. Upper Saddle River, NJ: Pearson/Prentice Hall, 2007.

Denny, Frederick M. *Introduction to Islam*. 3rd ed. Upper Saddle River, NJ: Prentice Hall, 2005.

Horwitz, Tony. *A Voyage Long and Strange: Rediscovering the New World*. New York: Henry Holt and Co., 2008.

Kee, Howard Clark, Jerry W. Frost, Emily Albu, Carter Lindberg, and Dana L. Robert. *Christianity: A Social and Cultural History*. 2nd ed. Upper Saddle River, NJ: Prentice Hall, 1998.

Ray, Benjamin C. *African Religions: Symbols, Myth, and Community*. 2nd ed. Upper Saddle River, NJ: Prentice Hall, 2000.

Scheindlin, Raymond P. *A Short History of the Jewish People: From Legendary Times to Modern Statehood*. New York: Oxford University Press, 2000.

2 European settlers increase religious diversity

In this chapter

This chapter looks at the religious aspects of European colonial conquest and settlement in North America before English colonization efforts got underway. It discusses the different religious styles of the French and Spanish and their interplay with Native American religions and cultures. It then directs attention to English colonies in Virginia and New England, demonstrating that even there, religious diversity was evident.

Main topics covered

- How the Spanish and French brought Catholicism to the Americas and their lack of understanding of Native American cultures
- The religious aspects of the first permanent English colonies in North America
- The variety of religious expressions always just beneath the surface in areas of English settlement, especially New England

The Spanish and French bring Catholicism to North America

The European religious tradition with the longest continuous history in the United States is Roman Catholicism, thanks to the efforts of the Spanish to exploit the New World to increase the power and wealth of Spain itself. Priests and monks came with the Spanish military, the famous conquistadors, first to areas in the Caribbean, South America, and Mexico. From Mexico, they moved into what is today the southwestern United States, with some exploratory ventures taking them through the Great Plains and even into what are now the southeastern states.

From the outset of Spanish conquest, sharp differences separated the military leaders from the priests. Governments and their armed forces did not hesitate to use ruthless military power to force the Native Americans to submit and work for them, if they did not enslave them. The Spanish military leadership had little interest in any aspect of native culture and rarely sensed that they were dealing with people whose common life had a rich integrity of its own. Indeed, because the Native American tribal societies were different from that in Spain, the people were often treated as less than human. Bartolomé de Las Casas (1474–1566), who served for a time as a colonial administrator in the Caribbean, objected greatly to the brutal treatment of the indigenous people and called for efforts to convert them to Christianity. Unfortunately, he also suggested at one point that the Spanish might bring slaves from Africa to replace the tribal peoples forced to do hard labor. Like other Europeans, Las Casas could not overcome the prejudice spurred by the visual difference between Europeans and Africans. Sometimes, however, the best intentions of the missionaries were thwarted by the alliance between the Spanish government and the pope. This agreement allowed the government, which saw itself as the protector of the Catholic heritage, to oversee the work of the church in colonial lands. That meant that often the local governors, with military backing, prevailed over the priests.

The priests and monks attempted to establish pueblos, something akin to self-sufficient agricultural compounds where natives were required to live, work, and receive religious instruction. Although religious leaders may have had better intentions than the conquistadors, by removing people from their tribal societies they were also helping to destroy those cultures. In addition, most of the Dominicans and Franciscans who came as missionaries to the tribal peoples still maintained a sense that they were superior to the natives simply because they were European Christians. Consequently, they often treated the natives as if they were young children who had yet to develop keen reasoning power. Even at their best, Spanish missions brutally undermined native life.

For more than two centuries, Spanish Catholics founded and staffed missions in what became the southwestern and western United States, from Texas to San Francisco. Perhaps the most famous of the Franciscans who ministered there was Junipero Serra (1713–1784). He spearheaded the move to bring a Spanish Catholic presence into California. Serra acquired a reputation for insisting on treating native peoples with dignity, yet he also, like most of the other missionaries, believed that this dignity was on a par with that accorded a young child.

One way in which even Serra subverted native life came in his approach to those Native Americans who sought to leave the missions after having been baptized. In such cases, Serra condoned forcefully restraining them, if necessary, and then additional punishment. Perhaps he knew that coerced conversions were not always sincere and that once a baptized convert returned to the tribe, the worldview and way of life that held the tribe together would prove more enduring.

Even in the twenty-first century, the impact of the Spanish missions and the vibrant Catholicism they brought with them is obvious across the religious landscape of the American southwest. Not only are some of the old missions and pueblos still standing, but the ties between Catholicism in the region and Mexico and even Spain appear, for example, in the architecture of many churches as well as in the ethos of Catholicism as it is practiced by many Americans whose ancestry goes back to the days of Spanish colonial conquest.

In New Mexico, for example, some Catholic men of Spanish–Native American stock refer to themselves by the Spanish *Penitentes* and engage in rather severe religious discipline, that may include self-flagellation on Good Friday, to cement their identification with the Christ, who was beaten and scourged prior to crucifixion. Such practices have endured in part because of the ways religious devotion fostered by orthodox Spanish Catholicism in the age of colonial expansion sometimes took on a distinct physical quality.

The Catholic missions of New France began just after Samuel de Champlain (1567–1635) founded the first permanent French outpost in North America in what is now the city of Quebec in Canada in 1608. They added another dimension to the Catholic presence in the New World. French explorers, trappers, and traders had made their way along the St. Lawrence River and nearby areas for decades before Quebec was established. Once there was a permanent settlement to support these economic interests, priests, monks, and scores of women religious or nuns accompanied those whose primary endeavors were in trapping or in trading with the native tribes.

The French may not have been as brutal as the Spanish in their treatment of indigenous peoples, but they were no less convinced of their own superiority and the religious duty they had to convert those with whom they did business. They, too, missed the way in which a religious dimension already penetrated every aspect of native cultures. Jacques Cartier (1491–1557), one of the earliest of the French explorers of the St. Lawrence River and surrounding land, was oblivious to the religious dynamic at work among the indigenous people he encountered, insisting that they were nothing other than beasts because they lacked true religion—in this case, Catholicism.

Spanish and French Catholics in North America

- Spanish military conquistadors and missionary priests frequently clashed because the military treated Native Americans so harshly
- Spanish priests and monks undermined indigenous cultures by moving Native American converts to their mission compounds
- Both Spanish and French religious and political leaders in North America believed native cultures to be inferior
- The French were less likely to destroy native societies, in part because they were intent on establishing a strong, permanent settlement of their own
- Women religious or nuns played key roles in founding and maintaining French Catholic institutions in Canada

At the same time, however, the French were never as intent as the Spanish on subduing or conquering the native tribes. Economic benefits resulting from trade generally trumped sheer conquest and control. Hence the French were less inclined to coerce conversion and more likely to use persuasion, education, and similar approaches to attract Native Americans to the Catholic faith. Nevertheless, French efforts also eroded native life, and occasionally there were violent confrontations between the French and tribal peoples.

The well-known French Jesuit Jacques Marquette (1637–1675), who was part of the expedition led by Louis Jolliet (1645–1700) that explored the Mississippi River, was not as dismissive as Cartier, but he was eager to present the French Catholic gospel to native peoples. Perhaps the most successful French Catholic Jesuit missionary was Jean de Brébeuf (1593–1649), who worked among the Hurons. Although he was somewhat more sensitive to the integrity of Huron and other indigenous tribal cultures, he, too, saw the Native Americans as savages who needed the redemption offered by the Christian gospel.

The French Catholic presence in North America differed from that of the Spanish in other ways. Some had to do with internal dynamics among native tribes in the regions where each concentrated its focus. The first permanent French settlers came to an area where considerable rivalry already prevailed among native groups such as the Hurons and the Five Nations of the Iroquois. Opportunities to ally themselves with the French against the Iroquois seemed attractive to some Hurons, for example, even if receiving instruction in the Catholic faith came along with the alliance.

Because the French were intent on having settlements, not just in conquest, they took greater pains to support religious endeavors among their own people. The story of French Catholicism in the colonial era involves efforts to retain traditional devotion among French settlers as much as to convert Native Americans. It also involves not just Franciscans, but also more particularly Jesuits and then Sulpicians, two orders intent on promoting a deep sense of faith among adherents.

French religious efforts also engaged women religious, especially those identified with the order known as the Ursulines. One French Ursuline nun, for example, devoted her work in North America to crafting a written form of several Native American languages and then producing books to teach the speakers of those languages how to write them, along with books of religious instruction. Other women religious helped found and staff schools, hospitals, and other agencies that served both the colonial population and sometimes the indigenous peoples. The net result was that even after the traditional hostilities between the French and the English resulted in English forces defeating the French and Canada's coming under British control, a vibrant and vital Catholicism had already been secured.

Not all the French who came to North America were Roman Catholic. After King Henry IV in 1598 granted some concessions to French Calvinists known as the Huguenots in a proclamation known as the Edict of Nantes, some of them also joined the colonial enterprise. However, by the 1630s the French government had rescinded liberties the edict granted to Huguenots in France for those residing in the Canadian colony, in order to assure that the Catholic expression of Christianity would retain dominant influence.

In time, French Catholic settlers and traders made their way into what is now the north central part of the United States and also down the Mississippi River and many of its tributaries, as far south as the Mississippi delta area from New Orleans to Mobile, Alabama. Combined with the French influence from areas bordering the St. Lawrence and into parts of New England, French entrenchment in the southern coastal region along the Gulf of Mexico guaranteed that Roman Catholicism would have a distinguished and enduring history in the United States, even though most of the English who settled in those colonies that declared their independence from Great Britain in 1776 were Protestants of one sort or another.

The Spanish and the French both planted Roman Catholicism in North America, but their styles of Catholicism—the mood of the religion, if you will—were different, as were the ways they went about relating to the indigenous peoples they encountered and building institutions to sustain the Catholic heritage over time. Both were staunchly Catholic, but there is a dimension of diversity even here because of this difference in style. Even more pronounced were the differences between either French Catholicism or Spanish Catholicism and the various strands of Protestantism that arrived in the Americas once the English had successfully established their own colonial outposts. Those strands of Protestantism were internally diverse, as we shall see, but they were united on one issue: They were suspicious of, if not hostile to, any form of Roman Catholicism. Coming from England, these settlers also harbored long-standing rivalries with both the French and the Spanish that reflected decades of political intrigue in Europe.

Varieties of Protestantism in the first English colonies

The English established their first permanent settlement in North America at Jamestown, Virginia, in 1607. Although the entrepreneurs backing this venture financially were interested primarily in gaining profit, they also almost from the start had a concern for religion, in this case that which was associated with the Church of England. In England, this body had a special relationship with government since it was what was called an established church. That meant that tax monies went for the upkeep and maintenance of church buildings and property and for salaries for priests and other clergy. It also meant that church officials, bishops, and the archbishop of Canterbury, the overall leader of the church, had public or political responsibilities. At that time, for example, bishops by virtue of their position were members of the House of Lords, the upper house of parliament, and were therefore involved in making laws that affected everyone. In theory, with a religious establishment, only the one religious group that received government endorsement was legal or formally recognized; everyone, regardless of personal preference, was expected to give at least token support to the one legally recognized church.

Plans for Jamestown included the expectation that the Church of England would receive the same favored treatment in the colony as it enjoyed in the mother country. But in the early years there was a profound Puritan impulse that lurked just beneath the surface at least in terms of a sense of religious discipline and formal standards of moral conduct. In 1610, for example, the deputy governor, Thomas Dale, announced a series of regulations that became known as Dale's Laws. They required everyone in the colony to attend religious services twice each day and placed heavy penalties on things like profane speech. Later, when the colonists received some latitude in formulating local laws through the House of Burgesses, the Church of England received official legal establishment in Virginia (1624).

The way the church developed in Virginia, however, was rather different from what prevailed in England itself. Because colonial settlement beyond Jamestown followed the rivers, which were natural routes of transportation, the population quickly dispersed along the river valleys, rather than being concentrated in towns and villages. In England, a parish was not just a church congregation, but could encompass an entire village or what we might think of as a neighborhood in a larger city. A priest served the parish, holding services, instructing the young in the faith, and performing baptisms, marriages, and the like. In Virginia, it was hard to form the same kind of parish, since the population was so dispersed.

In addition, relatively few priests were eager to migrate from England, where they had a more comfortable life, to Virginia, where they would be caught up in the struggle to survive. Throughout the colonial era, in areas where the Church of England enjoyed legal establishment, the shortage of clergy was always a problem, and it meant that religious life was likely to be more relaxed—despite legal expectations—than in England.

Another way the Church of England in a place like Virginia differed from what one found on the other side of the Atlantic was therefore an increased emphasis on lay control of what happened in a parish; if there was no priest, members of the congregation had greater power and were often reluctant to give up that power if a priest arrived. In England, bishops had oversight of much of what went on in the church, from ordaining priests to confirming those baptized in infancy as members once they had received proper instruction in the faith. Throughout the colonial period, there was never a bishop anywhere in the English colonies. The lack of a bishop meant that lay people always had a far greater voice in parish affairs than in England.

Nowhere did churches actually count a majority of the European colonists as formal members. The scattering of the population along the rivers, the expanse of territory comprising a parish, and challenges in providing clergy all contributed to an even smaller proportion of formal church members in the South than elsewhere.

To the north, the earliest English settlements drew from those who were discontent with the established church. Although it is convenient to label all of them Puritans, doing so obscures the differences among them. Even before embarking on colonial ventures, not all who thought the Church of England retained too many Catholic trappings agreed on how further to purify the church and bring it into line with what they believed to be more authentic New Testament Christianity. Some were convinced that the established church remained so corrupt that the only way they could practice their version of true religion was to separate from the church. By forming their own church, they could remain immune to the flaws and faults of the Church of England. Yet, because there was only one established church to which all were expected to give at least nominal allegiance, these separatists comprised an underground movement. For a time, some took refuge in the Netherlands, where there was somewhat greater freedom of religion than in England. But life there was less than ideal, so these separatist Puritans looked to the New World as a haven where they could live according to their understanding of scripture. They had intended to settle among the Virginia colonists, but wound up further north when they arrived in 1620. These separatists became the Pilgrims of popular legend.

Other Puritans, as intent on living according to their understanding of biblical precepts as the Pilgrims, continued to see themselves as part of the Church of England, albeit as a kind of purified leaven at work within the church. They, too, fell afoul of the law in England with their challenges to church authority. In particular, they held preaching services in addition to regular worship, emphasized Bible study, and insisted that while God alone determined who would receive salvation, all women and men should look within themselves to see if God had provided signs that they were among those elected to salvation. In time, they, too, looked across the Atlantic for a place to

Anglicans and Puritans
- English settlers who came first to Virginia were at least nominally part of the Church of England
- They granted the Church of England legal establishment in Virginia
- In Virginia, the scattering of the population along riverways and a shortage of priests hampered organized religious life
- The Pilgrims who came to Plymouth were Puritans who believed that they had to separate from the Church of England to assure their salvation
- Puritans, whether separatist or non-separatist, were committed to setting up church and society according to their understanding of what the Bible commanded; they were also intent on looking within to see if they saw signs that God elected them to salvation
- Puritans regarded other religious alternatives as dangerous to the purity or sacredness of their entire social order

Figure 2.1 Puritan meetinghouse in Massachusetts. In keeping with their aversion to elaborate decoration, Puritans gathered in unadorned buildings they preferred to call meetinghouses rather than churches (© Time & Life Pictures/Getty Images)

build their model society and ideal church, convinced that once they had done so, those back in England would see that they were right and then proceed to purify both church and state at home.

Like other Puritans, those who came to Boston in 1630, and those who were part of a large migration to New England when civil war erupted in England in the 1640s, believed that all of society should conform to biblical ideals. As a result, not only did they require all residents to attend worship—a move that was never entirely successful—but they also restricted the right to vote to male church members, convinced that only those who knew God had elected them to salvation could guide public life in a moral fashion.

What neither separatist Pilgrims nor other Puritans wanted was to allow alternative belief and practice in their midst, for doing so would endanger their own spiritual welfare and purity. Although later legend insists that all these Puritans came to the New World in order to have religious freedom, in reality they wanted that freedom only for themselves. Anyone who did not agree with them was welcome to leave. If they did not leave voluntarily, they would be required to leave by political authorities.

The religious mosaic of early New England

Four episodes early in the history of the Massachusetts Bay colony illustrate both the diversity that was always there and how the Puritan leadership (both civil and religious) took steps to contain what they saw as dangerous alternative religious approaches. The first centers around Roger Williams (1603–1683), a devout Puritan preacher who had come from England and settled first in Plymouth before accepting a call to pastor the Puritan congregation in Salem, Massachusetts. If anything, the passion for absolute purity consumed Williams more than it did those around him. Williams was a religious seeker, but in a sense different from persons in the twenty-first century who call themselves seekers. Williams believed there was but one truth, but that no one should be coerced into coming under the influence of the church. Coercion meant that people would lack genuine commitment; it would bring an impure element into a sacred body. So Williams disagreed with laws requiring church attendance. Forcing those who did not have a pure faith to worship with genuine believers polluted genuine religion. So too, forcing non-believers to adhere to moral codes that had the force of law when they did not accept their basis was, in his mind, absurd.

In addition, Williams insisted that Europeans had no legitimate claim to lands that were home to tribal societies. All of this made him seem a dangerous threat to public and religious order. Williams left Massachusetts in 1635, just before his banishment became official. Regarded as the founder of Rhode Island, where he went after leaving Massachusetts, Williams pursued his solitary quest for absolute religious purity. He attempted to respect the tribal cultures around him by learning their language. Popular lore also labels Williams as the founder of the Baptist movement in America, for Rhode Island early on became a center for congregations of English Puritans inclined towards Baptist ways. Unlike other Puritans, those inclined towards Baptist understanding wanted a clear separation between religious and political authority. They also baptized only believers who were sure of their salvation, not infants or children. In time Baptist influence fostered a kind of Puritan subculture throughout New England.

The second episode highlights both religious diversity and questions about gender roles in Puritan New England, for it concerns a woman named Anne Hutchinson (1591–1643). Hutchinson and her family had migrated to Boston after their Puritan pastor, John Cotton, had come to New England. Although practice at the time excluded women from formal leadership positions in Puritan congregations, Anne hosted devotional prayer and Bible study meetings in her home, primarily for women, as did women on both sides of the Atlantic. But Hutchinson ran afoul of authorities when she claimed that God, through the Holy Spirit, spoke directly to her. That claim seemed to deny the absolute authority of scripture and the authority of ordained male pastors to interpret and expound on scripture. When Hutchinson also taught a more radical idea of salvation by grace, political and religious leaders alike thought she had challenged all order and authority.

If every individual received direct communication from God and if God's grace were not linked to the ministry of church and clergy, then, there was no need for law and order at all, whether religious or political. In one sense, then, Hutchinson believed that grace could come directly to all people and did not require what others called "preparation" or reliance on preaching, pastors, and scripture for clues about God's presence. Hutchinson insisted that her views echoed those of her own pastor, John Cotton. Indeed, most Puritan pastors emphasized a long period of preparation before one might hope to experience grace and denied that grace could come directly and immediately to individuals.

In addition, when Hutchinson taught, she seemed to be preaching and thus taking on a role that Puritan culture of the day reserved for men. Later historians call what resulted the Antinomian Controversy. Antinomian means simply without any need for law. When Hutchinson refused in court to abandon her beliefs, she was banished from the colony in 1638. Given the expanse of land unsettled nearby, she and her family simply had to move outside the realm of Massachusetts political authority. They finally wound up in New York, where they met an unfortunate death in a hostile encounter with tribal people.

Controversy also surrounded the arrival in Boston in 1656 of spiritual cousins of the Puritans known as Quakers. Like others inclined to Puritan ways, Quaker founder George Fox (1624–1691) relied on a profound inner experience of the presence of God, given by God in an act of grace, as the basis for his approach. But he went further than most other Puritans in rejecting most expressions of formal worship, sacraments, and the right of clergy to be the primary—if not sole—interpreters of scripture. The inner light of God's truth came to each person directly.

Diversity and dissent in early colonial Massachusetts

- Puritan efforts to quash religious alternatives failed
- Roger Williams was exiled when he disagreed with efforts to impose Puritan religious ways even on non-Puritans
- Anne Hutchinson was exiled when, as a woman, she challenged traditional gender roles and claimed to receive direct revelation from God through the Holy Spirit
- Quakers were banished or put to death because they rejected the idea that religious leaders were absolute authorities in matters of faith
- Some who still believed that the world was full of supernatural powers accused others of being witches in the famous Salem Witch Trials

In England Quakers often spoke up after and sometimes during church services to explain why their way was more authentically Christian and why the more structured worship of the Church of England missed the mark. Often arrested for disturbing the peace for these disruptions of worship, Quakers spurred greater suspicion of all Puritans because of their "in your face" actions. Puritans in Boston were no more welcoming than English authorities, and after two Quaker women arrived in the colony, local leaders not only banished them, but also enacted legislation providing penalties for anyone who helped bring a Quaker into the colony or even who owned a book by a Quaker author. The Quakers, however, were used to this sort of treatment and, persuaded that truth was on their side, kept re-entering Massachusetts, even after local law provided for their execution. Between 1659 and 1661, four Quakers were put to death.

Yet the persistence of these colonial Quakers, along with their finding a less hostile reception in Roger Williams's Rhode Island, provides evidence of another strand of diversity within Puritan New England, one that has endured to the present. Their story also highlights an important subtheme in American religious history, namely the difficulties encountered by a minority group when there is another that has a solid majority. Dissent is an important part of the larger story of the ever-expanding religious options in English North America. But controversy and antagonism usually accompany dissent when a dominant group feels its power and influence challenged by alternative ways of being religious.

The final episode is well known and often misunderstood, for it focuses on those accused of witchcraft in Salem Village and the ensuing witch trials of 1692. Analysts have offered many theories for why witchcraft hysteria broke out then in Massachusetts. Some have suggested that the young women who made the accusations were hallucinating because they had eaten bread spoiled by a fungus; others have noted that the accusers were all women, excluded at the time from full participation in both church and society by custom and law. Yet others have stressed that among the first accused was an African slave who had come to Massachusetts from the Caribbean; prejudice and misunderstanding may have played a role.

What cannot be overlooked, however, is that Puritans were people of their times who were just becoming aware of a more scientific understanding of cause and effect that most people today take for granted. For them, the world was still a place where supernatural power was vital, and although they did not relate to that power in the same ways that Native American and African tribal peoples did, they were quite convinced of the reality of supernatural forces of evil that could thwart every effort to live according to biblical precept. For at least some of them, demonic powers were as real as the air that they breathed.

Many of those accused were what today we would call marginalized people; most were women—elderly, widowed, or otherwise on the fringes of the larger society. Although both civil and religious leaders regretted that they had approved death sentences for nineteen accused of witchcraft and had imprisoned around 150 others, the significance of the episode for our purposes lies in the way in which it suggests yet another dimension of diversity within the Puritan stronghold. What ordinary people believed and thought, in this case those who made accusations grounded in their sense of the supernatural, clearly lived out a religious style that deviated from the more reasoned, scripture-based theology of the colonial leaders. This passion for the supernatural explains as well why almanacs became bestsellers in Puritan New England; people wanted to consult the astrological information, precursors of today's horoscopes, found only in almanacs. So we have evidence for one more dimension of diversity, the variations in personal belief and practice that sometimes are at odds with those of recognized religious institutions, or at least are held in addition to whatever teachings are part of organized religion.

These four episodes indicate that, despite the best efforts of the Puritans of Massachusetts Bay to construct a colony where only their holy ways would prevail, strands of diversity were present from the start of the colonial enterprise. Some additional strands would become part of the picture when the English government issued a new charter for the colony in 1691, one that required colonial authorities to allow such freedom of religious expression in Massachusetts as was granted in the mother country. That meant not only that soon there would be Church of England congregations in Boston itself, but also that Baptists, Quakers, and others could not be dealt with as harshly as in the past. Their increasing presence and influence would remain part of the expanding religious diversity of the English colonies. Other expressions of diversity came as New England Puritans interacted more with Native American peoples and as English colonists everywhere in North America found their lives intertwined with those of African slaves. That story we shall explore in a later chapter, but it is a story that adds to the diversity developing in American religious life.

Key points you need to know

- The Spanish and French brought their own strains of Catholicism to the New World.
- Successful Spanish missions disrupted tribal life; French missions were more likely to build on tribal life.
- Neither the Spanish nor the French recognized the integrity of the religious styles of indigenous tribal peoples.
- The English added to the religious diversity when Anglicans settled in Virginia, but faced difficulties in organizing parishes and having priests to serve them.
- More diversity resulted when various kinds of Puritans came to New England.

- Puritans, a persecuted minority in England, tried to keep others from settling in their territories.
- A constant undercurrent of religious diversity challenged Puritan exclusivism.

Discussion questions

1. How did Spanish religious and political leaders differ when it came to relating to native peoples?
2. How did French Catholicism in the New World differ from Spanish Catholicism?
3. Why were the French more successful than the Spanish both in establishing Catholic religious institutions and in having positive relations with native peoples?
4. What was the religious character of early colonial Virginia?
5. What are the key features of Puritanism?
6. What different styles of Puritanism marked religious life in colonial Massachusetts?
7. What evidence suggests that there was considerable religious diversity in colonial Massachusetts despite the efforts of authorities to prevent it?

Further reading

Axtell, James. *The Invasion Within: The Contest of Cultures in Colonial North America.* New York: Oxford University Press, 1985.

Butler, Jon. *Awash in a Sea of Faith: Christianizing the American People.* Cambridge, MA: Harvard University Press, 1990.

Hall, David D. *Worlds of Wonder, Days of Judgment: Popular Religious Belief in Early New England.* New York: Knopf, 1989.

Lippy, Charles H., Robert Choquette, and Stafford Poole. *Christianity Comes to the Americas, 1492–1776.* New York: Paragon House, 1992.

Winship, Michael P. *The Times and Trials of Anne Hutchinson: Puritans Divided.* Lawrence: University Press of Kansas, 2005.

Woolverton, John F. *Colonial Anglicanism in North America.* Detroit: Wayne State University Press, 1984.

3 The expanding religious culture of English colonial America

In this chapter

This chapter focuses on the rather astonishing number of religious options that emerged in the middle colonies, especially Pennsylvania. Developments there foreshadowed much of what later became central to American religious life. The chapter also examines the role of English Catholics and Jews in adding to colonial religious diversity. It also looks at how an interest both in a more evangelical style of Protestantism and in Enlightenment rationalism increased religious diversity.

Main topics covered

- The Reformed and Lutheran presence in New York, New Jersey, and elsewhere
- The significance of William Penn's "lively experiment" for American religion
- The diversity that came to English colonies because of a growing presence of Roman Catholics and Jews
- The impact of the evangelical revivals of the eighteenth century and Enlightenment rationalism on religion and political culture

The importance of the middle colonies

Not all Europeans who staked their fortunes on life in the Americas came from England, Spain, and France. The age of exploration and colonial conquest stirred the interest of many others who also brought with them their own ways of being religious. As a result, the religious landscape of North America became increasingly diverse.

In September 1609, just two months after the French explorer Samuel de Champlain had engaged in military combat with the Iroquois while establishing a French outpost in Quebec, the Englishman Henry Hudson reached the river in New York that now bears his name. At the time, Hudson was employed by the Dutch East India Company, and by 1613 a few trading centers and crude homes began a Dutch presence in what became New Netherland until the English seized control of the colony in 1664 and renamed it New York. Because the Netherlands already offered more religious liberty than many other European countries, few Dutch people came to New Netherland for religious reasons when permanent settlers arrived, beginning in 1623. The Dutch Reformed Church, one forerunner of today's Reformed Church in America, did receive legal recognition, but Dutch colonial governors had little interest in promoting religion. They regarded the colony almost as a feudal barony, and their primary concerns were securing political power and then profit for the investors back home.

Consequently, the first Dutch Reformed pastor did not arrive until 1628 and faced an uphill struggle in creating viable congregations. As elsewhere, when pastors arrived, they were expected to devote some time to missionary work among the indigenous tribal peoples in the area, but as elsewhere, these efforts were sporadic and not very successful. Like the Puritan churches in New England, the Dutch Reformed Church bore the influence of the Calvinist wing of the Protestant Reformation. In Europe, the Dutch Reformed evidenced a concern for doctrinal precision. At a religious conference or synod meeting in the Dutch city of Dort in 1618–1619, the core doctrines of Calvinism received a classic statement. The synod emphasized especially the idea that all humanity was totally depraved or sinful, but that God unconditionally elected or chose some for salvation. That salvation resulted from the sacrificial death of Jesus, but the ministry of Jesus was effective only for those chosen or elected by God. At the same time, humans were powerless to resist this gracious action of God, who also granted them the power to persevere in their faith.

In New Netherland, doctrine at first did not matter all that much. In fact, when the English gained control of the colony, there was only a handful of struggling Dutch

Key doctrines of Calvinism
- **T**otal depravity or the utter sinfulness of all people
- **U**nconditional election by God of some for salvation
- **L**imited atonement or the view that Christ's death effectively restores a right relationship with God only for the elect
- **I**rresistible grace or the belief that no one elected by God can willingly refuse salvation
- **P**erseverance of the saints or the conviction that the elect will always have faith

Together, the first letters spell the word TULIP, a flower common to the Netherlands. At a church council in Dort in the Netherlands (1618–1619), these five doctrines were acclaimed as the foundation of the Calvinist understanding of Christianity.

Reformed congregations. But they did represent an alternative to the Church of England, which soon received legal establishment when English control was secure. By being ethnically Dutch and theologically Reformed or Calvinist, the Dutch Reformed experience added to the ethnic and religious diversity that was becoming more commonplace in English North America.

Just across the river, in what is now New Jersey, but was then known as East Jersey and West Jersey, other colonial communities brought additional and different ties between ethnicity and religion. Among English settlers there, most were either of Puritan or Quaker persuasion. In Massachusetts, as we have seen, Puritans regarded Quakers as dangerous enemies; in New Jersey, they managed to live side by side in relative harmony, perhaps because of the necessity of trying to survive as a colonial enterprise. In time, a small number of Scandinavians also made their way to Jersey. In most of Scandinavia, the established church had ties to the Lutheran wing of the Reformation, not the Calvinist heritage. In many cases, the Lutheran congregations were as much ethnic communities as religious ones, because the churches tended to use the first language of communicants in worship. Not until the twentieth century did some of those ethnically based Lutheran groups merge together, jettisoning the distinctive ethnic component.

But of the middle colonies, the one that proved a harbinger of what was to become the standard for later developments was Pennsylvania, with its premier colonial settlement at Philadelphia.

William Penn's experiment in religious diversity

William Penn (1644–1718) was a devout Quaker who believed strongly in the Quaker principle of pacifism. He also came from a prominent family and was thus able to secure from the English king a grant of land in the New World where he hoped to create a haven for his fellow Quakers—who were often persecuted and marginalized in England—once settlement began in 1681. A practical businessman, as a consequence of Quaker religious beliefs Penn called for a "holy experiment" in religious freedom in his colony. Quakers insisted that within all people there was a religious sensitivity—what they called the "inner light"—that God shaped in a variety of ways. That variety meant that for Quakers religious truth could take many forms and was not necessarily limited even to their own understanding of what was right and good.

It followed, then, that people of different religious viewpoints should not try to force others into agreement. They should recognize that religious belief was a matter of the inner life, not the public life or common life of a society. Penn's experiment was an effort to demonstrate that persons who held different religious views could live together in peace and harmony. Quakers were also more open than others to accepting the native tribal peoples, since they too could have truth within, but the quest for land often resulted in conflict. In addition, Quakers were critical of slavery.

Figure 3.1 A colonial Quaker meetinghouse. The simplicity central to the Quaker style of waiting quietly for the guidance of the inner light comes through in their meetinghouse architecture (© Lee Snider/Photo images/CORBIS.)

Penn had to welcome non-Quakers to the colony for a practical reason: Quakers were a relatively small group even in England, and for the colonial venture to succeed, non-Quakers would be needed to provide the necessary population base. Among those who accepted Penn's invitation were several clusters of German pietists. The pietist movement, although rooted in the Lutheran religious tradition, placed a strong emphasis on personal practice of prayer and devotion and generally rejected the idea of a religious establishment or state church. Pietists also had a rich tradition of hymnody, and some celebrated what they called love feasts as an alternative to what they saw as an arid sacramentalism in the state churches in the German states. Many, like the Quakers, were averse to bearing arms. Among the better known are the Moravians, who had more success than most in establishing a positive relationship with tribal peoples that included a quiet evangelization effort. Other German communities that migrated to Penn's colony included the Mennonites and their spiritual cousins, the

William Penn's "holy experiment"

- Quakers believed that there was an "inner light" in all people
- In addition to Quakers, Penn welcomed many German Pietists along with German Reformed to his colony
- Scots-Irish settlers brought Presbyterianism to Pennsylvania
- Philadelphia became an early center for colonial Catholics and Baptists
- Pennsylvania demonstrated that peace and harmony could prevail in society even if people followed different religions

Amish. With roots in the "left wing" or Anabaptist strand of the Reformation, these groups emphasized a devotion and simplicity even more rigorous than that promoted by the Quakers.

The Scots-Irish who came to Pennsylvania added another dimension to the religious diversity of the colony, for they brought with them a Calvinistic approach that gradually coalesced into the religious tradition known as Presbyterianism. By the eighteenth century, people known as German Reformed were also making their way to Pennsylvania; like the Scots-Irish, the early German Reformed were more inclined to Calvinist teaching than to Lutheran approaches, and like the Dutch Reformed, they affirmed the doctrinal principles set forth at the Synod of Dort. Other German Protestants who rejected the idea that God alone determined who would receive the grace of salvation, but argued that humans themselves could choose whether to accept or reject the offer of salvation, found a home in Pennsylvania.

Soon also there were Baptists in Philadelphia and elsewhere in the colony; the formation by Baptists in 1707 of the Philadelphia Associations ranks among the earliest efforts to bring Baptists in North America into an organized body. In time, some of the first independent African American religious groups would emerge in Pennsylvania, and by the time the American war for independence began, the colony boasted a substantial Roman Catholic population as well, although tradition has it that Maryland—just to the south of Pennsylvania—developed to provide a refuge for English Catholics.

Penn's experiment was not without its challenges, however, even as it was becoming a model for the wide-ranging religious multiformity that ultimately came to characterize all of American life. Although Quakers for many years dominated the political and economic life of Pennsylvania, non-Quakers objected to the rigid Quaker insistence on pacifism. Some who moved to the frontiers of central and western Pennsylvania had skirmishes with tribal peoples because of the European thirst for land that often resulted in violence. Then, when war erupted periodically between the French and the English over colonial dominance in North America, many non-Quakers believed that they needed a stronger defense than Quaker political leaders were willing to provide. At the same time, the Quaker emphasis on the "inner light" within each person sometimes led to an extreme individualism that resulted even in divisions among the Quakers themselves over just what to believe.

For the most part, Penn's holy experiment was a success. It demonstrated to skeptical Europeans and even to other colonists that persons of different religious persuasions could actually live in one society without having constant quarrels. It also reinforced the idea that was gaining more currency in the later colonial period that religious beliefs were a matter for the private sphere, a matter of personal choice that could be kept separate and distinct from the public or shared aspects of life.

Maryland and the Carolinas cradle more religious options

The religious upheavals in England, going back to King Henry VIII, the establishment of the Church of England, and the ongoing rivalry for generations between England and Catholic powers such as France and Spain, made life difficult for those who were still inclined to Catholic ways of thinking and the religious practices associated with Catholicism. Not until the early nineteenth century were English Catholics afforded full political rights, so strong was the suspicion of Catholics. But Catholic practice and adherence was never eliminated, despite the legal restrictions that tried to quash it.

The beginnings of English Catholicism in North America and the founding of Maryland are linked to this deep-rooted hostility towards Catholics. George Calvert (c.1580–1632), the first Lord Baltimore, had a political career that he had to abandon when he converted to Catholicism. He was not, however, forced to end his friendship with the English royal family, and hoped to secure from the king a grant of land in North America that might become a refuge for English Catholics. After his death, the grant passed to his son, who spearheaded the establishment of the proprietary colony that became Maryland. In one sense, then, Maryland and Pennsylvania have much in common in terms of their origins. Both were proprietary colonies; that is, both were initially the personal domains of individuals, in favor with the English king, who hoped to reap a financial profit from their colonies. The proprietors—William Penn and the two Lords Baltimore—were associated with religious communities marginalized in England, Quakers and Catholics. In time, both colonies became known for granting more religious freedom to European settlers than was commonplace, although the reasons for doing so were not the same and Maryland did not have the degree of religious diversity that quickly came to mark the Pennsylvania experiment.

When the first English Catholics arrived in the Chesapeake Bay area in 1634, their instructions indicated that although they were free to practice their Catholic faith, they should not discuss it publicly lest non-Catholics take offense. In addition, Jesuits soon launched missionary work among the indigenous peoples. Rather quickly Protestant settlers outnumbered Catholics in Maryland; as with the Quakers who came to Pennsylvania, the total number of English Catholics who might be able to migrate was so small that the colony would not have succeeded had it relied only on Catholic settlers. After Protestants became a majority, however, there was some concern that they might use their numerical strength to hinder Catholic practice, particularly after civil war in England placed political power there in the hands of Puritans, who were fiercely anti-Catholic.

In 1649 Cecil Calvert, the second Lord Baltimore, issued an act that later generations have often claimed provided for extraordinary religious toleration and assured the legal rights of minority religions. But the immediate concern was to protect Catholic practice, and the law itself was heavily Christian in focus, providing stiff penalties for those who blasphemed the Christian Trinity. Nevertheless, the provision did mandate that all Christians would have equal standing before the law in Maryland. It thus became an early harbinger of how American governments would deal with increasing religious difference, although in this case toleration extended only to trinitarian Christians and the diversity allowed was rather narrow.

More than a century after the initial settlement in Maryland, another issue brought the status of Catholicism in the English colonies to the fore and revealed that there remained a strong anti-Catholic prejudice among many colonial Protestant Christians. That prejudice came to light after the English defeated the French and their Native American allies in the Seven Years' War (1756–1763), the last of the so-called French and Indian Wars. As a result, Canada became part of the British colonial empire. Since the former French colony was overwhelmingly Catholic, English and colonial authorities had to deal with a vigorous Catholicism in Quebec, Montreal, and other areas of Canada. The English could not strip the Catholics of their religious identity if they hoped to impress their political control on the region. Many Protestants, especially in New England regions that shared a border with Canada, were apprehensive that England would give preferential treatment to Canadian Catholics in order to cement British authority over the territory.

Much further south, in the Carolinas, where permanent European settlement began around 1670, there were also early provisions that acknowledged religious diversity, even if there was no formal act of toleration as in Maryland. In the Carolinas, reasons for doing so had nothing to do with protecting a particular minority group, as was the case with Catholics in Maryland. The proprietors who spearheaded the Carolina colony—later divided into North Carolina and South Carolina—required only that settlers acknowledge belief in God in a document commonly called the "Fundamental Constitutions" of Carolina. Never endorsed by colonial legislative assemblies, the Fundamental Constitutions paved the way for considerable religious latitude, in South Carolina especially, even after the Church of England received legal establishment. Nearby Virginia had far stricter laws regarding religious dissent or non-adherence to the established church, and so many dissenters—Puritans, Baptists,

Religious diversity in Maryland and the Carolinas

- Maryland was founded as a haven for English Catholics, but Protestants quickly outnumbered Catholics
- An "Act of Toleration" in Maryland in 1649 is one of the earliest American legal moves to assure some degree of religious freedom
- The "Fundamental Constitutions" of Carolina was also religiously inclusive, opening the colony to all who acknowledged belief in God
- Consequently, South Carolina became home to one of the largest concentrations of Jewish settlers in the English colonies

Presbyterians—who first came to Virginia continued on to Carolina. Quakers and Moravians early on made a place for themselves in what became North Carolina. When, in 1685, the French government revoked the Edict of Nantes, which had granted limited privileges to French Calvinists or Huguenots, many as part of a larger migration came to the Charleston area. Although most of these Huguenots gradually made their way into the Church of England, one congregation in Charleston today still uses an English translation of the old Huguenot liturgy in its worship.

More stunning, perhaps, was the arrival of small but increasing numbers of Jews in Charleston. By 1750, Congregation Beth Elohim, which continues to serve the Jewish community in Charleston, was organized, becoming the second synagogue to form in the English colonies; a congregation had organized in New York City before the end of the seventeenth century. Part of the attraction of South Carolina for Jewish settlers stemmed from the broad provisions of the Fundamental Constitutions, for unlike the case in most of Europe at the time, in colonial South Carolina Jews were granted rights of citizenship, including the right to vote, since they acknowledged belief in God. By the time of American independence, South Carolina boasted one of the largest Jewish populations in the nation, with Charleston itself having then perhaps the largest of any city, both proportionately and in total numbers.

Religious diversity, although perhaps not as ethnically and theologically extensive as in Pennsylvania, became the norm in places like Maryland and the Carolinas, even if the intent had been for Maryland to be a haven for English Catholics, and even if the Church of England enjoyed legal establishment and its benefits in both North and South Carolina. By the middle of the eighteenth century, other forces at work in the English colonies were prompting the emergence of different forms of diversity, ones internal to some Protestant bodies that were already flourishing. They stemmed from two currents: evangelicalism and the Enlightenment.

The impact of the evangelical surge and the Enlightenment

The wide range of religious groups found in English colonial America by the middle third of the eighteenth century, the presence of established churches supported by tax monies in several of the colonies, and laws in some places requiring church attendance may overstate the power of organized religion in colonial life. To be sure, religious influence was pervasive and reached many who may not have had ready access to a congregation because of patterns of settlement and a shortage of clergy, or a burning interest in religious matters. But beginning in the 1730s and continuing in spurts over about two decades, there was an upswing in the religious life of most of the colonies. Some historians see this surge more as a time when colonists first began to have their religious sensibilities stirred. Those who are of this view emphasize that the number of actual church members was low—probably not much more than 10 percent of the population even by the time of the first national census in 1790—despite the prevalence of religious groups. However, those interpreters who recognize that a religious dimension to colonial society may be far more pervasive than numbers of members would suggest, view this time as one of religious renewal, revival, or awakening. Indeed, most look at the religious activity of the second third of the eighteenth century as a "great awakening" of interest in religion, but it was an interest in a particular style or way of being religious. Because that style emphasized personal religious experience—not belief, doctrine, or religious establishment—it is called evangelicalism.

Two preachers figure more prominently in the evangelical awakenings than any others: Jonathan Edwards (1703–1758), a Calvinist pastor in Northampton in western Massachusetts at the time, and George Whitefield (1714–1770), an English Calvinist and associate of John and Charles Wesley, the founders of Methodism. Edwards, often regarded as the greatest American theologian and philosopher, noticed a religious stirring among his congregation in the 1730s and went on to become a major analyst not just of the religious revivals, but also of the nature and character of religious experience. Whitefield made several trips to the English colonies, preaching to large audiences from Georgia to what is now Maine, although his initial purpose was to raise funds for an orphanage in colonial Georgia.

Figure 3.2 George Whitefield. Dynamic English revivalist George Whitefield made several preaching tours of the English colonies in the eighteenth century, dramatically urging listeners to examine their souls for signs that God had elected them for salvation (Courtesy of the Library of Congress.)

As Calvinists, both Edwards and Whitefield believed that God alone determined who would receive the grace of salvation and that humans themselves could do nothing to deserve that grace. However, just because all depended on God did not mean that ordinary people could not scrutinize their own experience to see if God had given them signs that they were elect or converted, signs more likely to become clear through prayer, reading the Bible, and attending preaching services. Sometimes men and women who heard evangelical preachers speak were seized by spiritual ecstasy; others became distraught as they looked inward and failed to see clear signs that they were among the elect.

From the outset, critics of the evangelical revivals saw the anxiety that some experienced as dangerous, and the ecstasy as excessive emotional display rather than genuine religious expression. When others mimicked Whitefield in travelling from place to place preaching, a practice called itinerating, some objected that these preachers were either intentionally or unintentionally condemning regular pastors of congregations who did not go from place to place.

The evangelical movement left its mark on colonial religious life and helped make religious options more diverse than they had been before. Because the mark of evangelicalism was inner, personal experience, the revivals gave greater influence to individuals than to churches and pastors in charting their own religious course. After all, only individuals could determine whether they knew with certainty that God had given them signs of their salvation. On a larger scale, because someone like Whitefield traveled throughout the English colonies, the revivals created a kind of common bond among Americans who were affected by the evangelical surge.

There were also parallels between the revivals in North America and movements in England and Scotland. About the same time as Edwards and Whitefield began to notice deeper religious stirrings in North America, John and Charles Wesley were inaugurating the preaching movement in England that became Methodism, with its emphasis on personal experience—but experience that required individuals to accept God's grace and not just look for signs that God had chosen them. In Scotland there was an evangelical movement that had a more Calvinist base, but also a sacramental element, as people came together to examine their souls prior to a religious festival that culminated in the celebration of the Lord's Supper.

The most significant aspect of the revivals was the way they made individual, personal experience the key to authentic religion. Although surviving church records indicate that for a time there was a general increase in church membership, greater growth came to those religious groups that emphasized personal experience. Among them were the Baptists and then the Methodists. Although the Methodist movement in England was underway by the later 1730s, it was not until the Seven Years' War that a distinctive Methodist presence in the English North American colonies can be found. That presence owes its beginnings in part to British soldiers who came during the war and then remained after the war ended. Like the Puritans, Methodists had roots in the Church of England. John Wesley, for example, was a priest in the Church of England until his death.

In North America, Methodist clusters began to meet separately from Church of England congregations, often at first in class meetings in homes where those inclined to the intense personal experience that lay at the heart of Methodist understanding could gather for prayer, mutual support, and Bible study. The Methodist style was especially attractive to women, who were denied positions of leadership and authority in virtually all organized religious bodies at that time. In a Methodist class meeting, even if class leaders were men, women were free to share their own personal stories of faith and gain a sense of self-worth that was frequently missing elsewhere. Indeed, anyone who could testify to an inner assurance of having accepted God's grace was allowed to speak. In time, this inclusiveness made the evangelical style in general, and the Methodist approach in particular, appealing to African Americans, who were generally ignored by other religious groups.

Another enduring consequence of the evangelical style was an increasing acceptance of the idea that becoming a church member should be a matter of choice, open to those who could testify to their religious experience. As membership became voluntary, individuals were free to choose which congregation to attend. In New England, for example, one might choose among not only traditional-style Congregationalists or the Church of England, but also from Baptists of various stripes, separatist Congregationalists, and more. The evangelical surge thus helped give birth to a broadening of the idea of denominationalism in American religious culture and helped break down what remained of the European notion of parishes that included all who lived in a particular geographic area.

Parallel to the evangelical surge was another movement that also promoted individual choice in matters of faith and belief, but one that at first glance seems rather different from evangelicalism. It stemmed from the Enlightenment or Age of Reason and thus emphasized reason or the role of the mind in determining what to believe and do in matters of faith. The rationalist impulse took many forms, with the most extreme rejecting religion and religious groups of the day, on the grounds that they depended on unprovable revelation for their beliefs. Rationalists insisted that the mind could determine for itself whether an idea was true and did not need a revealed sacred text like the Bible, or even clergy, to explain what it meant. Anything that reeked of the miraculous was suspect to some Enlightenment thinkers.

Others were more moderate, arguing that the mind could sort out from among the various doctrines and practices of different religious groups what seemed worth believing and doing—in other words, what made sense. If evangelicalism elevated the individual to a place of primacy in religion because of its emphasis on personal experience, Enlightenment rationalism did the same because of its emphasis on the power of the individual mind. There was also an assumption that exercising this right of private judgment, as Boston pastor Jonathan Mayhew (1720–1766) called

> **Evangelicalism and Enlightenment rationalism**
> - Evangelical revivals of the eighteenth century added an individual diversity to colonial religion by emphasizing personal experience
> - As a result, religious groups that stressed the importance of personal experience, such as Methodists and Baptists, began to grow rapidly, and congregations associated with denominations that one joined from choice began to replace the parish system transplanted from Europe
> - Critics of the revivals or awakening thought there was emotional excess and undermining of the work of regular pastors
> - The Enlightenment focused on the role of reason to find religious truth apart from revelation
> - Enlightenment rationalism also enhanced individualism in religion because of its emphasis on personal rational reflection
> - Both evangelicalism and rationalism challenged traditional authority and helped create a mindset that supported political independence from Britain

it in the mid-eighteenth century, would allow what was true to come to the fore, and everyone would pretty much agree. Of course, this confidence that minds would naturally agree about what was true in matters of faith and belief was much too naive and optimistic.

Many Americans of the later colonial period were drawn to rationalist ways of thinking, even if they remained members of a particular religious group. Among them were several figures prominent in later colonial public life, such as George Washington (1732–1799), Benjamin Franklin (1706–1790), and Thomas Jefferson (1743–1826). They all thought that reason would bring a shared identity to all who affirmed the same basic truths, with individuals adding to that basic core as they saw fit. The shared truths would concern morals and ethics, since there seemed some common agreement about what was right and what was wrong. For some inclined to Enlightenment rationalism, ethics became almost synonymous with religion; persons like Franklin and Washington, for example, encouraged organized religion not because they accepted its revealed doctrines, but because they believed that organized religion taught individuals ethics and morals so they could be good citizens.

The religion of reason left considerable latitude to the individual when it came to personal religious belief and practice beyond the basics of right and wrong. Enlightenment rationalists expected considerable diversity, and they recoiled from any efforts to force conformity to any one religious style or group. It seemed irrational to persecute others for their particular religious beliefs so long as they were upright citizens who promoted the common good. Rationalists also harbored qualms about a state church, for religious establishment put the power of government behind a single religious approach. That, too, went against reason. Many of those inclined towards rationalism are known as Deists, a designation that derives from the Latin word for god. The label is apt because Deism denoted a general belief in a providential God (deity) who is known primarily through rational deduction based on observation of the natural world, not through divine revelation, miracle, or even sacred texts.

Even before the American Revolution, rationalism and evangelicalism had started to come together in the tradition that later became known as Unitarianism. At first called Unitarian Christianity, this movement looked to figures such as the Puritan clergymen Jonathan Mayhew and Charles Chauncy as its theological precursors. What set early Unitarianism apart from much of the evangelical tradition also nurtured by Puritanism was its sense that a benevolent or good God would never consign anyone to eternal damnation. To do so would be inconsistent with a benevolent character. So universal salvation, as it was called, was one of nascent Unitarianism's major beliefs, one shared with a movement developing at the same time that was called Universalism. By the early nineteenth century, when the label Unitarian began to gain wider usage, some who were heavily influenced by rationalism began to question orthodox Christian ideas of the divinity of the Christ — preferring to regard the Christ as a moral exemplar and teacher—and Christianity's reliance on so-called miracles to support its teachings. Here, Unitarianism had common ground with Deism.

As these developments were taking shape, both evangelicalism and rationalism in different ways were also challenging fixed authority and emphasizing individualism. Both made it difficult to tie religion to government. Both emphasized personal experience, one stressing an inner, emotional or affective experience, and the other stressing a more intellectual reflection centered on reason and the mind. In many ways, evangelical and Enlightenment currents had a symbiotic relationship in that each thought it was recovering something lost and perhaps overemphasized by the other. Evangelicals believed they were restoring Christianity's core emphasis on the Bible, and the sense of the heart that formalism and rationalism had corrupted. Enlightenment advocates insisted that they were restoring the genuine moral core of Christianity that had been sacrificed to emotional excess and superstition. However, later historians would look back and see both as perhaps unwittingly contributing to the ethos that paved the way for political independence from England. The king and parliament, along with the established Church of England, came to represent that stagnant, oppressive authority whose foundations crumbled in the wake of evangelical personal experience and rational reflection. The idea of political independence almost naturally flowed from the power of inner experience and clear thinking. In some ways, then, the move towards independence traced some of its roots to colonial religious diversity.

Key points you need to know

- New Netherland and New Jersey added to the religious and ethnic diversity of the colonies.
- Pennsylvania's toleration of many groups made it a model for showing that religious diversity did not upset social order.
- English Catholics had an early haven in Maryland, while colonial South Carolina had a significant Jewish population.
- The evangelical revivals of the eighteenth century and Enlightenment rationalism increased diversity by making the individual the final authority in matters of religious belief and experience.

Discussion questions

1. What made the religious life of New Netherland and New Jersey different from the other colonies that became the U.S.?
2. Why did William Penn call his colony a "holy experiment"?
3. What brought English Catholics to Maryland?
4. Why did South Carolina have a large Jewish population in the later colonial period?
5. What were the evangelical revivals? How did they change colonial religious life?
6. How did Enlightenment rationalism promote religious diversity and religious toleration?

Further reading

Balmer, Randall H. *A Perfect Babel of Confusion: Dutch Religion and English Culture in the Middle Colonies*. New York: Oxford University Press, 1989.

Bonomi, Patricia. *Under the Cope of Heaven: Religion, Society, and Politics in Colonial America*. Rev. ed. New York: Oxford University Press, 2003.

Frost, J. William. *A Perfect Freedom: Religious Liberty in Pennsylvania*. University Park: Pennsylvania State University Press, 1993.

Gillis, Chester. *Roman Catholicism in America*. New York: Columbia University Press, 1999.

Holmes, David L. *The Faiths of the Founding Fathers*. New York: Oxford University Press, 2006.

Lambert, Frank. *"Pedlar in Divinity": George Whitefield and the Transatlantic Revivals, 1737–1770*. Princeton, NJ: Princeton University Press, 1994.

Marsden, George. *Jonathan Edwards: A Life*. New Haven, CT: Yale University Press, 2003.
May, Harry F. *The Enlightenment in America*. New York: Oxford University Press, 1976.
Sarna, Jonathan D. *American Judaism: A History*. New Haven, CT: Yale University Press, 2004.
Soderlund, Jean R., ed. *William Penn and the Founding of Pennsylvania, 1680–1684*. Philadelphia: University of Pennsylvania Press, 1983.

4 Religion in an age of revolution

In this chapter

This chapter looks at the religious culture of the English colonies and the new American republic during the era of independence. It looks at the impact of the war on religious institutions and examines some of the legal moves taken in the new nation to assure that religious diversity would prevail. Finally, it probes the birth of a form of religious organization unique initially to the United States, the denomination, and ends with some brief observations about religious life in areas not under English control at the time of independence.

Main topics covered

- The impact of evangelicalism in challenging colonial political structures just before the American Revolution
- How the Revolution itself received strong support from some religious groups and nearly demolished some others
- The importance of legislation in Virginia providing for religious liberty, and provisions in the U.S. Constitution and Bill of Rights regarding religion
- How the denomination emerged as a form of religious organization in a culture where diversity and separation of church and state created a "free market" for religions
- The religious pulse of areas where strong French and Spanish influences still predominated

Religious challenges in the late colonial period

After the close of the Seven Years' War, political tensions began to grow rapidly between the English colonies that were to become the United States and the British crown and parliament. Much of the political story related to taxation that British political leaders felt necessary to help pay for the cost of the war and for running an ever larger colonial empire. Increasing resistance to British control, however, was only part of a larger transformation underway that had implications for both political and religious life. That transformation also reflected the increasing religious diversity that was becoming a matter of course almost everywhere in English colonial America. Because the middle colonies had long demonstrated extraordinary religious diversity, attention here will focus on the southern colonies, where the Church of England enjoyed legal establishment, and New England, where the Puritan influence had long dominated religious life.

Some of the change that now seems so obvious had to do with three interrelated forces: increasing immigration, the movement of people to land that had not yet been settled by Euro-American colonists, and the religious styles that they brought with them. Much of that internal movement brought people further inland from the port cities along the Atlantic coast. For example, many Scots-Irish—the largest ethnic community among European immigrants in the eighteenth century—moved not only inland, but gradually south in areas along the eastern slopes of the Appalachian mountain chain. Movement further westward was at that time restricted by English policy. After the defeat of the French in the Seven Years' War, the English sought to have better relationships with many Native American tribal groups, especially those that had allied with France. Since Native American societies were feeling squeezed out of ancestral lands as the colonial population grew, the English government decreed that there would be no colonial settlement west of a line that went roughly along the western side of the Appalachian mountain chain.

For those who settled along the eastern side of the mountains, existing colonial governmental and religious patterns were just as oppressive as others found British policies regarding taxation and trade. Many of the Scots-Irish were inclined towards evangelical expressions of Christianity, not the Church of England. Although Presbyterian leanings were particularly strong among the Scots-Irish, others who came to the upcountry and piedmont regions were attracted to Baptist and Methodist ways of being religious. They, too, clashed with the established church. Those who migrated into the piedmont and upcountry areas increasingly resented their exclusion from the colonial political process. Those in the coastal areas retained control of the colonial legislative assemblies, for example; in some cases, they were considerably over-represented in terms of their proportion of the population and often adopted policies that favored their own interests. New variety came as more people who had little interest in the Church of England moved into the southern upcountry. They brought political as well as religious diversity. Slowly but surely, this multiformity was transforming the character of colonial life. In addition, those in the upcountry rankled at the idea of paying taxes to support an established church, especially when their own religious preference was decidedly different.

Along with an evangelical penetration from Maryland, south into Georgia came others. Moravians, for example, organized thriving communities in areas of western

North Carolina, while other German pietists found a home in the Shenandoah area of Virginia. Even in the areas of the southern colonies where the Church of England retained its prominence, there were signs of diversity. Some had to do with the genteel rationalism that attracted persons of the ilk of Thomas Jefferson and George Washington. Some were linked to the role lay vestries or church administrative boards had taken on because there was often a shortage of priests to serve parishes. When a priest might be available, he found that he had to tailor his theology to local tastes, which could be very different from what was assumed in England itself. So there was actually considerable difference even among congregations of the Church of England.

Added to all of this was the interaction with African American religion, that unique fusion of African tribal religious expression and dimensions of evangelical Protestant Christianity. Even if in some towns African American slaves attended services with their owners in the Church of England parish, African American religion and the religion of the slave owners were each influencing the other. Nor should one forget the Catholic presence in places like Maryland, and the thriving Jewish communities in Charleston and Savannah. Slowly but surely, the southern colonies were becoming as religiously diverse as the middle colonies such as Pennsylvania, even if the Church of England retained legal establishment.

Religious diversity was becoming more the order of the day in New England beyond Rhode Island, where the legacy of Roger Williams had perpetuated a stronger appreciation of religious pluralism, including welcoming a Jewish community in Newport. Differences among Puritan religious leaders over the evangelical awakening and its reliance on revivals and itinerant preachers were only one sign that not all came from the same mold. Some Puritan clergy, such as Jonathan Mayhew and Charles Chauncy (1705–1787), were absorbing rationalist thinking, shedding the rigid idea of election common to earlier Puritanism, and moving towards what shortly after the Revolution coalesced into the Unitarian tradition. In Boston itself, a congregation on Brattle Street founded in 1699 had long been a beacon for a more reasoned approach to faith. Then, too, for nearly three generations Church of England congregations had flourished, although without the prestige of legal establishment.

Religious issues at the time of independence
- Evangelicals, Moravians, and others moved into the southern upcountry
- They resented the political power of the coastal elite and the Church of England
- Baptist growth in New England challenged existing religious patterns, as did the growth of other non-Puritan groups
- New England Protestants feared the appointment of an Anglican bishop for the colonies and possible favoritism for Canadian Catholics

48 Religion in an age of revolution

Many Puritan Congregationalists, whether inclined towards evangelicalism or rationalism, feared that the Church of England's power would increase after the defeat of the French and that soon there would be an American bishop with both civil and religious authority to complicate religious matters even more. Anxiety continued over how English governmental representatives would try to accommodate the Roman Catholic population of newly acquired Canada. British control over Catholic Canada thus raised thorny questions about intolerance, even as it reminded people that not all Christians were Protestants. For generations, a grudging acceptance of diversity barely masked continuing and deep-seated anti-Catholic attitudes among many Protestants. Diversity did not necessarily mean harmony. Often controversy and conflict came with it.

As well, from the middle of the eighteenth century on Baptists were growing in strength, with their most well-known leader Isaac Backus (1724–1806) objecting strenuously to the idea of tax-supported churches—even if the money was remitted to Baptist congregations. Backus was also instrumental in moving many New England Congregationalists away from the practice of infant baptism, after he came to believe that the New Testament called for only baptism of adult believers by immersion, the position associated with Baptists. For colonial Baptists, the Puritan-dominated legislative assemblies seemed as tyrannical in their protection of the status quo as southern legislative assemblies appeared to evangelicals and others who had come into the upcountry. As mounting discontent with British colonial policy brought turmoil in the public sphere, religious life was exhibiting its own kind of turbulence as a consequence of ever-increasing religious diversity.

The impact of the American Revolution on religious life

When shots fired at Lexington and Concord, Massachusetts in April 1775 signaled the outbreak of a military conflict that would last more than six years before finally issuing in American independence, the diverse religious world of the former English colonies also experienced a revolution. On the one hand, many clergy, especially in New England, vigorously supported the rebellion, in part because they still believed that church and state were improperly intertwined in the British way of doing things (even if they did not reject using tax revenues to pay clergy salaries and such). Ironically, although they often proclaimed from the pulpit that British policy was itself a tyranny designed to enslave the colonists, they rarely spoke out against the institution of slavery that enchained thousands of African Americans throughout the colonies.

On the other hand, many clergy were reluctant to endorse rebellion and revolution. Some hesitated because they firmly believed, as had Puritans for generations because of their reading of the New Testament, that political power was ordained of God to preserve social order. Consequently, rebellion was akin to sin. For Church of England clergy throughout the colonies, loyalty to the Crown was often a matter of course, since in England the king was deemed the supreme governor of the church. Thus, when the war itself began, many Anglican priests fled—some to Canada, some to the Caribbean, and some back to England.

Disarray among many of the diverse religious bodies that had found a home in the colonies mirrored the political unsettledness brought by war. Many congregations were left without pastors, some for a time and some for several years. In North Carolina, for example, virtually no former Church of England parish had pastoral leadership when the war ended. Any group that had organizational ties to bodies across the Atlantic had to regroup, for severing political ties nearly always meant severing formal religious ties as well.

For Methodists, the years right after the war provided an opportunity to organize as a separate body distinct from the Church of England, in which its founders remained priests. Gathering in Baltimore, Maryland in 1784 under the leadership of Francis Asbury (1745–1816), representatives set up an organizational structure for the Methodist Episcopal Church, as it was called, that relied on itinerant circuit riders who would travel from place to place preaching and offering pastoral guidance. That mobility meant that the church did not rely on institutions, like church buildings, for its base, but went directly to the people. The remnants of the former Church of England came together under the banner of the Protestant Episcopal Church in 1789. Other Christian groups—the Baptists, Congregationalists, Presbyterians, Lutherans, and various Reformed bodies—had to rethink who they were now that they were operating in a new nation.

The Roman Catholic Church also took the opportunity to fashion an administrative structure that would link together all Catholics in the nation, even though ultimate authority still resided with church leaders in Rome. The war years provided some respite in the anti-Catholic sentiment that was always just beneath the surface in colonial life. Catholics themselves generally supported the cause of independence, and some colonial church leaders had gone to Quebec early in the war in an unsuccessful endeavor to persuade Canadian Catholics to join the move for independence from Britain. In 1789, the year that George Washington became the new nation's first president, John Carroll (1735–1815) was named bishop of Baltimore. He was the first American Catholic to hold that rank. Carroll, whose cousin had signed the Declaration of Independence, was pivotal in recruiting priests, especially in France, to come to the new nation to serve a Catholic population that was growing, thanks largely to immigration.

The move for independence had other religious ramifications. When the first census was conducted in 1790, figures indicated that only about 10 percent of the American people held church membership. That figure does not mean that only one in ten Americans had religious inclinations or participated in religious activities. Because church membership then often denoted a rather rigorous process, many whose lives were strongly influenced by religion never became members. Marginalized people,

> **The Revolution's impact on religion**
> - Many clergy and churches actively supported independence
> - Others, especially Church of England priests, were Loyalists and had to flee
> - The war disrupted religious life, leaving some congregations without pastoral leadership
> - Groups with ties to England, such as Methodists and Episcopalians, had to organize to adjust to the new national environment
> - Many political leaders used religious language and images to talk about the meaning of America and the corporate identity of the new republic

such as African American slaves, were likely excluded as well. But the figure is significant because it suggests that much of the apparatus of religion that we take for granted today—organized congregations, church facilities and buildings, a dazzling array of auxiliary programs and agencies—did not exist. In many cases, the lack of an organized institution simply had to do with the distribution of the population. If people were scattered over a relatively large area, it was unlikely that they would have the resources to organize a church or other religious institution; it was less likely, given the diversity that existed, that they would agree on what form or shape that institution should take and what beliefs it should represent.

At the same time, the use of religious language and images to talk about the meaning of the Revolution and the hopes for the new republic was widespread. Many political leaders, even those disinclined to traditional religious belief, often spoke in almost sacred terms about the new enterprise, for there was a broad sense that God, often denoted as Providence, had guided the independence cause and had called the American nation into being for divine purposes. As one later commentator expressed it, Providence was essential to the "invention" of America as a nation, and a key to the identity that political leaders sought to graft onto a people who had once labeled themselves as being from an individual colony, not one nation.

Many who study this link between nationalism and religion talk about a civil religion, or a religion that exists alongside more traditional forms of religious expression, but one that endows the public experience of the people with a sacred canopy of meaning. Others insist that there are religious aspects to nationalism that are part of our common life, but that they by no means constitute a religion on a par with, say, Christianity, Judaism, or Islam. What is clear is that many political leaders in the newly independent United States drew freely on religious language and religious images to frame their understanding of what the republic was all about. The Declaration of Independence, for example, although primarily the work of the rationalistically inclined Thomas Jefferson, claims that the Creator has endowed all men (and in this case he meant white men, not African Americans, Native Americans, or any women) with certain basic rights.

Figure 4.1 Reverse of the Great Seal of the United States. The Great Seal of the United States shows a providential eye watching over the nation, a key idea of civil religion (Courtesy of the Library of Congress.)

Many of the symbols associated with the new republic also had religious nuances. On the dollar bill, for example, there appears a pyramid with a single, all-seeing eye, suggesting that a beneficent Providence was looking after American interests. The Latin inscription, *novus ordo seclorum* ("new order of the ages"), beneath the pyramid suggests that in the American democratic experiment, the world—or at least the structure of human societies—had a fresh beginning; it was as if there was a new creation altogether, with the fledgling United States at its center. As well, rather quickly some of the battle sites became like places of pilgrimage in medieval European Christianity, though without the expectation of a new miracle to occur. Lexington, Concord, Valley Forge, Yorktown, and others became places where the faithful went to feel or sense the power of what had happened there in giving birth to the nation.

What was significant about this civil religion or this fusion of religious elements with nationalism was how it attempted to provide a single frame of reference for Americans who might have identified with a variety of different religions. Hence it had to draw on common experience, not the particular heritage of Quakers, Baptists, Presbyterians, Catholics, or anyone else. At the same time, this public religion really reflected the lived experience only of middle-class white men. Slavery was still a fact of life in the new nation; slaves were certainly not able to celebrate the right to life, liberty, and the pursuit of happiness. Nor were Native Americans part of the picture. And despite a frequently quoted letter from Abigail Adams to her husband John, a prominent Massachusetts political figure and later the second president of the U.S., in which Abigail urged her husband to insist that women and women's interests not be omitted in the moves the Continental Congress was taking towards independence, women were also outside the orbit of the civil religion of the American revolutionary era. Soon, though, women took advantage of the spirit of liberty to become more assertive in religious affairs.

This blending of religion and nationalism has endured to the present, at some times more effectively providing a sense of overarching meaning to the common life of most Americans than at others. Its genesis in the age of the Revolution adds to the variety within American religious life, for in this case there was an attempt to find sacred meaning in common life apart from organized religious institutions. One could harbor a personal faith or reject it altogether and still share in this civic piety. The most vital way that the age of independence influenced religious diversity in the U.S., however, came in some legal moves designed to assure a greater degree of religious freedom than was the case in most other western nations at the close of the eighteenth century.

Legal moves in the era of independence

Discontent with the idea of having a state church or established religion was widespread when the United States achieved its independence. Although New England Puritan Congregationalists were happy to levy taxes to support their own churches (and grudgingly some others), they strongly opposed the kind of arrangements that the Church of England had in Britain because they thought that those arrangements gave civil power to churches and religious power to the government. Baptists and others who thought that religion was a matter of personal belief that could not be dictated by government were also apprehensive about any legal ties between one religious body and any level of government. Those influenced by Enlightenment rationalism believed that favoring any one religion with legal establishment was absurd, for to them religious views were matters exclusively of private judgment, not the concern of government. As well, as Pennsylvania and several other colonies had already demonstrated, religious diversity did not bring social or political discord; people of different religious persuasions could live in harmony with one another, coming together in the public sphere when there were concerns that affected all people, not just those of one particular religious persuasion.

One of the earliest steps assuring that religious variety and freedom would characterize the new nation came in Virginia. Thomas Jefferson in 1779 first proposed legislation guaranteeing religious freedom, but his political ally James Madison (1751–1836) actually guided the moves leading to the adoption of Virginia's Act for Establishing Religious Freedom in 1786 while Jefferson was serving as American ambassador to France.

Fairly radical for the time, Jefferson's statute moved well beyond the idea of toleration, which implies that one religion could receive favor or endorsement, while others are allowed to exist. Rather, it provided that the state could not compel anyone to be part of any religion by requiring either attendance or financial support. The law also declared that individuals were free to believe or not to believe as they personally saw fit and that one's standing as a citizen had no relationship whatsoever to whether one did or did not have a religious affiliation or identity. In other words, religion was strictly a personal matter of the private sphere, devoid of any direct relationship to one's place in society, the public sphere. As well, every religious group was equal before the law, with none receiving preferential treatment. The Virginia approach reflected the principles of Enlightenment rationalism, but it also assured that religious diversity would flourish.

When delegates framed the U.S. Constitution in Philadelphia in 1787, they were well aware of both the broad discontent among Americans with the English religious establishment and the religious diversity that was constantly expanding in the new nation. Even if they had been inclined to designate a state church, they would have found doing so an impossible challenge, for no single religious group claimed a majority of American citizens as adherents, although if one put all Christian groups together, Christianity would be the dominant tradition. As originally crafted, the U.S. Constitution is virtually devoid of religious language and makes only one explicit reference to religion. Article VI provides that there could be no religious test or requirement for holding federal political office. By not mentioning religion elsewhere and most certainly by not designating any one religion or any single expression of Christianity as an established state church, delegates to the Constitutional convention believed that they had provided for a greater degree of religious liberty than existed in much of the western world and also had taken account of the reality of having a range of religious options.

As the various state conventions debated the merits of the proposed frame of government, it became evident that silence regarding a religious establishment was inadequate. There needed to be explicit prohibition of a religious establishment in order to assure that in the future no religious group could seek to claim special privilege and that the amazing diversity that abounded would continue.

In the first of the ten amendments to the Constitution, the Bill of Rights, those concerns come to the fore. In words (most likely coming from James Madison) whose full meaning remains contested today, the First Amendment specifically prohibited a state church: "Congress shall make no law respecting an establishment of religion or prohibiting the free exercise thereof." In time both clauses—the first prohibiting a religious establishment and

> **Religious liberty and the Constitution**
> - Widespread opposition to religious establishment existed in the new nation
> - No single religious group had a clear majority
> - The Constitution assures that seeking federal public office has no religious requirements
> - The First Amendment prohibits a national religious establishment
> - The First Amendment also assures extensive religious liberty
> - Both clauses stimulated the growth of religious diversity

the second guaranteeing free exercise—took on an importance that the framers did not envision.

At the time, though, the amendment applied only to the federal or national government. In theory, it did not prohibit individual states from giving a place of special privilege to one religion or one religious group. Few were inclined to be as expansive as Virginia, but most refrained from giving sanction to one religious body. Even in the New England states, where tax monies in some cases were still collected to pay salaries of religious teachers (pastors), those provisions were not limited to one group, although dissenters still argued that it was undemocratic, for those who wished to support no group and for those who believed that support should be voluntary even for members, to pay any religious taxes. Not until 1833 in Massachusetts were the last vestiges of this approach dismantled.

What did the First Amendment intend? The familiar phrase of later years, separation of church and state, nowhere appears here or elsewhere in the U.S. Constitution. It stems from a phrase used years later by Thomas Jefferson in a letter written during his presidency to a group of Baptists in Danbury, Connecticut, when he referred to a "wall of separation" between church and state. No one in the early Republic anticipated issues of later ages over whether prayer and devotional Bible reading in public schools, religious displays on public property at holiday time, or vouchers to help defray costs of sending children to private religious schools constituted even an indirect establishment of religion. Nor at the time did anyone ponder whether providing for free exercise extended to practices such as handling serpents in worship or refusing to work at one's employment on a day of the week held sacred by one's religious group. Such issues did arise because the amendment sought to provide basic religious liberty for all.

In the narrowest sense, the amendment meant simply that the United States would never designate a particular religious group as a national religion in the way the English parliament had so designated the Church of England. One implication of that rather direct understanding was that every religion would have equal standing in the eyes of the law; none would be favored over others. Another consequence is that formally affiliating with a religious group was a voluntary matter, an individual choice. In places like England, one was assumed automatically to be affiliated with the state church unless one intentionally sought membership in a different religious group. Also, because membership was voluntary, no one had to belong to a religious group; there could be no legal disabilities such as the loss of the right to vote if one chose not to claim religious membership.

Free exercise in its most basic expression meant that no government agency would tell religious groups or individuals what to believe, what practices to engage in, what kind of structure and organization to have, or, by contrast, what not to believe and do. All of that was left to the group or to the individual. In some ways, the "free exercise" clause was destined to have greater significance for sustaining and nourishing religious diversity than the establishment clause, even if the most well-known court cases of later years concerned establishment.

If religious affiliation was voluntary and if individuals and groups could have final authority over belief and practice, the realm of religion became like a free market, where different groups and their leaders competed with one another to persuade individuals of the benefits of belonging to one group or another. Since the government technically avoided regulation of religion, individuals were free to promote their own personal belief systems or to set up their own religions; if they attracted a following, then a new group would emerge. In this way the amendment opened the door for an explosion of religious experimentation in the early republic that continues to the present. It also gave birth to what was then a new form of religious organization, the denomination—a word that tends to describe an organized, structured religious body that functions like the older established churches, but without the benefits of a formal relationship with government.

Indeed, later generations have often forgotten another reason why the founders had reservations about ties between religion and government. Many believed that giving government power over religion would give it authority in areas that were not at all the legitimate domain of civil rulers. In one sense, then, religion could actually have a corrupting influence on government and detract it from its proper concern for the general welfare of all people. It was far better to leave issues relating to religious belief and practice to religious groups themselves than to mingle them with matters that related to every citizen.

The denominations and the explosion of diversity

Without any legal establishment to help or hinder them, American religious groups in the early decades of the republic had to contend with how a free, competitive market operated. Those who could adapt by framing their ministry in ways more consonant with the democratic impulses of the nation were likely to grow and gain numerical strength. Those that did not stood to be pushed to the religious periphery. There was at least one other way to grow, however, and that was through immigration. Since immigration was basically unregulated by the government, virtually anyone could come to the U.S. and promote their own religious views. And scores did just that.

Looking back, groups that emphasized experience over doctrine, had a flexible structure but with organizational controls, and relied on lay people as much as on clergy—in other words, groups that echoed the democratic spirit of the age—grew much more rapidly than others. Those wedded to Calvinistic teaching seemed to leave too little room for the lived experience and authority of ordinary people, while those tied to autocratic ways of doing things and those that expected leaders to be highly educated receded in importance. The age of the American Revolution was, in the words of historian Nathan Hatch, the age of the "democratization of American Christianity."

No doubt some of the growth of the evangelical bodies resulted from their allowing for greater involvement of women. Although Quakers provided perhaps the most opportunities for colonial women to exert religious leadership, in the years after independence as religion entered the marketplace, thanks to the First Amendment, women readily sought more active roles. In most cases, preaching and other clergy duties remained the reserve of men, but women began to organize auxiliary societies and agencies, especially as the new nation was swept by currents of social reform in the early nineteenth century. As in the colonial period, so too in the early national period: Women greatly outnumbered men when it came to Protestant church membership. There was also a growth in numbers of women religious or nuns who took increasing responsibility for practical ministry to a growing population of Catholic immigrants. As well, records indicate that once the war with Britain had ended and missions to Native Americans began afresh, hundreds of women offered themselves in the effort to bring the Christian message—usually in a Protestant form—to the various tribal peoples who lived within the borders of the new nation.

Other religious stirrings suggested that a republic providing for the free exercise of religion would constantly have fresh expressions of religion emerging, ever adding to its

The democratic spirit and denominations

- The denomination emerged as a distinctive form of religious organization in the revolutionary era
- Denominations that exhibited an evangelical style and a democratic spirit experienced stunning growth after the Revolution
- Religious experimentation flourished in the new nation in groups like the Shakers and others
- Some sought to experiment with restoring American Christian practice to what they thought characterized the New Testament church

Figure 4.2 Shaker Marching Dance. With separate lines for men and women, reflecting their emphasis on strict separation of men and women in all things, Shakers worshipped in a form that entailed Spirit-inspired song and dance (Courtesy of the Library of Congress.)

religious diversity. Roughly two years before military conflict with Britain began, the Englishwoman Ann Lee (1746–1784) and a few of her followers arrived in New York. Ann Lee had developed her own religious vision, based on her association with more radical English Quakers and on direct revelation from God. Lee and her followers, known as Shakers because their worship involved ecstatic dancing, believed that while Christ had come in male form in Jesus, she represented the "second coming" of Christ but in female form. Lee also traced human sin to sexual lust, so she demanded strict separation of the sexes among her followers and required all to be celibate. Living communally and sharing work responsibilities equally between men and women (though tasks tended to be assigned according to traditional gender roles), the Shakers were one of the earliest expressions of religious experimentation to leave a lasting imprint on American religious life after the Revolution. Attractive to many because they granted greater status to women than the culture at large and because their communities assured that all who lived there received the basic necessities of life, Shaker enclaves began to appear in the new nation from northern New England as far south as Kentucky.

The democratic spirit of the revolutionary era spurred other forms of religious experimentation that perhaps were more traditional in their outcome than the Shakers, but strikingly innovative for the time. Some of that innovation stemmed directly from elevating the individual as the final authority when it came to interpreting scripture. Even before the Revolution, in American academic circles a philosophy with roots in Scotland called Common Sense Realism had become fashionable. When applied to reading the Bible, Common Sense Realism decreed that the truth of the biblical text—its meaning—was self-evident as a matter of common sense. It did not require advanced education to read and understand the Bible.

In the early nineteenth century, this passion for an individual understanding of scripture would be one source of a religious movement called Restorationism, which sought to recapture or restore the character of New Testament Christianity on Christian belief and practice, based on the words of scripture understood and interpreted by ordinary people. In time, as we shall see, various groups ranging from the Disciples of Christ and the Churches of Christ to the Church of Jesus Christ of Latter-day Saints (Mormons) emerged from the broader Restorationist movement that profoundly captured the democratic spirit of the era.

The age of American independence was also a time of both political and religious transition in areas controlled by other European powers that would later become part of the United States. In Spain, early eighteenth-century conflict over succession to the throne resulted in a greater consolidation of power in the monarchy which was beginning to threaten the loyalty of colonists in Spanish America to their mother country. In many cases, the Spanish Catholic presence in North America suffered temporary setbacks when religious intrigue in Europe led to the expulsion of the Jesuits from both Spain and Portugal, a move that removed some of the personnel who had ministered in Spanish North America. Nevertheless, new mission efforts in what is now the southwestern United States were launched during the time leading up to the English American revolt against king and parliament, but, as before, the motives were mixed.

Spanish missions were less likely to be tied to permanent colonial settlement than they were to offer a way to protect Spain's claim to control. That was particularly true of missions in Texas, for example, where the perceived threat to Spanish dominance came from the French settlements to the east, along the Mississippi. During the course of the century, Spanish Franciscans planted missions in California that were always a combination of religious, military, and trading ventures, not places where appreciable numbers of Spanish colonists were urged to settle permanently.

In parts of North America once under French control, especially Louisiana, the Roman Catholic tradition also remained dominant. After the English defeated the French for control of Canada, hundreds of French Catholics decided to relocate because they feared repression should the Church of England receive legal establishment in British Canada. Their fear of Anglican dominance was as strong as the fear among New Englanders that the imperial government would be too eager to establish working relationships with French Catholics. Consequently, in 1764 many migrated to Louisiana, to what is now the Cajun belt west of New Orleans. The cultural influence that they layered onto Catholic practice provided an additional degree of religious diversity there. In 1803, when Thomas Jefferson's administration negotiated the Louisiana Purchase with Napoleon's government in France, the U.S. Catholic population suddenly skyrocketed. New dimensions of diversity marked the nation's religious culture.

Key points you need to know

- How evangelicalism challenged the colonial political process in the southeast.
- How and why more religious diversity came to New England late in the colonial period.
- Why the Revolution left much of organized religion in disarray.
- How religious language and images shaped American identity in the new republic.
- The significance of the Virginia Act for Establishing Religious Freedom.
- The meaning of the "establishment clause" and "free exercise clause" of the First Amendment to the U.S. Constitution.
- How "separation of church and state" fostered religious diversity.
- Why the denomination emerged as a distinctive American religious institution.
- What forces promoted religious experimentation in the new nation.

Discussion questions

1. How did religion challenge colonial political authority in the South as independence neared?
2. What stimulated greater religious diversity in the southern colonies and in New England at the time of American independence?
3. What impact did the American Revolution have on religious life?
4. How did religion and nationalism come together to help Americans fashion a new national identity after the Revolution?
5. How did the Revolution affect the religious life of women? of African Americans? of Native Americans?
6. What did the First Amendment mean when it prohibited a national religious establishment and allowed for the free exercise of religion?
7. Why are those issues still matters of controversy?
8. What is a religious denomination? How did the democratic spirit affect the birth and growth of denominations?
9. What kinds of religious experimentation flourished in the new republic?

Further reading

Albanese, Catherine L. *Sons of the Fathers: The Civil Religion of the American Revolution*. Philadelphia: Temple University Press, 1976.

Curry, Thomas J. *The First Freedoms: Church and State in America to the Passage of the First Amendment*. New York: Oxford University Press, 1986.

Gaustad, Edwin S. *Neither King nor Prelate: Religion and the New Nation, 1776–1826*. Grand Rapids, MI: Eerdmans, 1993.

Guyatt, Nicholas. *Providence and the Invention of the United States, 1607–1876*. New York: Cambridge University Press, 2007.

Hanley, Thomas O'Brien. *The American Revolution and Religion*. Washington: Catholic University of America Press, 1971.

Hatch, Nathan O. *The Democratization of American Christianity*. New Haven, CT: Yale University Press, 1989.

Holmes, David L. *The Religion of the Founding Fathers*. Charlottesville, VA: Ash Lawn-Highland, and Ann Arbor, MI: Clements Library of the University of Michigan, 2003.

Hutson, James H., ed. *Religion and the New Republic: Faith in the Founding of America*. Lanham, MD: Rowman and Littlefield, 2000.

Levy, Leonard W. *The Establishment Clause: Religion and the First Amendment*. New York: Macmillan, 1986.

5 Native Americans and African Americans challenge religious life

In this chapter

This chapter begins with a look at the attitudes of English settlers in what became the United States towards the native tribal societies they encountered and towards those they forced to come to North America from Africa as slaves. It then discusses how the evangelical style of Protestant Christianity had a major impact on religious relations between Euro-Americans and both African colonists (whether slave or free) and Native Americans. It also briefly sketches the impact of the Revolution on Native Americans and African Americans. Finally, it examines the emergence of revitalization movements among Native Americans and of separate African American denominations, additional signs of the growing religious diversity in the United States.

Main topics covered

- The broadening of colonial religious life because of the arrival of slaves from Africa and the interaction of English settlers with native peoples
- The interest of many African Americans in evangelical expressions of Protestantism
- The consequences of American independence for Native Americans and African Americans in the new nation
- The efforts of some Native Americans to revitalize tribal religious expressions
- The emergence early in the new republic of African American denominations separate from white-controlled groups

Early English colonists, Native Americans, and African slaves

Neither the English who first came to Virginia nor the various clusters of Puritans who arrived in Massachusetts Bay had as convoluted relationships with the Native American tribal peoples nearby as did the Spanish. The English, for example, generally were disinclined to attempt to conquer the natives, in part because they somewhat reluctantly recognized that they relied on tribal wisdom in terms of knowing the land and what it would produce in order to survive. As well, the English were less committed than the French in trying to organize lasting missionary efforts to convert the Native Americans around them to their own brands of Christianity, although proclaiming the gospel to them was part of their overall design.

In Virginia, the English wavered when it came to how aggressively they should seek to convert the natives. The colony lacked the resources to support missionary work; virtually all time and energy went into building the institutions that would ensure the colony's survival. Hence, for decades little was done to evangelize among the native peoples. At the same time, there was little recognition of the way religion penetrated every aspect of tribal life. When the Society for the Propagation of the Gospel in Foreign Parts (SPG) was founded almost a century after the Jamestown settlement, one of its primary goals was to proclaim the Anglican gospel to the Native Americans—and by then also among African American slaves. However, the agents supported by the SPG often found that ministering among the Anglo colonists was so time consuming that there was little they could do by way of evangelizing among either the indigenous people or the slaves. More sustained efforts to do so in the southern colonies would, for the most part, not come until around the middle of the eighteenth century.

The Puritans in Massachusetts were at first somewhat more zealous in trying to convert the Algonquian tribal peoples who lived near their settlements than were the Anglican colonists to the south. John Eliot (1621–1657), for example, learned the tribal language and translated the Bible into Algonquian in order to be able to teach the Algonquians how to read and to instruct them in the Christian faith. He then organized those who converted into "praying towns" where Christian, rather than native, influence would prevail. Of course, the result would be that those who lived in the "praying towns" would ultimately give up all tribal practices and become like the Puritans. Later in the seventeenth century, as the number of Puritan settlers mushroomed and conflicts both with and among some of the neighboring tribal peoples escalated, these early efforts foundered. Only some missionary endeavors on Martha's Vineyard survived these times of turmoil. Hence in New England, as in Virginia, colonial ministry to native peoples was more an eighteenth-century matter.

In neither case, though, did English colonists regard the indigenous peoples as their peers or equals. Even in the feeble, sporadic efforts to convert Native Americans to Christianity that were the norm for the early years of English colonization, at least part of the rationale for promoting conversion was the belief that if Native Americans became Christians, they would become more "civilized"—a term that really meant they would begin to abandon traditional tribal patterns of life and adopt those that the English saw as the norm. The long-term consequence, as noted before, would be the erosion of the integrity of tribal cultures and the imposition in their place of a European way of life that was in essence completely alien to what native peoples had known and nurtured for centuries.

English relations with Native Americans and slaves
- English colonists tended to be less aggressive than French and Spanish Catholics in seeking converts among Native Americans
- Puritans in Massachusetts were more active than Virginia Anglicans in trying to start missions to Native Americans
- English settlers regarded African slaves as pagans and sometimes as not even human
- English religious and political leaders were hesitant to try to convert African slaves because some thought that Christian baptism would require granting slaves their freedom
- Traditional tribal rites associated with divination and conjure flourished alongside Christian expressions among slaves
- Native American tribal cultures and expressions of African religious life among slaves added to the religious diversity in English colonial America

More perplexing and problematic was how English Protestants, whether Puritan or Anglican, should respond to the religious life of those forced to come to America from Africa as slaves. The first Africans arrived in Virginia in 1619, probably as indentured servants rather than as slaves. But quite quickly, most likely because of the visual difference, Africans were regarded as slaves, not indentured servants who would earn their freedom after a fixed number of years of labor. Just as quickly, the slave trade became a major component of the colonial economy from New England to Virginia, and in the southern colonies especially, reliance on slave labor became central to the plantation system that grew rapidly as the demand for its major agricultural product, tobacco, increased in Europe.

For the most part, English settlers remained content to regard Africans as pagans whose inferior social status was such that even offering them religious instruction was fruitless. Everywhere European colonists misconstrued African tribal religious expression as something other than religious, even as African song and dance—especially the well-known ring shout—somehow spanned tribal barriers and provided some sense of common identity among slaves. Often the response of Anglo settlers was to try to quash such activity, perhaps out of fear that the excitement and frenzy generated in enthusiastic ritual performance could easily get out of control, lead to rebellion, and upset a fragile colonial social order.

Religious reasons also made English people reluctant to seek converts among the slaves. For all Christian groups, despite their differences from each other, when conversions occurred, those who were new to the faith were baptized. Baptism was a rite of passage that signaled movement away from one's former way of thinking and believing into a Christian way of thinking and believing. The issue, for Anglo colonists, had to do with the consequences of baptism. Among the early English colonists, whether Anglican or Puritan, baptism had a symbolic link to freedom. The baptized were, in a sense, free from the negative effects of sin or misguided behavior. But did it mean that they were also free in a more absolute sense? That is, did baptism mean that African slave converts were no longer slaves once baptized, but free and thus equal to their owners/oppressors in societal terms? At the same time, baptism may well have had an appeal to African Americans, who found in the practice echoes of African water rituals.

One way to sidestep this contentious and complicated issue emerged in the ministry of the Anglican Francis Le Jau (1655–1717) in South Carolina early in the eighteenth century. By 1700, there were more slaves in colonial South Carolina than there were colonists of European stock, so the white fear of slave revolt was vivid and concern about the status of baptized slaves very real. Le Jau therefore insisted that slave converts make a public statement that they would not use their Christian baptism as an occasion to demand their freedom from the bonds of slavery. Gradually, in codes regulating slavery, Southern colonial legislative assemblies sought to resolve the dilemma by including provisions stating directly that conversion and baptism did not alter the legal status of a slave. But for the most part, Christians of every stripe, in the early years of the English colonies, tended to refrain from serious efforts to secure slave converts, despite the insistence of some that Christian slaves would labor more diligently than others because their toil was a divine calling. It is also clear that Christian slaves consistently understood their faith to be a challenge to the slave system itself, not a device to make slaves docile and content.

At the same time, regardless of whether Christians presented a message of gospel obedience to slaves, practices coming from the African tribal past continued to endow life with meaning for slaves, despite the ravages to African American culture brought by slavery. Life experiences such as childbirth, marriage, and death were marked by traditional tribal rites, even though, for example, marriage among slaves lacked legal standing in the colonies. Birth and burial especially were celebrated, yet slave owners and masters repeatedly failed to see the religious dimensions of these vital rites and treated them as exhibitions of exuberant behavior or custom.

Divination and conjure, ways of seeing spiritual power in natural phenomena and of invoking spiritual forces through practices like incantation, also had deep African roots. Both continued to inform African American life, adding to the world of meaning on which slaves drew to gain some sense of identity, when the society around them attempted to deny that meaning, for divination and conjure brought the realm of supernatural power into daily life in a way abstract doctrine never could. In many cases, even after slaves gave some affirmation to Christianity, traditional practice continued. Tribal heritage and Christianity merged together to fashion a slave spiritual expression that was, in essence, a religion of its own, not completely identical with either the tribal religious tradition or Christianity. As such, it represented another dimension of diversity within the larger religious culture of the English colonies and then of the fledgling United States. It was a greater challenge for those Africans whose religious identity came from Islam actually to engage in practices associated with that tradition. In most cases, it proved impossible for slaves to transmit Islam from one generation to the next, for there was no reinforcement from the larger culture that would help lend credibility and support to Islamic belief and practice.

The presence of Native American tribal peoples, and then of Africans, whether slave or free, added to the religious mix that marked early colonial life in the English colonies. Anglicans may in theory have believed that they were the only authentic expression of Christianity; Puritans themselves had diverse ideas about what made up authentic Christianity. Yet interaction with native and African tribal religious expression had an impact on all forms for Christian expression, sometimes enriching spiritual sensibility and sometimes by showing an alternative way of being religious. That reciprocal impact would become more pronounced when European settlers and Africans would worship together or hear dynamic preaching—sometimes by slave exhorters—as the evangelical movement gained momentum. The interaction changed and challenged both European Americans and African Americans. Examples of that interplay also marked the Catholic experience in Florida and Louisiana, where some Africans identified with the religion of the Spanish and French colonial powers. Indeed, some Catholic parishes were more likely to record African American baptisms and even marriages than most Protestant churches in areas controlled by England.

Evangelical missionary efforts among African Americans and Native Americans

Euro-Americans were not the only ones who found in colonial evangelicalism a religious style that brought fresh meaning to their lives when revivals and religious awakening spread through the colonies in the middle third of the eighteenth century. If most Christian groups in the English colonies had waffled when it came to seeking converts among those they forced into slavery, the evangelical stirrings of the eighteenth century reached deeply into the slave communities and in time, particularly in cities where there was a free African American population, gave birth to congregations and then denominations that were predominantly African American. Several features of the evangelical movement help explain why this style resonated with the lived experience of African Americans, whether slave or free. Because evangelically inclined preachers were often itinerants who moved from place to place, they did not need church buildings or other formal apparatus like that in order to proclaim their understanding of the gospel. That meant, for example, that evangelical preachers were more inclined than settled pastors to preach to slaves on southern plantations. Related to this mobility is the evangelical emphasis on a personal experience of conversion. That experience gave one the credentials to preach, not formal education or other learning. Up until the evangelical awakenings, most colonial religious groups had relied on what was called a "learned clergy" or pastors and preachers who were formally educated in theology, the biblical languages of Hebrew and Greek, and other related subjects. After all, if the clergy were to interpret scripture correctly, they needed proper training to understand the Bible. For many evangelicals, it was what one felt in one's heart—one's personal experience of conversion—not what one knew in one's mind that enabled one to preach powerfully and sincerely. Many slaves, for example, who were moved to conversion through the preaching of an itinerant or even perhaps of a settled pastor like the Presbyterian Samuel Davies (1723–1761) in Hanover county, Virginia, themselves became preachers because they felt the power of God's spirit within. It did not matter whether they could read or write; they had something more spiritually potent than education, the assurance that came when they accepted the gift of God's grace.

African tribal religious expression, as noted earlier, centered on song and dance, on enthusiastic exercises that inspired emotional response. Evangelical preaching evoked a similar reaction. So there was a congruence between the evangelical and tribal ways of expressing religion. One result was the emergence among southern African American slaves of what has become known as the "invisible institution" or the gatherings in forest arbors after labor ended, and without white owners or overseers present, where slaves would preach and pray, sing and dance, in a dynamic fusion of evangelical and tribal practices. As well, particularly dynamic African American evangelical preachers often gained a hearing among white audiences eager for the powerful presence of spiritual energy. Little wonder, then, that evangelical bodies such as the Methodists and Baptists quickly made greater headway in bringing African Americans into the Christian fold than had Anglicans or other religious groups, albeit with a unique style that blended things tribal and things Christian. Little wonder, too, that the first independent African American congregations, when they formed, were Baptist and Methodist in orientation. Slave Christianity was in some ways an extraordinary expression of religious diversity because of how it joined together aspects of the tribal heritage with features of Protestant Christianity.

Not all Euro-American Christians applauded evangelical inroads among the African American population, particularly among slaves. From the outset, concern centered on whether religious frenzy could become transformed into revolt against white control and whether slave preachers, even though they might seem to be proclaiming the gospel, were not incendiaries promoting uprisings against white masters. After all, the liberty that came with the gospel had larger implications for freedom. Just as some Euro-American women found the evangelical style empowering because it gave them a link to a supernatural realm that transcended gender roles, so some African American slaves found release and a powerful spiritual freedom in the gospel that had broader implications. Indeed, the fear of revolt among religiously enthusiastic slaves occasionally proved true. Most of the attempts at slave rebellion either in the English colonies or in the antebellum United States had religious overtones, inspired by dynamic African American slave preachers.

Some whites remained uncertain about whether African Americans who became Christians could still be held as slaves, although, as noted, colonial slave codes sought to resolve that dilemma by insisting that conversion and even baptism did not alter one's slave status. Others welcomed evangelizing efforts, convinced that slaves who accepted the gospel message would in turn accept their situation in this life, be more inclined to obey their masters and overseers, work more diligently because their labor would yield future heavenly reward, and therefore be less likely to revolt. But as some Euro-American evangelicals sanctioned slavery and used the gospel to manipulate slaves into submission, they were themselves distorting the gospel message and compromising their own religion. Looking back, it seems clear that they were using Christianity to justify an inhumane racism and thereby corrupting the Christian message.

Some evangelicals and a few others also engaged in mission work among indigenous tribal peoples in areas controlled by the English. But everywhere Europeans settled—whether in territories claimed by the Spanish, the French, or the English—more significant in the long run was the encroachment on tribal lands, for much of tribal culture was intimately linked to the land. So every movement of tribal peoples from ancestral lands whittled away at the integrity of tribal society with its deep religious dimension. As European powers sought alliances with tribal peoples in their own contests for colonial empire, those alliances also undermined the fabric of native life. These arrangements not only pitted tribe against tribe, but also lured native peoples into thinking that the colonial power they favored would help assure the survival of tribal life.

Those in areas under English control who attempted to form missions among various tribes were less ambivalent about accepting converts among Native Americans than they were about accepting African American slave converts. Among the more sustained efforts were those of the Congregationalists who received some support from the Society in

Evangelicals, African Americans, and Native Americans
- Evangelicalism, with its emphasis on experience and emotional expression, resonated with aspects of African tribal religiosity
- African Americans drawn to Christianity were more attracted to evangelicalism than to other styles
- The combination of evangelicalism with tribal religiosity produced a unique African American Christianity centered around the "invisible institution"
- Some whites feared that evangelicalism would encourage slaves to rebel; others thought that it would produce "better" slaves who would now be obedient in hopes of gaining heavenly reward
- Moravians and Congregationalists also had missions to Native American tribal groups that brought educational opportunities as much as religious conversion to those interested

Scotland for Promoting Christian Knowledge and those of German Moravians. The former concentrated their labors in areas of western New England and New York; among the better known in the eighteenth century is David Brainerd (1718–1747), mostly because he died while at the home of the renowned Jonathan Edwards, who later published Brainerd's diary, which became something of a spiritual classic inspiring others to work in religious and humanitarian ways among Native Americans. Moravians had missions that stretched from Pennsylvania into what is now Ohio and, by the early nineteenth century, down along the Appalachian mountain chain as far south as Tennessee and Georgia. In many cases, the missions assisted tribal people in learning how to deal with Europeans when it came to business and trade. That effort often involved teaching an oral people how to use a written language. Most such missions had to deal with prejudice on the part of European settlers who remained ignorant of the vitality of indigenous culture and regarded native peoples as hindrances to European colonial expansion, not as fellow members of a larger human community. Hence, when there was conflict over control of land, or war among European powers, the missions suffered. When the American move towards independence from England led to a military confrontation that lasted for more than half a decade, the vast majority of missions folded. Few long-term converts to a European form of Christianity remained, as virtually none of the missions attempted to train natives as religious leaders who could then serve as bridges between two religious and cultural worlds.

We are mistaken if we overlook how profoundly even this interaction contributed to the religious diversity in the English colonies. The tribal cultures always stood in contrast to European ways of life, but the religious culture of European colonists took shape in America with native culture as a backdrop. At times simply because they were "other" or different, tribal religious ways became a way by which Europeans could define their own styles. They might not be able to explain fine points of Christian doctrine and practice, but they could at least say they were not the same as the tribal peoples, native or African. Unfortunately, too often Europeans assumed that their ways were, by definition, superior, and anything that was different—anything that was "other" than European—was thus inferior. That posture also contributed to the erosion of Native American tribal life wherever Europeans settled, for it was always seen as less worthy.

Revolution and revitalization

The Revolutionary War years disrupted whatever efforts existed in English America to evangelize among Native American societies. After hostilities with Britain ended and renewed attempts at missions among Native Americans got underway, other factors undermined both the missions and the integrity of Native American culture, with all of its deep religious undertones. Once American independence was secure, Euro-Americans began rather quickly to move further westward, crossing over that line set in 1763 when Britain, in its efforts to have peaceful relations especially with tribes formerly allied with the French, restricted settlement to areas east of that line, which meant essentially east of the Appalachian mountain chain.

As Americans moved westward, their passion for land continued to strain relations between them and tribal peoples; they just did not appreciate how Native American culture was entwined with the land. Throughout the new nation, tribal life generally entered a time of gradual disintegration in terms of being able to sustain tradition and thus the religious dimensions of tribal identity. In turn, by the early nineteenth century, some efforts attempted to revitalize or give new life and energy to traditional native ways. Among the most well known is that associated with Handsome Lake (1735–1815) from the Seneca tribe of the Iroquois in what is now central New York, but in an area west of that line separating colonists from native peoples. In 1799, Handsome Lake reported having several visionary experiences that empowered him to call for a restoration of traditional Iroquois ways by abandoning some social practices introduced by the French and English. Among them were the use of alcohol and engaging in any activity that brought evil to individuals, or particularly to the tribe. Among some of the Iroquois, Handsome Lake's teaching became the major means by which pre-conquest traditions survived. Handsome Lake's preaching is but one example of yet another expression of diversity, for it represented an effort to maintain but update Native American tradition—threatened with extinction because of its association with Christianity and the cultures of the colonial conquerors.

As well, by the opening decades of the nineteenth century, in many areas, an almost religious sense of American destiny was feeding into calls to relocate Native American peoples to territories further west in order to allow Euro-Americans access to the land occupied by tribal societies. In the southern United States, the increasing hostility between the indigenous peoples and those eager to move in and take over more land ultimately led to the policy adopted during the presidency of Andrew Jackson that required all tribal people to embark in 1838 on what is called the "trail of tears" and relocate to reservations in the Oklahoma Territory. There, with nothing familiar at hand and ancestral land far distant, tribes began a daunting effort to rebuild their lives as a people and to sustain their traditions against great odds. But even before this forced relocation got underway, however, there was a sign of resistance in another revitalization movement, this one among the Cherokee. In 1811–1812, at least one Cherokee prophet, Tsali (also called "Charlie"), claimed that the Great Spirit had allowed the declining fortunes of the Cherokee to occur because they had abandoned the age-old religious traditions of their people. This revitalization effort called upon the Cherokee to give up everything that they had acquired or learned from the Euro-Americans, from use of plows in cultivating crops to books and other printed material. and again participate in the traditional ritual dances, sometimes called a Cherokee "ghost dance." Once they returned to the old rituals, they could anticipate a specific apocalyptic event, a hailstorm, that would not only destroy the Euro-American conquerors but also restore to its former abundance the wildlife that was in increasingly short supply. Although

> ### Revitalization and new calls for freedom
> - Handsome Lake led an effort to revitalize Native American tribal culture and religion among the Iroquois
> - Among the Cherokee in the south, early in the nineteenth century a different sort of revitalization movement centered around the "ghost dance" (which later took different forms among other tribal peoples)
> - Both movements called for a rejection of all aspects of the white culture
> - African Americans linked the revolutionary call for freedom to a desire to end slavery in the "invisible institution"
> - In the northern states, African Americans also began to form their own denominations, separate from white groups

there was widespread interest in this Native American expression of diversity, when the predicted defeat of the invaders did not transpire, the revitalization movement lost its momentum, and the devastation of removal in 1838, in which at least 4,000 Cherokee lost their lives, effectively ended the hope for revitalization and renewal.

Among African American slaves, the age of independence highlighted the disparity between the rhetoric of freedom and equality and the brutality of the slave system. By the time of the Revolution, evangelical expressions of Protestant Christianity had made such inroads into slave culture that, even with war-time disruption of ministry to slaves, the "invisible institution" assured that slave religion would continue to provide an alternative to the diluted Christianity of slave owners. One need think only of the spirituals beginning to take root in slave culture to see how African Americans had made the Christian message their own, for the spirituals were calls to freedom as much as they were folk representations of biblical stories.

Spirituals represented one way in which African Americans combined the Christian message with forms familiar from the tribal cultures left behind in Africa. Song was central to much tribal ritual celebration; here was an adaptation of song to a different environment. Slaves might sing what came to be familiar spirituals as they labored and also as they gathered in brush arbors at night. The rhythm as well as the content provided a bridge between what was in the collective unconscious and what was the lived reality of existence under slavery. The yearning for freedom always remained at their core. Over generations, the spirituals provided one source for the emergence of the blues as a distinctive genre of American music even as they continued to fuse biblical messages with the realities of daily life.

The spirituals first emerged primarily among slaves on plantations, but another concrete way African Americans acted on the rhetoric of freedom and equality came more among free blacks in the north, when they formed separate denominations that were independent of white control. These new denominations in turn added to the religious variety that was already a hallmark of the American nation. Prior to their formation,

> **One well-known spiritual powerfully captures both the cry for freedom as well as the heart of a biblical story:**
>
> When Israel was in Egypt's land—
> Let my people go—
> Oppressed so hard they could not stand—
> Let my people go.
> Go down, Moses, way down in Egypt's land.
> Tell old Pharaoh
> To let my people go.
>
> On the surface, the spiritual retells the saga of the ancient Israelites who yearned to leave the bondage of slavery in Egypt under the leadership of Moses. But few slaves, if any, would not have also heard these words as calling for an end to the slave system that existed in the United States.

most African Americans who attended religious services or who were themselves church members were part of biracial congregations, whether slave or free and whether in the north or in the south. In at least one case, a free African American became a pastor in a predominantly white denomination. In 1785 Lemuel Haynes (1753–1834) most likely became the first African American ordained as clergy when the Congregationalists granted him ministerial standing. He went on to serve as a pastor in Massachusetts for around three decades, until even there mounting racial prejudice forced him into retirement.

The move to form separate denominations likewise stemmed from racial prejudice. One of the more well-known episodes occurred around 1787 in St. George's Methodist Episcopal Church in Philadelphia, when some African American worshipers were forced while praying to move from a section of the church supposedly reserved for whites to an area set aside for blacks. As a result, Richard Allen (1760–1831), a former slave and longtime Methodist exhorter then active at St. George's, spearheaded the formation of a separate congregation by 1793, now known as "Mother" Bethel African Methodist Episcopal Church. Although for some years the white congregation from which Bethel emerged sought to control its affairs, court action in 1816 gave the African American members of Bethel that right. By then a new denomination was already in the making. Similar moves in other cities were also underway, with New York becoming the center for the developing African Methodist Episcopal Zion Church. Independent African American Baptist congregations formed in New York, in other northern urban centers such as Boston and Philadelphia, and even in a few places in the South, where law and custom made organizing an independent congregation much more difficult. Among the earliest independent African American Baptist congregations in the south are Silver Bluff in South Carolina, not far from Augusta, Georgia, and a church in Savannah. In some areas there were also

Figure 5.1 Mother Bethel AME church. Mother Bethel AME church represents one of the earliest congregations formed by African Americans free from white control or dominance (Courtesy Mother Bethel African Methodist Episcopal Church collection.)

congregations among Episcopalians and Roman Catholics that were predominantly African American, although these never coalesced into independent denominations in the way many of those emerging from the Methodist and Baptist traditions did.

In terms of formal beliefs and organization, African American Baptist and Methodist denominations generally echoed their parent bodies. Both clusters, for example, continued to place strong emphasis on personal religious experience, on a style of religion that was felt, more than one that was argued in terms of theological doctrine and formal belief. The African Methodist Episcopal (AME) Church and the African Methodist Episcopal Zion Church, like white Methodism, relied on a structure that saw bishops overseeing denominational organization, and pastors who would move about to serve different congregations following annual meetings. The new denominations also formed auxiliary agencies that reflected the ways in which the white denominations that gave them birth organized for ministry. Rather quickly, for example, these fledgling denominations and congregations set up mission boards, Sunday schools, and in some cases even publishing houses. Soon they were dispatching preachers elsewhere, including missionaries who went to Africa to proclaim the gospel there. In some cases women, although denied ordination, traveled extensively, preaching and exhorting as dedicated lay persons. Among the first and perhaps better-known is Jarena Lee (1783–?), an associate of Richard Allen who was a popular and widely traveled AME preacher. As with other denominations, women outnumbered men as formal members in the new African American bodies, and they often provided the volunteer labor that kept local congregations flourishing and growing.

The separate denominations, concentrated in the north in the antebellum period, also became key institutions providing opportunities for leadership for African Americans in a nation where racial inequality was the norm. Popular practice continued to blend aspects of tribal religiosity, such as conjure, with Christian affirmation. As well, the African American clergy often combined the role of preacher and pastor with that of the conjurer and the shaman whose extraordinary abilities made him an adept at making a realm of supernatural power real and accessible. Yet the denominations attracted some of the most dynamic and gifted African American men into the ranks of the clergy. Generations later, African American churches and their pastors would draw on this heritage of leadership and charisma to launch and guide the civil rights movement of the twentieth century.

With some Native Americans attempting to revitalize tribal religious expressions, albeit in modified form, and African Americans sensing a religious cry for freedom in their amalgamation of African tribal and European Christian notions, dimensions of diversity cascaded through American religious life even on the margins. The emergence of separate, independent African American religious groups only added to them. They had their roots in the evangelical traditions, such as the Baptists and Methodists, that were growing most rapidly everywhere in the years immediately after the war for independence. The era of independence highlighted the ever-expanding diversity of America in ways that went well beyond what the First Amendment envisioned. When the nineteenth century began, that diversity would grow by leaps and bounds.

Key points you need to know

- The English, whether Anglican or Puritan, were not very successful at evangelizing among native tribal peoples.
- Tribal religions represent another aspect of colonial diversity.
- More diversity came when African slaves brought their own tribal religious expressions to the New World.
- How evangelicalism resonated with African American tribal religiosity and blended with it to create a distinctive African American religious style.
- The consequences of the American Revolution for Native American tribal life and African American religious life.
- The nature or revitalization movements and their impact on Native American tribal societies.
- The significance of the founding of independent African American denominations.

Discussion questions

1. Why were English colonists ambivalent about evangelizing among Native Americans and Africans who were slaves?
2. Why did the evangelical style fit so well with the religious experience of African Americans?
3. What was the nature of English colonial efforts to convert Native Americans to Christianity?
4. What is a revitalization movement? What efforts were made to revitalize Native American religious life in the early republic?
5. What led to the founding of independent denominations among African Americans? How were they similar to and yet different from the white denominations from which they emerged?

Further reading

Bowden, Henry Warner. *American Indians and Christian Missions: Studies in Cultural Conflict*. Chicago: University of Chicago Press, 1981.

Mathews, Donald G. *Religion in the Old South*. Chicago: University of Chicago Press, 1977.

McLoughlin, William G., with Walter H. Conser and Virginia Duffy McLoughlin. *The Cherokee Ghost Dance: Essays on the Southeastern Indians, 1789–1861*. Macon, GA: Mercer University Press, 1984.

Melton, J. Gordon. *A Will to Choose: The Origins of African American Methodism*. Lanham, MD: Rowman and Littlefield, 2007.

Mitchell, Henry H. *Black Church Beginnings: The Long-Hidden Realities of the First Years*. Grand Rapids, MI: Eerdmans, 2004.

Raboteau, Albert J. *Canaan Land: A Religious History of African Americans*. New York: Oxford University Press, 2001.

——. *Slave Religion: The "Invisible Institution" in the Antebellum South*. New York: Oxford University Press, 1978.

Sobel, Mechal. *Trabelin' On: The Slave Journey to an Afro-Baptist Faith*. Westport, CT: Greenwood, 1979.

Wheeler, Rachel. *To Live Upon Hope: Mohicans and Missionaries in the Eighteenth-Century Northeast*. Ithaca, NY: Cornell University Press, 2008.

6 *Evangelical America*

In this chapter

This chapter explores the diversity prevailing as evangelical Protestantism provided a framework of unity to much of American religious life. It looks at the frontier camp meeting and its impact in making revivalism an ongoing feature of American culture. It then examines how the camp meeting style influenced religion in northern urban centers. Next it looks at how those groups most influenced by evangelicalism and revivalism experienced rapid growth in antebellum America. Finally, it discusses various movements promoting social reform, particularly the abolition of slavery.

Main topics covered

- The rise of the camp meeting on the southern frontier and how it helped diverse evangelical forms of Protestantism to become dominant
- How northern Protestants adapted camp meeting methods for an emerging urban culture
- Why denominations closely identified with revivalism grew quickly in antebellum America, gradually undermining the Calvinist thought that had shaped much of earlier American Protestantism
- The ways in which broad-based efforts at social reform gave a veneer of unity and common purpose to the diverse denominations

Evangelicalism's harvest time: the frontier camp meeting

After independence, people began to cross the Appalachians to what was then the western frontier of Kentucky and Tennessee, facing conditions in many ways similar to those that the first Europeans coming to America encountered. There were no towns or villages, no institutions like churches to serve the people, and often no neighbors near at hand to provide social contact and a sense of community. Religious people coming into the area noted the rawness of life and hoped that a renewed interest in religion would assure the eternal destiny of those brought into its orbit and bring civility to the frontier. The agency that helped do both was the camp meeting.

When and where the first camp meeting occurred is lost to history. Presbyterian pastor James McGready (c.1758–1817), as early as 1797, was urging his struggling congregation in Logan County, Kentucky, to pray for a revival of religion. In August 1801 what became a model for other camp meetings developed at Cane Ridge in north central Kentucky, when hundreds came together from miles around for an extended period of preaching and socializing before they returned to harvest their crops. The intense religious fervor at Cane Ridge echoed earlier Scottish gatherings that brought people together for a time of soul searching prior to celebration of the Lord's Supper or Communion; it also had roots in the enthusiasm marking the eighteenth-century revivals known as the Great Awakening.

Ideally suited to frontier conditions, the camp meetings' results stunned even the most ardent travelling evangelists—whether Baptist, Methodist, or Presbyterian—who regularly helped organize them and who went from one to another stirring religious fires within people often starved of any human interaction. Methodist preacher Peter Cartwright (1785–1872) recorded in his diary powerful descriptions of the camp meetings. Under the spell of dramatic preaching, sometimes with evangelists from different denominations speaking from different preacher's stands at the same time, throngs of men and women both black and white (though often seated or gathered separately) would be seized by spiritual forces beyond their control, an example of what analysts call ecstatic religious experience. Cartwright wrote, for example, about

Figure 6.1 Cane Ridge meetinghouse. This meetinghouse commemorates the site of one of the first and most famous frontier camp meetings, held in Cane Ridge, Kentucky (Courtesy of www.TheRestorationMovement.com.)

a barking exercise when the repentant would sound like dogs while in the throes of conversion; he also described a jerking exercise when the arms, legs, and sometimes entire bodies of those possessed by divine power would thrash about.

In tracts of land roughly cleared of trees and brush to accommodate the crowds, an area in front of the preacher's stands would be set apart where those most fervently scrutinizing their sinful lives could come and await spiritual power to take control of their minds and bodies. Called "the pen" because of the way the space was marked off, the area for a time became holy ground, with the movement of people into that sacred turf foreshadowing the altar call of later evangelism. At times, preachers from different denominations vigorously debated with each other over particular doctrines and practices, a sign of the diversity always in the background. When all the activity was combined, the camp meeting was both an extraordinary religious phenomenon and a kind of popular entertainment, with the socializing dimension lending credence to detractors' observations that at camp meetings as many souls were conceived as were saved.

In one sense, the frontier camp meetings were a corporate rite of initiation or rite of passage from one identity to another for those whose lives underwent transformation. Many years ago, the Belgian anthropologist Arnold van Gennep suggested that such rites have three clearly discernible stages. The first, separation, comes when an old identity is left behind. In the camp meeting, separation occurred quite literally when one moved physically from where one lived to the camp meeting ground, space transformed from wilderness woods to holy ground for the duration of the meeting.

Peter Cartwright describes a camp meeting

In his autobiography published in 1856, Methodist evangelist Peter Cartwright wrote about what happened at one camp meeting:

> Just in the midst of our controversies on the subject of the powerful exercises among the people under preaching, a new exercise broke out among us called the *jerks*, which was overwhelming in its effects on the bodies and minds of the people. No matter whether they were saints or sinners, they would be taken under a warm song or sermon, and seized with a convulsive jerking all over, which they could not by any possibility avoid, and the more they resisted the more they jerked ... The first jerk or so, you would see [the young ladies'] fine bonnets, caps, and combs fly; and so sudden would be the jerking of the head that their long loose hair would crack almost as loud as a wagoner's whip.

From William G. McLoughlin, ed., *The American Evangelicals, 1800–1900* (New York: Harper & Row, 1968), 49.

Van Gennep identified a second stage that followed called liminality. An "in between" moment, liminality in the camp meeting came most forcefully when those under conviction moved to the pen (another visible way of leaving behind an old self) and were perhaps seized by the jerking or barking exercise, behavior in which one would not ordinarily engage. Casting aside uncivilized, irreligious selves, those converted emerged with new identities, a new life in Christ, as they returned home after the camp meeting to resume their daily lives. This third and final stage of a rite of passage or initiation Van Gennep called reintegration; one returns to the mundane tasks of daily life, integrating one's new identity with the tasks and responsibilities there before, but with a new perspective.

From another vantage point, camp meetings promoted a facade of unity amid the diversity represented by the different denominational backgrounds of the preachers and evangelists. Many ended with all attending sharing in a celebration of the Lord's Supper or Holy Communion, another connection to Scottish religious festivals in the heritage of those of Scots-Irish ancestry now living on the American frontier. An additional dimension of unity came in the emphasis camp meetings placed on personal religious experience, echoing the revivals associated with Jonathan Edwards and George Whitefield before the American Revolution. The long-term result was that an evangelical style, a religious style stressing inner experience, became the norm among most American Protestants, regardless of differences in their theological and historical backgrounds.

The Calvinist idea that God alone determined who would receive salvation faded as more and more saw the religious life as a choice made by individuals in response to the gracious work of God. At the camp meetings, too, religious passion temporarily eclipsed the social distinctions and other cultural patterns that divided people. Rich and poor, educated and illiterate, black and white, male and female—all came together during that sacred time when the annual camp meeting occurred, though when people returned home, what divided and separated resurfaced. The camp meetings thus became a symbol of evangelical unity, even though they had many dimensions.

For some, the enthusiasm and the ecstasy of the camp meeting recalled the outpouring of the Spirit marking the biblical account of the Day of Pentecost described in the second chapter of the New Testament book of Acts. As we shall see, this view combined with the democratic spirit and the principles of Common Sense Realism, described earlier, to feed the hunger for American Christians to abandon denominational structures that promoted division and diversity and come together as one religious people who had recaptured and restored the essence of New Testament Christianity.

Even in areas of the new nation far from the frontier both geographically and spiritually, the opening years of the nineteenth century generated a concern for religious renewal. In New England, where the Great Awakening of the eighteenth century had waxed strongly, some believed that revival and renewal were again needed. Churches and pastors might abound, but religious vitality had waned, often replaced by a stark rationalism influenced by both the Enlightenment and the attacks on faith marking the extreme of the French Revolution. Infidelity, literally a lack of faith, appeared on the rise. Among those who longed for renewal was the pastor, theologian, and educator Timothy Dwight (1752–1817), whose sermons preached primarily to students at Yale College where he was president resulted in many coming to conversion and then carrying the banner of revival with them as pastors and preachers intent on combating infidelity in whatever form it took.

As interest in revival of religious commitment grew in more established areas of the early republic and camp meetings brought religious zeal to the frontier, some linked the surge in faith to democratic ideals, becoming convinced that, when considered together, American religion and public life were moving towards what Christians called the millennium, that mythic time when Christ would return to usher in God's final reign. Others were content to believe that a "second" Great Awakening, akin to that of the eighteenth century, was transforming American society. In either case, when evangelists adapted the tools of the camp meeting for the towns and factory villages developing along the western frontier in the north, not only would new expressions of religion mushroom, but also the evangelical style would become entrenched as a framework for a common religious expression among American Protestants.

Revivalism cements the evangelical style on American Protestantism

Although camp meetings began on the southern frontier, many of the techniques that made them successful proved adaptable to other contexts. Especially important was the transformation that came when Charles Grandison Finney (1792–1875) refitted much of the camp meeting apparatus for use in reinvigorating the religious life of more recently settled areas in central and western New York. There were many who became itinerant revivalists, but Finney was perhaps the most well known, and in many ways his own life illustrates the dynamics beginning to cement the evangelical style on American Protestantism. Born in Connecticut, Finney started out as a schoolteacher in New York and New Jersey and then embarked upon the study of law while living in Adams, NY. Following a dramatic conversion in 1821 that he described as being overcome by "wave upon wave of liquid love," Finney abandoned legal pursuits to become an evangelist and pastor. Even so, the fluidity prevailing among Protestant denominations echoed in Finney's life. Ordained as a Presbyterian, Finney served both Presbyterian and Congregationalist churches and eventually became president of Oberlin College in Ohio, which then had Congregationalist ties. Although both groups had roots in different strains of Calvinism, Finney was anything but a Calvinist when it came to his own religious position. His conversion experience convinced him that ideas of election and predestination were flawed and that humans were active agents in accepting the grace offered by God in Christ.

That view undergirded his approach to religious revivals, beginning in 1830–1831 in Rochester, NY, then an emerging urban center. Like many nearby towns and villages, Rochester experienced dramatic population growth after the Erie Canal opened in 1825 and made central New York a major area moving people and products from east to west. Unlike the evangelists of the eighteenth-century Great Awakening, Finney organized his revivals to span several weeks or more, with daily preaching services and home-based prayer meetings. These "protracted meetings" paralleled camp meetings in terms of duration. Finney also set apart what he called the "anxious bench" where those under conviction could pray and examine their souls, an urban adaptation of the pen in front of the preacher's stand at a camp meeting. Finney's revivals, again like the camp meetings, challenged traditional gender roles, for women might pray aloud, minister to other women in the throes of conversion, or even mobilize to support the revival through prayer meetings and Bible study—some of which the evangelist's wife led. Finney called these techniques "new measures" in revivalism, but most stemmed from the frontier camp meetings. Many remain central to revivalism in the twenty-first century. As revivals spread through central New York, not all led by Finney but many following his model, the region became known as the "burned-over district" to denote how the fires of religious enthusiasm burned so brightly. There would be other consequences of that fervor as well.

Finney's reputation took him to major northern cities such as Boston and New York, where special auditoriums were constructed for his protracted meetings. Often criticized by settled pastors still wedded to the idea of a learned clergy and caught up

---

How Charles Grandison Finney viewed revivals

Although many people believed that genuine revivals resulted from divine intervention, Charles G. Finney, who developed "new measures" to promote revivalism, startled many when he wrote in 1835 in his handbook or series of lectures on how to conduct revivals, that:

> A revival is not a miracle, nor dependent on a miracle, in any sense. It is purely a philosophical result of the right use of the constituted means—as much so as any other effect produced by the application of means ... [M]eans will not produce a revival, we all know, without the blessing of God. No more will grain, when it is sown, produce a crop without the blessing of God. It is impossible for us to say that there is not as direct an influence or agency from God, to produce a crop of grain, as there is to produce a revival ... A revival is as naturally a result of the use of the appropriate means as a crop is of the use of its appropriate means.

Charles G. Finney, *Revival Lectures* (Old Tappan, NJ: Fleming H. Revell, n.d.

in a modified Calvinist ideology, Finney dismissed attacks by pointing to the success of his approach. He went so far as to claim, in a handbook based on lectures about how to organize a revival, that revivals were the result of human effort and mastery of the right techniques, not the miraculous work of God mysteriously stirring human religious sensibilities, as Jonathan Edwards had claimed during the Great Awakening. Finney and some of his associates—particularly Asa Mahan (1799–1889), who was also involved in the establishment of Oberlin College—raised more eyebrows when they began to talk about Christian perfection as a state of holiness that one might experience in this life, an idea also popular in a slightly different form in some Methodist circles at the time. By perfection, Finney did not mean that one would never make mistakes or be wrong. Finney saw perfection as the goal of growth in faith after conversion, as one intentionally sought to give control of one's will entirely to God or to make one's will be perfectly (totally) conformed to God's will.

From Kentucky and Tennessee to New York, camp meetings and revivals enlivened an evangelical style among diverse denominations. The denominations did not cease to exist; in many locales Congregationalists, Baptists, Methodists, Presbyterians, and others engaged in friendly competition. Groups such as the Episcopalians and Lutherans, whose orientation focused more on liturgically ordered worship and sacramental devotion and who in some cases depended on ethnic constituencies, generally were less taken by the evangelicalism promoted by revivals. Nonetheless, an evangelical style penetrated the popular religious consciousness among antebellum American Protestants, so much so that historian Catherine Albanese has called this cross-denominational evangelical Protestantism "America's religion," in the sense that its impact was felt everywhere and its assumptions were intertwined with the very fabric of the culture, layering an evangelical spirit on diverse denominations. The ramifications of this "second" Great Awakening for the larger culture would be legion.

Evangelical Protestants and the erosion of Calvinism

Many Protestant bodies benefited from the surge of evangelicalism that swept across American religious culture in the first half of the nineteenth century, but none more than the Methodists and Baptists and then, to a lesser extent, some Presbyterian groups. Despite the evangelical overlay, denominational diversity remained the norm when it came to institutional or organized religion. As noted in Chapter 4, American Methodists balanced a hierarchical structure and the democratic ethos of the new nation with an organizational format style that centered around bishops as administrative leaders and an annual conference or gathering of all preachers (hierarchy) and the preachers themselves as they went from place to place (democracy). Having a mobile cadre of preachers who regularly made a circuit of the various preaching stations assigned to them gave Methodists a decided edge as the American people themselves began to move ever further westward.

The rapid growth of American Methodism stemmed as well from at least two other factors. One was the Methodist emphasis on some sort of inner experience of conversion. This emphasis meant that Methodists were particularly taken with revivals, camp meetings, and other gatherings that looked to powerful preaching to stir listeners to examine their own lives and feel the power of God convicting them of sin and reorienting them to a life of holiness. Methodists thus played down particulars of belief or doctrine. Conversion also empowered its subjects, for they saw themselves as no longer enslaved to sin, even if they lacked power within society. For example, women, increasingly seen as innately more religious than men but denied positions of power within church and society, often found the Methodist approach compelling, for it gave them a superior power, a spiritual power, transcending all earthly power. African Americans, whether slave or free, also found the Methodist message attractive for much the same reason. They, too, were often marginalized when it came to economic, political, or other kinds of social power and influence.

In addition to empowerment grounded in personal experience, Methodism's rejection of many ideas integral to Calvinism became a great advantage. Calvinists such as the early Puritans and their heirs among Congregationalists and Presbyterians insisted that God alone was responsible for human destiny and that people themselves could do nothing to earn or deserve divine grace. They talked about predestination or election to describe how God freely chose (predestined or elected) some for salvation. Methodists—and, in time, more and more of those who believed that revivals and the evangelical style had greatly enhanced the influence of religion in American life—saw predestination or election as denying any human responsibility or choice in matters of faith. Calvinism seemed to make God a puppeteer and humans the puppets. For non-Calvinists, or Arminians as they were sometimes called (after an earlier Dutch thinker who had challenged Calvinist thinking), the individual willingly and freely chose to accept (or reject) the gift of grace offered by God in salvation. This approach also seemed more in keeping with notions of individual responsibility at the heart of the democratic ideal. So a democratic individualism, combined with a mobile yet structured organization, allowed Methodists to seize opportunities for expansion in the new nation.

Baptists were also well poised for growth, although within the Baptist tradition there was wide-ranging internal diversity. Some Baptists, reflecting the origins of Baptist ways within English and New England Puritanism, retained much of their Calvinist underpinnings, including a firm belief in predestination. They distinguished themselves primarily by questioning whether there should be any formal ties between religion and government, insisting that local congregations rather than any larger association or denominational body determined belief and practice, and generally refusing to baptize infants but reserving that rite of initiation into the Christian life for those old enough to give an accounting of their faith and submit to full immersion.

Other Baptists recognized that rejecting ties to government and the authority of associations or denominational assemblies likewise empowered individuals to pursue

> ## Why evangelical denominations grew so rapidly
>
> In antebellum America, Protestant denominations that identified with the evangelical style and promoted camp meetings and revivals grew quickly because:
>
> 1. They emphasized personal experience or inner feeling over formal doctrine and belief.
> 2. In doing so, they empowered individuals, because only individuals could have this intense personal experience.
> 3. Consequently, evangelicalism appealed to many who were otherwise on the margins of a white male-dominated society, especially women and African Americans.
> 4. Evangelical denominations that relied on itinerant or travelling preachers, who went from place to place rather than preaching only in a church in one town or village, grew the most rapidly, because they went to the people instead of waiting for the people to come to them.
> 5. Often these groups did not require lengthy formal education for persons to become preachers; their own religious experience and their ability to talk about it persuasively were more important than theological training.
> 6. This approach undermined the Calvinist heritage important in much of colonial America and echoed the democratic spirit of the new nation with its emphasis on the "common" person.

their own salvation. Baptists inclined to this way of thinking, like Methodists, were often zealous supporters of revivals and camp meetings because they made individual experience foundational. As well, Methodists and Baptists alike made formal training for clergy less important than whether those called to preach could speak clearly and forcefully about their own personal experiences of conversion.

In time, even in Presbyterian circles, adherence to some core ideas of Calvinism became less important. On a popular level predestination was becoming almost synonymous with the belief that an all-knowing God understood whether an individual would accept or reject the grace of salvation, not whether God alone chose some for grace. Lyman Beecher (1755–1863), who served as pastor of both Congregationalist and Presbyterian churches in New England and Ohio and later as president of a theological seminary in Cincinnati, at first was suspicious of Finney's "new measures" revivalism. He thought it undercut Calvinist belief and substituted sheer emotion for reasoned examination of the soul. In principle, though, he believed revivals were beneficial because they could arouse the religious sensibilities of those whom God had elected, not because they summoned individuals to make a decision to accept or reject the grace of salvation. In time, his position softened, for he recognized that revivals generally advanced the cause of religion and morality in American life. More than Beecher feared excesses of evangelical emotion, he feared other expressions of religious diversity then making their way into American life, particularly Unitarianism and Roman Catholicism. So Beecher tempered his critique of revivals and even joined with other clergy to invite Charles Finney to conduct a protracted meeting in Boston.

How more evangelical bodies capitalized on the revivals and camp meetings comes through when one looks at numbers. Some estimates suggest, for example, that while Methodists accounted for less than 3 percent of those identified as adherents of a specific religious group in 1776, by the middle of the nineteenth century they claimed just over one-third. Baptists, accounting for about one-sixth of adherents when war with England erupted, were not far behind, with about one-fifth of all religiously affiliated Americans by 1850. Congregationalists, the heirs of the Puritans, plummeted from around one-fifth as the Revolution began to a mere 4 percent by 1850, and the Church of England, which had enjoyed establishment in several colonies, saw its share drop from just under one-sixth of religious adherents to less than 4 percent during the same period. Roman Catholics were showing steady growth, but largely because of immigration rather than because of echoing the democratic spirit.

Within those evangelical groups growing by leaps and bounds considerable diversity flourished. In addition to that prevailing among Baptists and Presbyterians, already mentioned briefly, by the middle of the nineteenth century much internal diversity was brewing in Methodist circles. One strand emerged among those who believed that the Methodist emphasis on personal experience and individual choice in matters of faith was correct, but found the blend of individualism and hierarchical authority in the structure of the denomination—pastors and circuit riders empowered by their own personal experience and then bishops who seemed sometimes to exercise almost dictatorial authority in administrative matters—to be increasingly out of step with democratic culture. Some of those in 1830 organized the Methodist Protestant Church, a denomination that had no bishops and granted a greater voice to lay people in running church affairs than its Methodist Episcopal Church parent. It exemplified the republican ethos that first nurtured American Methodism.

Another strand of diversity came in what is known as the Holiness Movement. Although only men could serve as clergy in the Methodist tradition, women outnumbered men among American Methodists, as they did in virtually every group, and women's leadership propelled Holiness. Devout Methodists Phoebe Palmer (1807–1874) and her physician husband had experienced devastating loss as three of their children died at early ages. Consequently, Phoebe Palmer became absorbed with Bible study and prayer. She soon believed that the experience of conversion, although deep and emotional, was only the beginning of what a believer might expect. Recalling Methodist founder John Wesley's passion for holiness or what theologians sometimes called sanctification, she eagerly sought another intense experience beyond conversion, a "second blessing" to confirm that her will had become one with God's will and that genuine holiness infused her life. With her sister, she organized meetings in her home, at first primarily of women, although men attended as time passed, where through prayer, devotional Bible study, and a sharing of personal testimony those present received encouragement in their own pursuit of holiness. In time Palmer became a popular speaker at summer conferences that had evolved from camp meetings and at revivals in both the United States and England. Many of those took place in rural, bucolic settings, providing a retreat from urban life and stirring nostalgia for a mythic, more agrarian past.

Palmer's journey illustrates what happens when an intense personal experience lies at the center of the religious life. As the intensity fades, one seeks another experience that not only restores the fervor and energy of the original experience—in this case the experience of conversion—but pushes it to a new level. For many drawn to Holiness as Palmer described it, traditional Methodist ways had become static, losing the spiritual edge of an earlier day. Holiness was thus a revitalization movement. Some moved to establish denominations that would promote that primal holiness—the Wesleyan Methodist Church and the Pilgrim Holiness Church (which much later merged to form the Wesleyan Church), the Church of the Nazarene, and a host of others. Some got caught up in a fresh approach to the idea of perfection. If they echoed the perfection of Charles Finney and his "new measures" revivalism, they also had roots in Methodist teaching about the gradual attainment of spiritual perfection. That came only when the divine will had completely taken over an individual's life. Refitted camp meetings, especially after the formation of the National Campmeeting Association for the Promotion of Holiness in 1867, provided venues to promote holiness revivals. One of the better-known that still exists, albeit in much changed form, is the Methodist-oriented enclave at Ocean Grove, NJ.

Even as evangelicalism gave a common veneer to much American Protestantism, it also bred its own kind of diversity. Some came with the formation of new denominations. Some came with movements within denominations to recapture ideas that seemed to have gone by the wayside. Some came because individual experience remained at the heart of the evangelical style, and no two individuals have experiences of faith that are completely identical. Evangelicalism had an abiding influence on the larger culture not only because of this common sensibility, but also because many influenced by evangelicalism sought to reshape and reform the entire society so that it, too, would be more ideal and holy.

The evangelical vision of a moral society

Evangelical Protestant Americans recognized that there was diversity among the various denominations when it came to fine points of belief, styles of worship, ways of organizing religious groups, and other practices. Yet many shared a vision for the larger society, one that presumed there was a common moral base more important than the differences. The first half of the nineteenth century witnessed such an array of cooperative ventures at social reform that later commentators have described them as creating a benevolent or righteous empire. Although various organizations tackled different dimensions of the larger task of fashioning a nation that was moral at its core and promoted what was good and right, they presumed that through voluntary, cooperative endeavors, the American nation would come as close to being the perfect society as any human construction could be. Although that optimism seems naive, the labors that went into trying to reach the goal were formidable. These cooperative efforts to infuse the larger culture with an undercoating of evangelical spirituality and values were part of a larger Anglo-American surge of benevolent or charitable activity. In almost every case, there was a British organization paralleling an American counterpart. In some cases, the British provided an earlier example that an American group would emulate.

In the United States, rapid growth, both in terms of population and in terms of geographic expansion westward, stirred Protestant leaders to work together to create a better society. If organized religion was a civilizing influence, as the frontier camp meetings demonstrated, assuring that religious influence penetrated newly settled areas was critical. The earliest associations operated on a state or regional level. In 1808, for example, a Bible society organized in Philadelphia drew support from individuals from a host of Protestant denominations. Its goal was to provide the Christian scriptures at low or even no cost to persons living in areas where organized churches were few in number. The following year saw several similar groups founded in New England states and New York. Then, in 1816, the American Bible Society formed to distribute Bibles on a national basis, especially in newly settled areas to the west. Seven years later, the American Tract Society became the successor to the New England Tract Society, founded in 1814. Its aim was to produce not only tracts or pamphlets with a moral or religious message, but magazines, books (especially to nurture children in the moral and religious life), and other literature designed for use in the home, recognizing that in areas where there were few religious institutions, the home was the primary place to instill values in children and youth.

Denominations, both acting alone and cooperating together, also launched numerous educational enterprises. The American Sunday School Union (1824) set out to publish material to be used for religious instruction. Throughout what is now the midwestern region of the United States, countless colleges owe their origins to religious denominations whose leaders believed that education was essential to sustaining the kind of citizenry needed to keep the American democratic experiment on a moral course. Alongside these were numerous missionary societies, the earliest of which was probably the Connecticut Missionary Society, which emerged in 1798

> ## Why voluntary societies were important
> Robert Baird (1798–1863) went to Europe in 1835 as an agent of the American and Foreign Christian Union. He revised lectures about American religion that he gave in Sweden in 1841 and published them in Scotland the next year. Other editions followed, in both Europe and the United States. When he described the voluntary principle vital to evangelical influence, he recognized both the extent of religious diversity in the United States and the ways evangelical cooperative societies hoped to create a moral nation:
>
>> This inability to support the public preaching of the Gospel often arises from the number of sects to be found in new settlements and even in some districts of the older States. In this respect diversity of sects sometimes causes a serious though temporary evil, not to be compared with the advantages resulting from it in the long run. It is an evil, too, which generally becomes less and less every year in any given place: the little churches, however weak at first, gradually becoming ... strong and independent ...
>>
>> The most obvious way of aiding such feeble churches is, to form societies for this express object among the older and more flourishing churches ... The faithful men sent by these societies into the wilderness were greatly blessed in their labors, and to them, under God, many of the now flourishing churches of those regions owe their existence.
>
>> Robert Baird, *Religion in America*, ed. Henry Warner Bowden (New York: Harper & Row, 1970), 126

with the goal of carrying the evangelical Protestant Christian message to areas of the United States where churches were few. Soon some had a more global sense of where American Protestant Christianity could leave its mark. In 1810, clergy from Massachusetts and Connecticut launched the American Board of Commissioners for Foreign Missions.

Others targeted specific issues or even specific aspects of individual behavior that seemed to require adjustment in order to make the United States a righteous nation. Some Massachusetts people dedicated to mission work in 1826 formed another outfit called the American Society for the Promotion of Temperance; a decade later the American Temperance Union, which advocated total abstinence, came into being. Behind both was the conviction that high levels of consumption of alcoholic beverages hindered the American nation from being all it could be. A complete list of all such agencies would take pages, but perhaps the one in antebellum American destined to have the most profound impact was the American Antislavery Society, organized in

Figure 6.2 Certificate of temperance. Early efforts to link religion to social reform that cut across denominational lines highlighted the need for temperance (Courtesy of the Library of Congress.)

Philadelphia in 1833. As moral and religious indignation over the brutality and inhumanity of the slave system mounted in the United States, the American Antislavery Society kept the horrors of slavery before the public, pressured denominations to denounce chattel slavery, and urged the government to make slavery illegal. Moral and religious debates over slavery antedated the organization of such societies; colonial Quakers, for example, had early on condemned slavery on moral and religious grounds. But these debates highlighted another dimension of diversity. Not only did religious people disagree, but in time, as we shall see, several Protestant bodies divided along regional lines, paving the way for civil war and making regional identity another component of religious identity.

Although social custom in antebellum America decreed that men would be at the forefront of official leadership of virtually all these cooperative ventures, with individuals often serving in formal capacities in more than one, American Protestant women provided the grass-roots labor and support for them. A "cult of domesticity" that promoted strict gender roles that made home the sphere of women and anything public the sphere of men was taking root. Thus, although women may have been denied opportunities to speak at the annual conventions when leaders of such societies gathered, without the commitment of Protestant women to moral and social reform, none would have survived. For hundreds of women, moral leadership in the home stimulated vigorous engagement in moral reform in society.

As well, women increasingly took the lead in using materials published and distributed by groups such as the American Tract Society and American Sunday School Union to instruct children and youth in the home. If this role cemented perceptions that women were more religious by nature than men and that the home, increasingly the domain of women, was vital to religious nurture, it also paved the way for a broader involvement in the larger society. Many women who recognized that their work had larger implications began to combine their social reform efforts with calls for women's rights in the political sphere, stirring controversy there. Women were also at the forefront in launching many new religious movements in the decades just before and after the Civil War, ranging from spiritualism to Christian Science. In scores of ways, women's refusal to accept a place determined by male control added countless layers of diversity onto American religious life, often highlighting the stark inequity reinforced by social custom.

The evangelical vision for a moral society created a veneer of common identity among many Protestant Americans, yet diversity flourished as individual denominations went about their business. At the same time, the new nation was witnessing many kinds of transformation, for the same political and cultural environment that spawned cooperative ventures for social reform also spurred countless efforts at religious experimentation and the formation of scores of new religious movements. Increasing immigration likewise augmented diversity as groups outside the orbit of evangelical Protestantism began to grow rapidly. Immigration solidified the ways ethnicity brought its diversity to American religion; in many cases the religious style of immigrants was intertwined with the ethnic cultures of their lands of origin. Despite an evangelical united front to create a moral America, then, diversity remained alive and well.

Key points you need to know

- The camp meeting emerged as a way to bring religion to frontier regions in the early nineteenth century.
- Besides being religious events, camp meetings had important social dimensions.
- Northern preachers adapted techniques developed at camp meetings for revivals in growing urban centers.
- Denominations emphasizing the kind of conversion experience central to camp meetings and revivals grew rapidly, although they remained organizationally and theologically diverse.
- Regardless of denominational background, antebellum Protestant evangelicals shared a common vision that the United States should be a moral or righteous nation.

- Despite diversity, evangelical Protestants worked together to reform the American nation through groups like the American Bible Society and the American Antislavery Society.
- Women played increasingly important roles in evangelical efforts to create the ideal society and to nurture the religious lives of children and youth.

Discussion questions

1. Describe the frontier camp meeting. What brought camp meetings about? What was their impact on American religion and culture?
2. How did the style of the camp meeting become adapted for use in urban revivals?
3. How did camp meetings and early nineteenth-century revivals lead to the rapid growth of evangelical Protestant denominations?
4. In what ways did the surge of evangelicalism mask continuing religious diversity in American Protestantism?
5. How was evangelicalism connected to shared visions of the United States as a moral nation?
6. Explain ways in which evangelicals worked together, despite their differences and diversity, to reform American society. What role did women play in these efforts?

Further reading

Albanese, Catherine L. *America: Religions and Religion*. 4th ed. Belmont, CA: Thomson Wadsworth, 2007.

Bruce, Dickson D., Jr. *And They All Sang Hallelujah: Plain-Folk Camp-Meeting Religion, 1800–1845*. Knoxville: University of Tennessee Press, 1974.

Conkin, Paul K. *Cane Ridge: America's Pentecost*. Madison: University of Wisconsin Press, 1990.

Hambrick-Stowe, Charles E. *Charles G. Finney and the Spirit of American Evangelicalism*. Grand Rapids, MI: Eerdmans, 1996.

Handy, Robert T. *A Christian America: Protestant Hopes and Historical Realities*. 2nd ed. New York: Oxford University Press, 1984.

Hatch, Nathan O. *The Democratization of American Christianity*. New Haven, CT: Yale University Press, 1989.

Schmidt, A. Gregory. *The Way of the Cross Leads Home: The Domestication of American Methodism*. Bloomington: Indiana University Press, 1993.

Wigger, John H. *Taking Heaven by Storm: Methodism and the Rise of Popular Christianity in America*. New York: Oxford University Press, 1998.

7 Religious experimentation brings more diversity

In this chapter

This chapter examines how religious diversity expanded rapidly in the nineteenth century. It looks first at different strands of the Restorationist movement, especially the wing that gave birth to the Latter-day Saints. Next it examines the fascination with communitarian or utopian groups. Intrigue with adventism and millennialism forms the basis for another section. Then attention turns to other impulses, such as Swedenborgianism and Christian Science, which show how widespread religious experimentation was.

Main topics covered

- How a passion to recover New Testament Christianity led to a religious movement known as Restorationism
- Joseph Smith's experience that drew on Restorationism but gave birth to a new religion that is uniquely American, the Church of Jesus Christ of Latter-day Saints
- The scores of religious utopian and communitarian experiments that took root on American soil in the antebellum period
- The fascination Americans had in predicting when the Second Coming of Christ would occur and religious groups that emerged from this adventist impulse
- Other movements looking to mental power and to science to create the ideal life

Recapturing original Christianity

The belief among some Americans in the new republic that ordinary people could readily understand the meaning of the Bible had many implications. One comes to light when the conviction that authentic religion was accessible to anyone joined with the religious fervor coming from frontier camp meetings. The result was an interest in restoring or replicating the actual beliefs and practices of the Christian movement as they were in the time of the New Testament. Like the Puritans who regarded their experiment as a city on a hill, a model for the world, most of those who launched new religious movements in the nineteenth century had a vision of some kind of ideal community or ideal life. The details, however, varied widely. And while all of them added to the diversity within American religious life, virtually all also encountered strident opposition and aroused controversy—some more so than others. Together, they highlight parallel impulses in American religious life that often are in some sort of combat—reaching for a new ideal and a fear of what is different or unknown. Here, too, strides towards diversity did not always come easily.

One such vision is generally called Restorationism because of its explicit effort to tie beliefs and practices to those thought basic to earliest Christianity. The movement sometimes takes its name from two of the key figures associated with it, Barton W. Stone (1772–1844) and Alexander Campbell (1788–1866), and is known as the Stone-Campbell Movement. Stone was associated with James McGready and the Cane Ridge camp meeting in 1801. He soon became convinced that true Christianity did not require denominations; he found no mention of them in the Christian scriptures. So he and some others who believed as he did decided to call themselves simply "Christians" without any denominational label and to have no formal doctrine other than the Bible, understood simply by using common sense. Stone also rejected the idea of predestination or election, believing that this aspect of Calvinist teaching had no basis in scripture.

Campbell, born in Ireland of Scottish ancestry, arrived in what was then a frontier area of western Pennsylvania around 1812, where he joined his father Thomas in a parallel effort to restore American Christianity to its New Testament foundations. Campbell, like Stone, thought different denominations represented a corruption of genuine Christianity. He referred to himself and his followers as Disciples of Christ, not imagining that in time they would become a denomination alongside the scores of others that flourished in the U.S. Around 1830, Stone and Campbell joined forces, both eager to use the revivalistic spirit and their shared commitment to restoring New Testament Christianity to revitalize American religious life.

For a generation, congregations forming this loose connection grew rapidly. Campbell and the later movements that emerged from this one used the press and other publishing media to forge links among the people and promote the Restorationist perspective, while still insisting on the autonomy of local congregations. Campbell was also drawn into the orbit of those intrigued by millennial expectation or the hope that Christ would soon return to earth. He even named one periodical the *Millennial Harbinger*. Although he did not fall into the trap of setting a date when the millennial age would begin, he did believe that the restoration of simple, biblical, apostolic Christianity was a sign of its dawning.

The Stone-Campbell Movement found a warm reception in areas of the old southern frontier where the camp meetings had first flourished and then in what was to become the midwestern region of the United States. By the end of the nineteenth century, the movement was itself dividing. Some of those who saw the Disciples of Christ gradually metamorphosing into a denomination coalesced into the Churches of Christ, even today a cluster of different congregations that refuse to accept denominational labels or structures, with individual congregations determining with which other congregations they will be in fellowship through several networks of periodicals, lectures, schools, and other connections.

Restorationist currents of a different ilk came to the burned-over district of New York. In the 1820s, Joseph Smith (1805–1844), who today would be called "a religious seeker," experienced religious visions leading him to believe God had called him to restore the church to its primitive ideal. Citing guidance from an angel named Moroni, Smith claimed to have found golden plates buried on Hill Cumorah in central New York not far from Syracuse. Other spiritual guides empowered the uneducated Smith to translate the text on the plates, published in 1830 as the *Book of Mormon*. What set Smith's Restorationist ideal apart from others was its insistence that Christ had made post-resurrection appearances in North America and that the continent had once been populated by peoples with a heritage akin to that of ancient Israel in terms of being those chosen by the Almighty to bring pure truth to all humanity. By giving the American land a mythic history, Smith also gave it a sacred past.

As he organized his followers, Smith developed a distinctively American religion with a theology that expands on the Bible. Especially significant is Smith's conviction, still vital to the tradition, that revelation is an ongoing, continuous phenomenon; God may choose to impart new truth at any time—through Smith and then through his successors. Most Christian groups do not hold such an open-ended understanding of revelation. One well-known example came in 1843, when Smith received a revelation calling for reinstituting the practice of plural marriage or polygamy, which some had already adopted. Smith rightly noted that having multiple wives was common in ancient Israel as well. In addition, because they insist that God is a physical as well as spiritual being, Latter-day Saints believe that those who accept the truth revealed to Smith and his successors also have the capacity to become gods.

The Latter-day Saints, popularly still called Mormons, early adopted communitarian principles. These also stirred suspicion among outsiders or Gentiles, but not to the extent that in time plural marriage did. Moving to Ohio, then to northern Missouri, and on to a community along the Mississippi River in Illinois called Nauvoo, the Mormons grew rapidly as they sought to build their own Zion, their own ideal community. Hostility also mounted. Many opponents thought plural marriage would undermine society. Some thought Smith an arrogant shyster who fabricated his claims to direct inspiration. Others resented the freedom from state control that the Latter-day Saints had secured in their charter for Nauvoo. After Smith was arrested for a minor offense, a mob broke into the jail in Carthage, IL, and shot both Smith and his brother to death.

> ### Latter-day Saints believe Christ appeared to Israel's Lost Tribes
>
> The *Book of Mormon*, which Joseph Smith claimed to have transcribed from golden tablets, describes what happened in North America at the moment of the birth of Jesus told in the New Testament gospels of Matthew and Luke:
>
> And it came to pass that there was no darkness in all that night, but it was as light as though it was mid-day. And it came to pass that the sun did rise in the morning again, according to its proper order; and they knew that it was the day that the Lord should be born, because of the sign which had been given.
>
> And it had come to pass, yea all things, every whit, according to the words of the prophets.
>
> And it came to pass also that a new star did appear, according to the word.
>
> (3 Nephi 1: 19–21)

The assassination of their founder did not deter the Latter-day Saints for long. Although some looked to Smith's blood relatives for leadership and remained in the Missouri–Illinois region (where they became known first as the Reorganized Church of Jesus Christ of Latter-day Saints and today as the Community of Christ), the majority accepted Brigham Young (1801–1877) as their prophet. In 1846, Young spearheaded the movement of the main body of Latter-day Saints westward to land then part of Mexico. Like earlier exiles such as Roger Williams and Anne Hutchinson, the Latter-day Saints hoped that by removing to a distant wilderness they would be free to live according to the truth revealed to their own prophets. But shortly after they arrived at the Great Salt Lake in what is today Utah, the territory became part of the United States. Fear of persecution returned, even though Young became the first U.S. governor of the territory. Occasional direct conflict and much indirect confrontation ensued, some even after a later revelation rescinded the command to practice plural marriage and Utah became a state. Even today some Mormon splinter groups attempt to practice plural marriage and hold to what they believe is the original vision of Joseph Smith.

The Mormon restoration of apostolic Christianity thus took quite a different form than that of Barton Stone and Alexander Campbell. Yet both illustrate a recurring theme in the history of religions generally and the history of religion in America in particular. That theme is what Mircea Eliade called the "myth of the eternal return" or the conviction that by returning to or restoring what existed at the creation, one received fresh life and power. By going back to the first forms, time itself begins anew

Figure 7.1 Mormons reaching Utah. Led by Brigham Young, the Latter-day Saints or Mormons arrived in Utah, where they sought to build their ideal Zion, then called Deseret, near the Great Salt Lake (Courtesy of the Library of Congress.)

and all is regenerated or born again, for the corruptions of time disappear. To be sure, in one sense one can never duplicate exactly what existed at any moment in the past, whether in the apostolic age idealized in the Stone-Campbell Movement or in the pre-history of America encapsulated in the *Book of Mormon*. But the symbolic return endows power. Restorationist efforts thus form an integral pattern in American religion that adds to the richness of its diversity.

Bringing heaven to earth

When Joseph Smith first gathered his followers together, they attempted to live in a communitarian fashion, sharing goods and property. Earlier, a group such as the Shakers had also created utopian or ideal communities where members had no private property but all was held in common (hence communitarian). The first half of the nineteenth century witnessed an explosion of such idealistic experiments in the United States. Many had religious foundations, although some had roots more in various economic theories and some in philosophical or intellectual visions of the ideal society. These groups are in one sense tied to the larger Restorationist impulse, but in this case what is being restored is the kind of society that people envisioned might have developed if we still lived in the Garden of Eden, the original creation. They are also tied to the adventist and millennialist intrigue, since many of the groups that emerged out of a Christian context looked ahead to a new creation, a new Eden, that would come in the millennial age. They were thus trying to bring heaven to earth. Scores of communitarian or utopian ventures were attempted; most were short lived, with many fading after a founder figure died and the inspiration behind the community vanished.

Three illustrations of different communitarian styles will highlight this aspect of the growing diversity in American religious culture.

John Humphrey Noyes (1811–1886), like many who explored new religious possibilities in the early nineteenth century, had deep New England roots. While studying for the ministry at Yale, however, he had a profound experience that moved him away from traditional Protestant Christianity and towards yet another expression of perfectionism in American religion. Noyes became convinced that the heart of the gospel message was salvation from sin and that the faithful could live now as life would be in the heavenly kingdom. Not only would heavenly life be free from sin, it would also be free from the trappings of society, including personal property and marriage. All such phenomena bound humans to corrupt social institutions. Calling his followers to adopt a communitarian lifestyle, where goods and property were held in common and exclusive relations between men and women were forbidden, Noyes quickly aroused hostility. What he called complex marriage (regarding all the women in the community as wives of all the men and men as husbands of all the women) seemed to promote "free love" and sexual excess. Noyes and his early followers left Vermont, where they initially formed a community, and relocated in 1848 to Oneida, in New York's burned-over district, not too far from where Joseph Smith had received the visions that launched the Latter-day Saints.

Oneida Perfectionists, however, were hardly hedonists. Sexual relations were strictly regulated to prevent exclusive relationships from competing with loyalty to the community, and a unique form of birth control called "male continence" was practiced. The attempt to live a heavenly existence on earth began to crumble when selected couples were allowed to have children, although those born were raised by the community, not by their parents. The hope was that children born to those already free from sin, already living in heaven on earth, would themselves be perfect. In other

Oneida's practice of male continence

Although the Oneida community of Perfectionists reaped scorn as a haven for sexual excess, within the community sexual relations were highly regulated, although frequent. The community practiced a form of birth control called male continence that founder John Humphrey Noyes believed was natural. In this practice, although the man would penetrate the woman, he would not move towards ejaculation.

Noyes thought this practice promoted good health. "In the first place," he wrote, "it secures woman from the curses of involuntary and undesirable procreation; and secondly, it stops the drain of life on the part of man." (John Humphrey Noyes, *Male Continence* [Oneida, NY, Office of the *Oneida Circular*, 1872], 13) words, this experiment, called stirpiculture, was a form of eugenics. Not surprisingly, the authorizing powers granted Noyes the privilege of fathering more children than other males. Resentment against Noyes mounted, as did criticism from outsiders who thought complex marriage and stirpiculture undermined the family. By the late 1870s, with Noyes in Canada, the community dissolved as a religious entity and became a joint-stock company akin to a modern corporation, building on its success in manufacturing traps and then silver-plate flatware. In Oneida's case, heaven on earth lasted but a generation.

Several other utopian experiments drew on the German pietism that had brought some migrants to Pennsylvania during the colonial era and illustrate the second style. One of the more well-known, today still functioning as an incorporation with a cooperative foundation, is the Amana Society, also called the Community of True Inspiration. This group had already formed in the Rhineland area of Germany before coming to America in 1843. The first home for the society in the United States was on the western edge of the burned-over district near Buffalo, New York, where the community called their settlement Ebenezer. Because the devotional tradition of pietism seemed to flourish when exposure to the temptations posed by urban, industrializing locales was minimal, Amana's people preferred to live apart in their own rural communities. But nearby Buffalo began to encroach on the purity of their spiritual discipline. In the 1850s, rural Iowa seemed a safer haven, and the society moved there, where the cooperative still retains large land holdings. Amana never reaped the hostility that Oneida faced. Although remaining aloof from the larger society as much as possible, Amana at least did not challenge Victorian ideas of the monogamous family but seemed intent on promoting a quiet devotion whose heritage stretched back to the age of the Reformation.

Some communitarian clusters fused a religious vision with an economic one, the third style of utopian endeavor. For Hopedale and Brook Farm, for example, the religious base emerged from Transcendentalism, a movement with an enduring impact on American literary and intellectual life. Transcendentalism is most often associated with a cluster of writers centered in and around Boston, including one-time Unitarian pastor Ralph Waldo Emerson (1803–1882). Influenced in part by an early American intrigue with Asian philosophy, Emerson and his circle were drawn to the idea of a universal spirit or mind, whose presence infiltrated every aspect of reality from the natural world to human life. There was a correspondence between this single spiritual essence and everyday life, known more by intuition than traditional religion based on revelation and sacred texts like the Bible. While not all drawn to Transcendental thought sought to translate its implications into a communitarian experiment, some did, including another discontented Boston Unitarian pastor, George Ripley (1802–1880).

Reworking ideas developed by several other utopian communities, including the Shakers, Ripley and just over a dozen others in 1841 pooled their resources to purchase some acreage in West Roxbury, just outside Boston, that they named Brook Farm. At one point the renowned author Nathaniel Hawthorne served on Brook Farm's agricultural committee. For a time both Orestes Brownson (1803–1876) and Isaac Hecker (1819–1888), who later became prominent converts to Roman Catholicism, had close associations with Brook Farm. This utopian venture quickly became known for its heady intellectual atmosphere (including an elite school) based on Transcendental ideals and philosophical currents associated with Kantian thought. With a small printing industry, woodworking, and some other business efforts, Brook Farm also developed a stable economic foundation.

But economic experimentation would also prove the undoing of Brook Farm. During this age of probing alternative visions for an ideal society, some groups formed based on socialist economic principles advanced by the French thinker Charles Fourier (1772–1837). Fourier called for the formation of different workforces within a single community that he called a "phalanx." By 1844, Ripley and some of the other leaders at Brook Farm desired to transform their community from a Transcendentalist haven to a Fourierite phalanx. For a couple of years, while the transition from utopian commune to socialist phalanx was underway, Brook Farm seemed about to meld religious idealism with an economic vision. But when a disastrous fire destroyed some of the buildings central to the economic reorganization, several key people left the community. Reservations soon developed about whether socialist economic ideals were completely compatible with the Transcendentalist religious vision, the economic base of Brook Farm disintegrated, and in 1847 the community dissolved.

These various efforts to construct the perfect society, even if in miniature, demonstrate something of the creative religious genius that erupted in the first half of the nineteenth century, stimulated by the spirit of democracy and protected by the freedom offered by the First Amendment. Although most religiously inclined Americans remained associated with more traditional churches and related religious institutions, these attempts to bring heaven to earth demonstrate the rich diversity that was expanding in American religious culture. They also reveal a willingness to move in bold, new directions as Americans sought to bring meaning and purpose—perhaps even an eternal purpose—to their life together.

The adventist impulse

The conviction that the American democratic adventure represented a decisive turning point in human history had implications that went well beyond trying to recapture original Christianity within nineteenth-century culture or to bring the structures of heavenly life to earth in utopian communities. Centuries earlier, the first generation of Christians developed a lively belief not only that Jesus the Christ had conquered death through his resurrection, but also that he would soon return to earth to vindicate his followers and establish divine rule. Expressions of this hope always endured just beneath the surface, but in nineteenth-century America they emerged in a dramatic way in a variety of religious forms. Some gave birth to movements clustered under the label of adventism because they emphasized the belief that the second advent, the long-awaited second coming or return of Christ to earth, was about to occur, leading to the events that would bring history to a close with the final triumph of good over evil. The technical term for this position is premillennialism. Closely related are those groups and movements sometimes called millennialist or millenarian. That label refers to the idea that there would be a thousand-year period or millennium before history drew to a close. This position is formally called post-millennialism. Although there may not always be precise distinctions, here the term "adventist" will refer to those who generally hold to a premillennialist view, while "millennialist" will take in those who generally espouse a post-millennialist view. Many of those drawn to adventist and/or millennialist thinking found the inspiration for their views in the biblical books of Daniel and Revelation, both noted for their highly symbolic texture and both popularly perceived to offer a reliable guide to when Christ's return would occur or when the millennium would begin. The faithful wanted to crack their symbolic codes and match the predictions about the end of all things with current events. This hope stirred especially those who were adventists or premillennialists.

Much of the adventist and millennial fervor centered in the northeast, in places like New York City and the burned-over district of central New York that also gave birth to groups like the Mormons and a host of other religious ventures. Among the more well-known voices for adventism in the first half of the nineteenth century was William Miller (1782–1849), a New Englander who left his farm in Vermont for one in New York in 1815 and, following a conversion experience the next year, became a preacher for the adventist cause until his death. Thanks to publicity efforts spearheaded by his associate Joshua Himes, Miller quickly emerged as a popular speaker on the revival circuit. Himes also promoted Miller's views in the rapidly expanding world of newspapers and periodicals, especially in *Signs of the Times* and the *Midnight Cry*.

Much of the fascination with Miller stemmed from his claims to have correlated the apocalyptic messages of Daniel and Revelation with actual events so completely that he was able to fix a precise date for the return of Christ to earth, the long-awaited Second Advent. When the proposed date passed without dramatic divine intervention in human affairs, Miller revised his calculations, finally insisting that Christ would return on 22 October 1844. Although hundreds eagerly anticipated the end of history, they experienced instead what became called the "Great Disappointment." Not all abandoned adventist thinking, however. Among them was a former Methodist attracted to Millerite teaching, Ellen Gould Harmon (1827–1915), who in 1846 married adventist preacher and publisher James S. White.

White became convinced that the delay in Christ's return resulted from a lack of attention among the faithful to the conditions necessary to prepare for history's concluding moments. Among them were a return to worship on the Sabbath, the

> ### Ellen White calls for a return to Sabbath practice
> Seventh-Day Adventist founder Ellen White insisted that Christians should return to worship on the Hebrew Sabbath rather than on Sunday in order to prepare for Christ's second advent. In *The Great Controversy between Christ and Satan*, first published in 1886, she wrote:
>
>> Many urged that Sundaykeeping had been an established doctrine and a widespread custom of the church for many centuries. Against this argument it was shown that the Sabbath and its observance were more ancient and widespread, even as old as the world itself, and bearing the sanction both of angels and of God. When the foundations of the earth were laid, when the morning stars sang together, and all the sons of God shouted for joy, then was laid the foundation of the Sabbath. Job 38: 6, 7; Genesis 2: 1–3. Well may this institution demand our reverence; it was ordained by no human authority and rests upon no human traditions; it was established by the Ancient of Days and commanded by His eternal word.
>>
>> ([Mountain View, CA: Pacific Press, 1971], 400)

seventh day, rather than Sunday and adherence to many of the ancient Hebrew dietary guidelines found in the biblical book of Leviticus. Related to that was a growing concern for health matters in general, for White herself faced serious health problems. By 1863, her followers coalesced into the Seventh-Day Adventist denomination. White's concerns continued among Seventh-Day Adventists with the establishment of a sanitarium in Battle Creek, Michigan, which also became an early home of a cereal industry that reflected White's interest in dietary reform.

The Seventh-Day Adventists represent only one expression of the diversity that ongoing millennialist thinking added to American religion. Another strand developed around the teaching of Charles Taze Russell (1852–1916). Although he lacked formal theological education, Russell became a keen student of scripture, writing extensively and speaking widely across the nation. Consequently, his followers called him "Pastor" Russell. The unique twist that Russell gave to adventist teaching came in his conviction that Christ had actually returned to earth in 1874, but in spiritual rather than physical form. In 1914, according to Russell, Christ's invisible reign began. Increasing conflict between good and evil would follow (after all, World War I erupted in 1914), but good would finally triumph. Then God's faithful few would enjoy a thousand years (millennium) of prosperity, before evil as represented by Satan returned to test humanity. Those who remained true would in turn thrive in an earthly paradise for eternity. Although Russell in 1884 called his movement simply the Watch Tower Bible and Tract Society, it has become known more commonly as the Jehovah's Witnesses, especially after Russell's

Figure 7.2 Pastor Russell. Charles Taze Russell energized his followers in the Watch Tower Bible and Tract Society, better known as Jehovah's Witnesses (Courtesy of Pastor-Russell.com.)

successor as leader of the group, "Judge" Joseph Rutherford (1869–1942) gave more institutional structure to the Witnesses.

What made adventist passion powerful and the message of people like Miller, White, and Russell compelling? Some, of course, has to do simply with a fascination with end times that has been an undercurrent in the Christian tradition since its beginnings. As well, linking current events to biblical apocalyptic prophecy serves to give profound meaning to what may otherwise seem challenging to explain; it helps people make sense out of what otherwise might seem to lack any sense at all. In the 1840s, when adventist fervor peaked, the American nation was expanding rapidly, sectional controversy over slavery was mounting, and the economy was emerging from a period of serious depression. All that was familiar seemed in transition.

In that context, the adventist excitement stirred by Miller and then institutionalized in the movement that gathered around White helped put all that political and economic turmoil into a larger framework leading up to the end of history itself. Russell's adventism took shape as the nation was recovering from Civil War, immigration was swelling the ranks of Catholics and other non-Protestants, and rapid urban and industrial growth were transforming the larger culture. In the midst of such unsettledness, linking daily life to a divine scheme culminating in history's end was a striking way to endow life with meaning. The turmoil of postbellum American society became a stepping stone to an apocalyptic future that was already coming into view for those who could see beneath the surface. Millions continue to find in millennial expectation the key to the present and hope for the future, particularly when the pace of social change seems overwhelming. Adventism thus remains a vibrant and dynamic current within the diverse religious culture of the American peoples.

Exploring new religious worlds

Not everyone looked to an apocalyptic end to history to help make sense out of life in the United States in the decades just before and after the Civil War, any more than they looked to restoring the ancient past as the key to finding meaning in life. Part of the story of religious diversity in this epoch concerns a variety of efforts to look within the human mind itself to uncover a larger frame of meaning for all of life. In one sense, most of these movements had a vision of an ideal personal life that was marked by health in both mind and body. Many believed that the mind actually determined whether the physical body would be healthy. There were others, of course, who were primarily concerned with what in time became known as divine healing, or the direct healing of physical ailments and conditions through faith. Here, we shall look just at those that saw the mind and mental power as foundational for all human well-being.

Some of this "looking inward" into the mind had roots in ideas formulated by Emanuel Swedenborg (1688–1772), a Swedish religious mystic and scientist who constructed a world of religious meaning based on visions of the heavenly realm, spiritual conversations he reported having with renowned figures long dead, and a conviction that the mind could discern a clear correspondence between physical reality and the heavenly reality described in scripture. His Church of the New Jerusalem, whose first congregation was organized in London, made its way to American shores shortly after the American Revolution and had its inaugural general convention in 1817 in Philadelphia.

Swedenborgians in America have never attracted a large following, but the idea that the material world had reality only because of its correspondence with a spiritual reality took hold in many different ways. It provided, for example, one of the foundations for what is now called homeopathic medicine, which emphasizes the healing power of the mind itself, as well as for much religious experimentation. Much of that experimentation became known as metaphysical religion because of the intellectual way it presumed that a spiritual dimension hidden in the material or physical was the foundation for what was truly real. Another European thinker who elevated the power of the invisible mind above that of material things was the Austrian Friedrich (Franz) Mesmer (1733/34–1815). Not only did he dabble in astrology, but he also developed techniques that became the basis for hypnotism (then called mesmerism), which he believed could unleash the mental power to bring about physical healing.

In the United States, two religious seekers who absorbed this way of thinking had particularly enduring influence, although neither one is well known today. They are Phineas P. Quimby (1802–1866), from Portland, Maine, and Warren Felt Evans (1817–1889), a one-time Methodist pastor who lived for a time in Portland and who

Figure 7.3 Mary Baker Eddy. Mary Baker Eddy, the founder of Christian Science, was one of many female religious leaders in the nineteenth century to launch a new religious movement (Courtesy of The Mary Baker Eddy Collection.)

at one point was also a Swedenborgian minister. Quimby concluded that if the invisible mind represented the only true reality, then problems in the physical realm, such as disease, represented the temporary triumph of some sort of mental disorder or wrong way of thinking. Here one can see the influence of both Swedenborg and Mesmer. But Quimby took his belief and fashioned it into a technique to bring about physical healing. Today one might talk about psychosomatic illness in which profound and powerful thought processes result in the actual physical symptoms of particular illnesses or diseases that do not respond to traditional medical treatment. Like the cause, only a thought process that presumes mind is more potent than matter can effect a cure. Or one might think of chronic depression, today a genuine mental illness, that conventional medicine controls, but does not seem able to cure. For Quimby and Evans, only the mind itself could cure, whatever the ailment. Evans became convinced of this understanding when, in 1863, he sought help from Quimby to get relief from continued sickness that kept him in a state of ill health.

Evans wrote extensively about this method of healing, convinced that it represented a new scientific understanding of how the mind and body, the spiritual and the physical, were related. In terms of religious belief, he also insisted that God was the only true reality, a reality that existed only in spiritual but not physical form. With right thinking, individuals would come to recognize that they, too, were part of this same spiritual reality, that they, too, had their being in the very being of God.

Figure 7.4 Mother Church of Christ Scientist, Boston. The Mother Church of Christ Scientist in Boston remains the symbolic center for one of the distinctive new religious movements to begin in America in the later nineteenth century (© Angelina DeLioncourt.)

At one point, Evans even referred to his way of understanding the world as "Christian science," long before that phrase became popular through the teachings of Mary Baker Eddy (1821–1910). They provided the foundation for what later became called New Thought (with the emphasis on "thought" because of the reliance on mental power to influence material or physical reality).

An experience of healing at the hand of Quimby had initially propelled Evans. It was also central to Eddy. Like Evans, Eddy for years lived with a feeling of desperate malaise, finding some relief and a new direction in life after Quimby worked with her. She was so taken with Quimby that she spent part of two years studying with him. Within a decade of Quimby's death, her own understanding of health and healing combined with her earlier evangelical Christian background shaped by New England Congregationalism. The result was the Church of Christ, Scientist or what is still popularly called Christian Science.

For Eddy, the physical world, the realm of sense experience, is unreal; hence disease and even pain and death are ultimately not real but the result of misdirected thinking that sees matter and spirit as two separate and distinct phenomena. God, the Eternal Mind, empowers individuals to cast aside wrong thinking and with it the illusions of sickness and sin, through harnessing their own mental energy. For Eddy, this was science at its best, for it was a logical way of thinking that echoed the way scientists used the mind to understand the more technical aspects of the world and measured results through experiments. It was

> **Mary Baker Eddy describes how to treat disease**
>
> In her classic 1875 work expounding the principles of Christian Science called *Science and Health with Key to the Scriptures*, Mary Baker Eddy devoted one chapter to the practice of the religion she founded in which she wrote about rejecting traditional medicine:
>
>> "Agree to disagree" with approaching symptoms of chronic or acute disease, whether it is cancer, consumption, or smallpox. Meet the incipient stages of disease with as powerful mental opposition as a legislator would employ to defeat the passage of an inhuman law. Rise in the conscious strength of the spirit of Truth to overthrow the plea of mortal mind, *alias* matter, arrayed against the supremacy of Spirit. Blot out the images of mortal thought and its beliefs in sickness and sin. Then, when thou art delivered to the judgment of Truth, Christ, the judge will say, "Thou art whole!"
>>
>> ([Boston: First Church of Christ, Scientist], 1994, 390–91)

also Christian at heart because, in her reading of the New Testament, Eddy found in Jesus one who was united with Eternal Spirit in every aspect of life. She collected her teachings in *Science and Health with Key to the Scriptures*, a work first published in 1875, and then in a newspaper, the *Christian Science Journal* (1883), and then the *Christian Science Monitor*, a daily founded in 1890 in Boston, home to the First (Mother) Church of Christ, Scientist.

Eddy's teachings appealed particularly to women, who have long accounted for the majority of Christian Science practitioners—despite Eddy's own hesitation to welcome women into the ranks of leadership of her movement. Constrained by the ethos of the Victorian world, women often had few opportunities to assume positions of authority and leadership outside the family circle and home. Christian Science gave its practitioners, especially women, a superior power that was both in keeping with and ahead of its time with its emphasis on science. Popular culture might see women as the "weaker sex," but within Christian Science they had a superior strength because they had a knowledge that transcended anything material or physical.

Over the decades that followed, these metaphysical approaches branched out in many different directions. Ralph Waldo Trine (1866–1958), named for the Transcendentalist writer whose own thought echoed some of this metaphysical understanding, claimed that ultimate happiness could come to anyone who realized that they were part of a single Infinite Power (God) undergirding everything. His *In Tune with the Infinite*, first published in 1897, remains in print today. Strong traces of this approach appear in the teachings of Charles (1854–1948) and Myrtle (1845–1931) Fillmore, who started the Unity School of Christianity. Principles of tapping an inner reservoir of mental power to overcome physical problems informed Alcoholics Anonymous when it was founded in 1935 and continue to guide countless "anonymous" self-help groups. In the middle of the twentieth century, Norman Vincent Peale (1898–1993) adapted some of the foundational ideas of metaphysical religion when he promoted what he called "the power of positive thinking" in a book by that title that remained on the best-seller list for two years in the early 1950s. It took fresh shape in the "possibility thinking" of televangelist and pastor Robert H. Schuller (1926–) later in the twentieth century, and it remains basic to a host of highly personalized and idiosyncratic religious practices often clustered together under the label of "new age" religion.

The popularity of "mind over matter" understanding and of the scores of diverse religious groups that it has spawned suggests the continuing appeal of belief in an invisible spiritual realm that is more powerful and thus more real than anything material or physical. After all, everything that is material or physical ultimately decays and dies; that which is truly spiritual endures eternally. At the same time, the mythic tradition of rugged individualism and the democratic impulse give credibility to any religious view or group that places ultimate authority in the power of the individual mind. Here the truth is within; one needs no external authority—not even church or priest or scripture—in order to arrive at absolute truth that will endure long beyond this life. Formal education and other trappings of social class and cultural standing pale in comparison to the spiritual force that makes those who really know and can draw on inner power an elite who have the key to happiness now and forever. With roots in European mystics like Swedenborg and Mesmer, the broad tradition of metaphysical spirituality and self-help illustrates the explosion that came to American religion as the ideological frontiers of the nineteenth century moved in new directions. Also significant in advancing religion in the nineteenth century was the growth of American Catholicism and Judaism.

Key points you need to know

- Social unsettledness and the conditions of frontier life (and the expansion of the frontier to the west) stirred much religious experimentation in nineteenth-century America.
- One response to that social climate was to try to recapture or restore New Testament Christianity in actual practice.
- The Church of Jesus Christ of Latter-day Saints or Mormons emerged as a distinctively American "new" religion as part of the larger Restorationist movement.
- Others tried various forms of utopian or communitarian religious expressions to bring meaning and stability to life.

- In addition, especially during times of seemingly rapid social change, Americans have shown a lively interest in adventism or millennialism or looking to the end of time when Christ would return to earth.
- Other religious innovators looked to the power of the mind and to putatively scientific ideas to craft new religious alternatives.
- Such experimentation reveals that religion moved in many directions in nineteenth-century America.

Discussion questions

1. What led some religious leaders to think that they could actually change Protestant Christian practice and go back to the way things were in the time of the New Testament apostles?
2. How did Joseph Smith's religious vision lead to the development of a uniquely American religion?
3. What accounts for America's fascination with adventism and millennialism?
4. What gives credibility to various metaphysical religions? How and why do they claim to be more scientific than other forms of belief?
5. Why do new religions generate opposition and hostility? Is such hostility justified?
6. What role did women play in the development of nineteenth-century new religious movements? How did utopian groups try to alter the status of women in society?
7. What do new religious movements add to the story of religions in the United States?

Further reading

Albanese, Catherine L. *A Republic of Mind and Spirit: A Cultural History of American Metaphysical Religion.* New Haven, CT: Yale University Press, 2007.

Foster, Lawrence. *Religion and Sexuality: The Shakers, the Mormons, and the Oneida Community.* New York: Oxford University Press, 1981.

Gottschalk, Stephen. *Rolling Away the Stone: Mary Baker Eddy's Challenge to Materialism.* Bloomington: Indiana University Press, 2005.

Hughes, Richard T., and C. Leonard Allen. *Illusions of Innocence: Protestant Primitivism in America, 1630–1875.* Chicago: University of Chicago Press, 1988.

Numbers, Ronald L. *Prophetess of Health: Ellen G. White and the Origins of Seventh-Day Adventist Health Reform.* Knoxville: University of Tennessee Press, 1992.

Shipps, Jan. *Mormonism: The Story of a New Religious Tradition.* Urbana: University of Illinois Press, 1985.

8 Catholic and Jewish growth stretch diversity

In this chapter

This chapter traces the growth of Roman Catholicism and Judaism in the new republic. It looks at the Catholic presence in the nation just after independence and then at the rapid increase in the Catholic population. The chapter explores how women contributed to Catholic stability and well-being. Then it focuses on Catholic concerns about whether the American environment would allow Catholicism to flourish and a Protestant backlash to this expression of diversity. Next it examines the story of Jewish growth. Finally, it discusses the relationship between ethnicity and religion.

Main topics covered

- How Catholicism developed in the new nation
- The impact of Irish immigration on American Catholicism
- The way women, both lay and religious, helped shape the character of American Catholicism
- Why some Catholics wondered whether democracy could provide a good home for Catholic practice
- Why Protestant Americans, especially those in the "nativist" movement, found Catholicism a threat
- The slower, but significant growth of Judaism before the Civil War
- The place of ethnicity in sustaining religious identity

Catholics in the new American nation

In 1789, the year that George Washington became the first U.S. president, John Carroll (1735–1815) became the first Roman Catholic bishop in the nation. Carroll, who was from Maryland and a cousin of a signer of the Declaration of Independence, had his "see" or base of operations in Baltimore, MD. Founded as a place where English

Catholics could live and worship without adverse political repercussions, Maryland was home to the majority of the nation's Catholics, although Philadelphia, especially, also had a thriving Catholic community. By the middle of the nineteenth century, Roman Catholicism had become the largest single religious group in the United States. A few thousand Catholics became part of the United States at the time of the Louisiana Purchase in 1803, but most of the growth came from immigration and built on the foundations laid by Carroll.

In Carroll's day, many Protestant Americans were suspicious of Catholics because of the mistaken idea that Catholics could never be good citizens or patriots since they were loyal to the pope, at the time both the political ruler of part of the Italian peninsula and spiritual leader of the church. This suspicion had deep roots in English life, for in the later sixteenth century there had been widespread fears of Catholic plots to overthrow Elizabeth I and restore Catholicism as the established church as it had been under her half-sister, Mary Tudor. Also feeding that prejudice were rumors concerning Mary Queen of Scots, who was thought to be poised to take the English throne as a Catholic while she had political refuge in England. Also, Protestants regarded some Catholic beliefs as akin to superstition, particularly the idea of transubstantiation. This doctrine held that when the priest consecrated the bread and wine in the mass, they became the actual body and blood of Christ. In other words, their substance was transformed, even though they still appeared as bread and wine. Most Protestants saw the change as symbolic, not literal, although they interpreted that symbolism in many ways. As well, Protestants thought it strange that Catholics used the Latin language in worship, since few people actually understood it, and presumed that priests exerted unusual, if not dangerous, power over lay people. They also were wary of celibate priests and especially of celibate women religious or nuns, living in convents and wearing distinctive garb known as a habit. Carroll tried to soothe some of these fears in 1784 when he wrote a short book called *Address to the Catholics of the United States*. Despite the title, the book really targeted Protestant readers who looked down on Catholics, and tried to reassure them that Catholics were loyal citizens.

Carroll also spearheaded efforts to give better organization to the American Catholic Church. He had to deal with some Catholic churches that spurned church authority, imitating patterns more common among Protestants. Also, there were no American schools to train men for the priesthood. Carroll, for example, had studied in France with English Jesuits and remained for many years in Europe. So he recruited priests there to come to the new nation to provide pastoral leadership. Carroll was especially successful in arranging with the Society of Saint Sulpice to secure help. Sulpicians, for example, organized St. Mary's Seminary just outside Baltimore and in 1808 set up Mount St. Mary's College in Emmitsburg, MD. Carroll also encouraged the founding of what is now Georgetown University in Washington, DC. Although the most significant growth in parish or parochial schools came later in the nineteenth century, Carroll urged churches to found schools where Catholic children could receive instruction in traditional subjects and in Catholic ways of being religious. He recognized that most

> ## A shortage of priests in the early republic
>
> Writing to the Prefect of Propaganda at the Vatican in Rome in 1785, Bishop John Carroll commented on the shortage of Catholic priests in America, but argued that having parishes without priests was better for Catholics than having priests not committed to serving in the new nation:
>
> > ... for I am convinced that the Catholic faith will suffer less harm, if for a short time there is no priest at a place, than if living as we do among fellow-citizens of another religion, we admit to the discharge of the sacred ministry, I do not say bad priests, but incautious and imprudent priests. All the other clergymen lead a life full of labour, as each one attends congregations far apart, and has to be riding constantly and with great fatigue, especially to sick calls.
>
> (From H. Shelton Smith, Robert T. Handy, and Lefferts A. Loetscher, eds., *American Christianity: A Historical Interpretation with Representative Documents*, vol. 1 (New York: Charles Scribner's Sons, 1960), 463)

American education presumed Protestant, not Catholic, ways of thinking. That bias towards Protestant assumptions in education became even stronger after public schools began to develop in New England in the middle third of the nineteenth century.

Formally, the American Catholic Church was classed as a mission enterprise, a designation it retained until 1908. The priests who served faced many obstacles, and often parishes lacked regular priestly and pastoral leadership. But without the labors of European-born or educated priests, American Catholicism would have foundered badly. By 1808, signs of their success were clearly evident. Carroll was elevated to the position of archbishop, with Baltimore becoming a metropolitan see. In addition, bishops were appointed in Philadelphia, New York, Boston, and Bardstown, Kentucky. By the time the leaders of the American church gathered for their First Provincial Council in 1829, the nation counted around 300,000 Catholics, with ten bishops overseeing the work of the church. Roman Catholic Christians had a secure place for themselves, adding to the religious diversity that was a hallmark of the nation.

Immigration spurs rapid Catholic expansion

At the time of the First Provincial Council, most American Catholics outside of Louisiana were of English or perhaps German ancestry. Within two decades, however, Irish immigrants identified with the Catholic tradition outnumbered all others. The full story of Irish immigration to the United States is still unfolding. For many years, those who told that story insisted that during the colonial era most Irish or Scots-Irish who came to American shores were Protestant and provided the foundation for the emergence of the Presbyterian tradition in America. Then, the standard accounts continue, the disastrous famine that followed when adverse weather conditions and disease repeatedly destroyed the potato crop propelled millions of Irish to immigrate to the United States, with most of the "famine Irish" being Catholic. Analysts now realize that this story is too simplistic and that many Irish immigrants had no strong allegiance to any religious group until after they arrived in the U.S. Prior to the immigration that followed on years of famine, those Irish who took on a religious identity made their way into Protestant bodies, perhaps because of the dominance of Protestant groups in the larger culture. Those who came in the years following the famine gravitated towards the Catholic heritage largely because they were familiar with that tradition and the church moved aggressively to link an Irish identity with a Catholic affiliation. Hence the Irish came to dominate American Catholicism as a product of their American experience. Yet the Irish impact on American Catholicism endures into the twenty-first century, since for nearly a century and a half Irish leaders have dominated the ranks of Catholic bishops, and it was Irish American Catholics who engineered the creative ways the church responded to a later wave of immigration that came between the end of the Civil War and the outbreak of World War I.

Numbers tell one part of the story. In the two decades after the First Provincial Council, the Catholic population swelled to 1.75 million, growing at a rate nearly triple that of the nation as a whole. Then, between 1850 and 1860, while the number of Catholic adherents doubled to around 3.5 million, the national population increased overall by just over one-third, according to census figures. How American Catholicism accommodated that growth and dealt with all the internal pressures that accompanied it is a remarkable tale in itself. In turn, that extraordinary growth prompted a backlash of opposition that sometimes turned violent. The expanding religious diversity of the United States was not without its growing pains.

Much of the growth was concentrated first in cities and developing urban areas along the east coast, although immigrants quickly found their way to cities further inland, such as Cincinnati, Chicago, and St. Louis. The heavy concentration of immigrants in cities allowed for religious groups like the Catholic Church to organize new parishes to serve the people. Population density in cities thus facilitated church organization. But because the "famine Irish" arrived as westward movement was mushrooming, the American Catholic Church moved quickly into the Midwest, and in the 1840s Canadian Catholic bishops helped organize parishes and missions in Oregon and Washington that complemented the missionary endeavors of the Belgian-born Jesuit Pierre Jean DeSmet (1801–1873) among Native American tribal communities in the region. As the nation purchased, annexed, or otherwise

A call for Catholic schools

As the Catholic population grew and Protestant hostility mounted, Catholic leaders urged parishes to set up schools for Catholic children. In words that foreshadow concerns of many religious people, Christian and non-Christian alike, in the twenty-first century, the American bishops gathered at the First Plenary Council in 1852 wrote:

> ... give your children a Christian education, that is an education based on Christian principles, accompanied by religious practices and always subordinate to religious influence. Be not led astray by the false and delusive theories wh[i]ch are so prevalent, and which leave youth without religion, and, consequently, without anything to control the passions, promote the real happiness of the individual, and make society find in the increase of its members, a source of security and prosperity.

(From H. Shelton Smith, Robert T. Handy, and Lefferts A, Loetscher, eds., *American Christianity: A Historical Interpretation with Representative Documents*, vol. 2 (New York: Charles Scribner's Sons, 1963), 107)

gained lands in the west, other ethnic strains of Catholicism added to an internal diversity within the Roman tradition in America. That ethnic variety in turn made it more challenging for the church to insist that it was one church, not many—a view that reflected its being a European-based expression of Christianity that tended to see the world from the perspective of a centralized bureaucracy headquartered in Rome.

If urban clusters and steady geographic expansion contributed to American Catholicism's growth and stability, so, too, did the ways in which women were drawn into a life of Catholic devotion invigorate a tradition that remained "other" to American Protestants. Sociologist Michael Carroll, for example, has shown that immigrant women were largely responsible for cementing the ties between the famine Irish and Catholicism. Often finding domestic work in Protestant households, women saw their employers involved in organized religion, believed that living a religiously centered life was thus one means of displaying an American identity, and became immersed in Catholic practice as a way of both sustaining their Irish heritage and demonstrating their ability to be good Americans. Their devotion in turn carried over into their home life as they sought to raise families who were both good Catholics and good Americans. Among Cajun Catholics in Louisiana, who became part of the United States with the Louisiana Purchase, women fused folk practices with Catholic devotion to sustain a distinctive style of Catholicism among those forced to leave Acadia and come to western Louisiana in the eighteenth century.

In addition to the profound way in which lay women promoted Catholic identity, women religious or nuns also helped assure that Catholic ways would become a significant component of American religious life. Elizabeth Ann Seton (1774–1821) left the Episcopal Church to become a Catholic after visiting Italy with her ailing husband and finding the aura of Catholicism personally attractive. After the death of her husband, Seton moved to Baltimore, started a school for young women with help from Sulpicians, and went on to found the Sisters of Charity, an order of nuns that has provided thousands of teachers for Catholic schools in the U.S. Seton, beatified in 1963, became the first American-born saint named by the church in 1975. As early as 1818 the French nun Rose Philippine Duchesne (1769–1852) spearheaded the establishment of the first convent of the Society of the Sacred Heart in St. Charles, Missouri, not far from St. Louis. In some areas, such as Louisiana, women religious exercised chief responsibility for ministry among African Americans, bringing scores into the church in a culture where many leaders, Catholic and Protestant alike, avoided ministering to the slave and free black population. Altogether, by the time of the Civil War, more than fifty religious communities of women were ministering to American Catholics, white and black, immigrant and native-born. Without their dedication, the church could not have reached the millions of Catholics, native and immigrant alike, who were planting the church on Protestant soil. After the Civil War, Katherine Drexel (1858–1955), the daughter of a wealthy Philadelphia Catholic banker, extended the church's work among minority communities when she founded the Sisters of the Blessed Sacrament for Indians and Colored People. Drexel served as mother superior of that order from 1891 until 1937.

Catholic doubts about America amid nativist backlash

As Catholicism was becoming central to American religious culture, some church leaders doubted whether the American environment was conducive to Catholic ways of being religious. Most of those leaders, because they remained in Europe, were not familiar with the American ethos, particularly the idea of separation of church and state and the democratic spirit that made religious belief and practice matters of personal choice rather than expressions of a single absolute truth binding on all. In the European context, the Catholic heritage was most comfortable functioning in nations where it enjoyed privileged or legally established status, with other religions outlawed or at least restricted in some way. Because the official view of the church was that the Catholic tradition alone contained God's truth, the idea that religious diversity was healthy for society was taboo. As well, at least until the time of the French Revolution, most of the areas of Europe where Catholicism was entrenched had some form of monarchical government. Parallels between the idea of power from the top down in politics, which was key to monarchy, and the way the church was organized, with religious power trickling down from popes and priests to the people, seemed obvious. Separation of church and state made little sense, since it was the duty of the state to endorse and support Truth, not to allow for diverse expressions to compete in an open religious marketplace.

Nor were the Enlightenment idea of the right of private judgment and the sense that final authority in matters of belief and practice was grounded in individual inner experience, so vital to evangelical Protestantism, easily reconciled with Catholic sensibilities. If there were but one Truth and the church had responsibility for protecting and teaching that Truth, religious diversity was dangerous. It could pollute church teaching and undermine truth. Even though Catholics had become the largest single religious community in the nation by mid-century, they were still a minority of the population. It was hard for a church that saw itself in sole possession of religious truth to acquiesce to minority standing, even if the government gave no official sanction to the majority. From the Catholic perspective, the diverse Protestant bodies represented temptations to the faithful, and the fear always lurking behind even the phenomenal growth of Catholicism was that Catholics would be lured to Protestant falsehood and thus lose their own salvation, which was found only within the Catholic fold. The situation was complicated by claims among some Protestants that their way alone captured the truth of God. Having competing absolute truths invited conflict and controversy.

Interestingly, one of the most vibrant voices claiming that the American context provided a hospitable environment for Catholicism was that of a convert, Orestes Brownson (1803–1876). A religious seeker attracted first to the Presbyterian tradition and then to Universalism, Brownson became a Unitarian after becoming friends with William Ellery Channing (1780–1842). An interest in social reform drew him into the orbit of Boston Transcendentalists before he was finally received into the Roman Catholic Church in 1844. Although Brownson continued to speak out on social matters, such as labor issues, in Catholic circles he became an advocate for what was called "Americanism" or the view that Catholicism as a religion represented the epitome of the values and ideals associated with American democracy. Brownson was so outspoken that church leaders feared he would provoke even stronger resistance to the growing Catholic presence. Articles he penned for his well-known *Quarterly Review* also revealed a kind of elitism that seemed to look down on immigrants, who were the major cause swelling the ranks of Catholicism.

Within the developing structures of American Catholicism came less radical ways of trying to demonstrate to both Catholic believers and Protestant skeptics that Catholicism and democracy were compatible and that Catholics were loyal, patriotic Americans. Among the most significant is the Catholic newspaper, the *United States Catholic Miscellany*, which first appeared under the editorial leadership of Bishop John England (1786–1842) in Charleston, South Carolina. It was joined by a host of other papers as well as pamphlets and shorter pieces published by the American Catholic Tract Society. Regardless, Catholic leaders had to contend with an increasingly shrill, but irrational, hostility on the part of the Protestant rank and file and in some cases on the part of Protestant leaders.

> ## Why Catholicism and democracy go together
>
> A convert to Roman Catholicism, Orestes Brownson aggressively tried to convince both American Protestants and Catholics that the Catholic faith and American democracy were compatible and that Catholicism was really the ideal religion for a democracy. He wrote the following in 1845:
>
>> The Roman Catholic religion, then, is necessary to sustain popular liberty, because popular liberty can be sustained only by a religion free from popular control, above the people, speaking from above and able to command them, and such a religion is the Roman Catholic ... Not dependent on the people, it will not follow their passions; not subject to their control, it will not be their accomplice in iniquity; and speaking from God, it will teach them the truth, and command them to practise justice.
>>
>> ("Catholicity Necessary to Sustain Popular Liberty" (1845), Edwin S. Gaustad and Mark A. Noll, eds., *A Documentary History of Religion in America to 1877*, 3rd ed. (Grand Rapids, MI: Eerdmans, 2003), 444)

Three examples will illustrate how this hostility presented extraordinary challenges to American Catholicism. The first relates to a genre of literature designed to provoke horror and fear among non-Catholics by recounting lurid tales of what supposedly transpired in Catholic convents. Many told similar tales of nuns serving as concubines to priests, giving birth to illegitimate children, baptizing them before slaughtering them, and then burying them in the convent basements. Even before the most well known appeared in 1836 under the title *Awful Disclosures of the Hotel Dieu Nunnery of Montreal* (with the author, a sometime prostitute, using the pseudonym Maria Monk), popular suspicion of what "really" went on inside convents had tragic consequences for the Ursuline convent and school in Charlestown, Massachusetts, just outside Boston. Fueled also by prejudice against the increasing number of Irish immigrants coming to the Boston area, a mob invaded the convent in August 1834, searching for graves of infants in the basement. When they found none, the mob burned the convent to the ground. Especially tragic was the loss of the Ursuline school. There young women, many non-Catholics, received a solid formal education traditionally accessible only to men.

A second illustration concerns presumed Catholic plots to establish a base of power in the Midwest that would allow Catholics to overthrow the American government and transform the nation into a Catholic state. Lyman Beecher (1775–1863), who had been a pastor in Connecticut and then in Boston, gave credence to this paranoia after he became president of Lane Theological Seminary in Cincinnati, Ohio, then an important center for the movement of both goods and people into the Midwest and regions beyond. An heir to the best in New

Figure 8.1 Ursuline convent. Roman Catholic nuns, including the Ursulines, whose convent or place of residence is shown here, helped plant a vibrant Catholicism in the U.S. (© Alexey Sergeev.)

England Puritan theology and a critic of some of the emotional excesses associated with evangelical Protestant revivals of the day, Beecher launched an anti-Catholic tirade in his *Plea for the West* published in 1834, the same year the mob burned the Ursuline convent in Massachusetts. In this work, Beecher constructed a mythic vision of American democracy that saw the nation as a harbinger of the millennial age. That vision was under attack, Beecher continued, because swarms of Catholic immigrants intended to seize control of the entire Mississippi Valley and from there engineer a plot to turn over the entire nation to the pope through the (Catholic) Austrian emperor. Samuel F.B. Morse (1791–1872), known for inventing the telegraph and the code that made telegraphic transmission possible, further fanned such prejudice in a series of letters to the editor published in the *New York Observer*, collected in his *Foreign Conspiracy against the Liberties of the United States* (1834).

Morse also illustrates the third aspect of this irrational hostility, for he later decided to use the political arena as a forum to promote anti-Catholic and anti-immigrant sentiment, also known as nativism. Morse entered the mayoral race in New York City in 1836 as a nativist candidate. Although he lost, nativists coalesced into groups such as the American Republican Party and then the more well-known Know-Nothing Party. Pledged to support only "native-born" (meaning white Protestant) candidates for office, nativist political groups were responsible for burning Catholic churches and homes of Irish-Americans in the Philadelphia area in 1844, an episode that brought several days of mob rule in the City of Brotherly Love. Fears that the tumult would spread to New York City led the Roman Catholic bishop there, John Hughes

(1797–1864), to surround every Catholic church in the city with armed men to thwart a similar attack.

In the political arena, nativist impulses began to wane as the nation moved towards civil war. That regional division illuminates some of the challenges American Catholicism faced. In the South, where pro-slavery sentiment prevailed, rank and file Catholics tended to support the pro-slavery cause, perhaps in the hopes that by echoing the social views of the white Protestant majority they would seem less alien and more like fellow citizens. Few Catholics became part of the antislavery movement as it gained momentum, although outside the South many Catholics echoed popular sentiment in opposing slavery. Remaining aloof from involvement in a controversial social movement like antislavery and quietly supporting the views of the Protestant majority, regardless of region, became a calculated strategy that helped assure the survival of a minority, even though numerically large, religious group. At the same time, with the mushrooming of sectional division, whether rooted in the conflict between the urbanizing, industrializing north and an agrarian south or between a "free" north and a "slave" south, violent anti-Catholicism receded. That division was more serious and had greater potential to destroy the nation than did immigration and the rising strength of a religion that was still "other" to most Protestants. Undercurrents of religious pluralism, despite the tensions that erupted, flowed less swiftly than those that would lead to civil war.

Jews find a home in America

Jewish immigrants coming to the United States before the Civil War were far fewer than Catholic immigrants, but they added yet another dimension to the fabric of American religion. As with American Catholics, Jews would find their own ranks swelling rapidly in the decades between the Civil War and World War I. Yet the foundations for much that transpired then and efforts to secure a place for Judaism in the U.S. are anchored in the antebellum era. In the first years after independence, the largest concentration of Jews was found in South Carolina, centered around Charleston. There the oldest synagogue or Jewish place of study and prayer in continuous operation in the United States survives into the twenty-first century, although a synagogue was founded even earlier in Newport, Rhode Island.

The core of the colonial Jewish population identified with the Sephardic tradition, meaning that its style of religious practice went back to the Iberian Peninsula, to Spain and Portugal. There thriving Jewish communities creatively interacted with both the Muslim and Christian traditions prior to the late fifteenth century, when Jews were required to convert to Christianity, leave Spain and Portugal, or face possible death. Some made their way to England; most English Jews coming to America in the colonial era were Sephardic. So, too, were those whose journeys took them from the Iberian

Peninsula to other places in Europe and even to South America before they arrived in what became the U.S. After independence, most Jewish immigrants had ties to the Ashkenazi heritage, centered around Jewish life in Germany, but in actuality reflective of the Jewish experience in much of western Europe other than where the Sephardic way had flourished. Because many European governments had long placed restrictions on their Jewish populations, the Ashkenazi heritage was less expansive and certainly less cosmopolitan than the Sephardic, often more deeply rooted in the Hebrew past. Hence there was diversity within even the small American Jewish population in the antebellum period, sometimes leading to synagogues offering multiple services, some reflecting the Sephardic approach and some the Ashkenazi.

The German influence, though, came to dominate American Jewish life in the first half of the nineteenth century, and that influence was itself coming to reflect a different kind of diversity within the larger Jewish tradition. That new twist stemmed from the impact of the Enlightenment on German Jewish life, which in turn propelled considerable rethinking about what it meant to be Jewish in the modern world. The result was the emergence of what became known as Reform Judaism, a movement that developed first in Germany and then flourished in the United States, thanks to immigrants and spiritual leaders (rabbis) committed to this way of being Jewish.

One key figure in both Germany and the U.S. is David Einhorn (1809–1879), a rabbi who immigrated from Germany in 1855 and who served congregations in Baltimore, Philadelphia, and New York City. The other major force behind Reform Judaism in America was Isaac Mayer Wise (1819–1900), born in Bohemia but rabbi at congregations in Albany, New York and Cincinnati, Ohio after coming to the United States in the 1840s. Wise later served as president of Hebrew Union College in Cincinnati, a central institution promoting Reform.

At the heart of Reform was a rationalistic impulse stemming from the Enlightenment. In this case, reason required examination of all belief and practice, jettisoning what was irrational or so bound to a past era or culture that it made no sense in the modern world. Then one could determine what was essential or foundational to Judaism and recast it in a way that made sense to rational men and women. For example, what set Jews apart from others in both Germany and the U.S. was their use of Hebrew in prayer and worship as well as their following a dietary regimen based on guidelines in the biblical book of Leviticus. Some advocates of updating Jewish practice even called for eliminating the centuries-old requirement of circumcision for males. Reform wondered if any of this was essential to the inner nature of Judaism.

Even before coming to the U.S., Einhorn had revised the standard Hebrew prayer book and services, translated them into German, and made the services shorter. Much of his work was later translated into English for use in American Reform synagogues. Wise, somewhat less radical than Einhorn, encouraged other changes. Some reflected practices common among Christians, such as not requiring men and women to be seated separately during prayer services, having organs provide musical accompaniment, and offering religious instruction for both girls and boys at Sunday schools (although efforts of some Reform advocates to change the day of prayer from the traditional Sabbath to the Christian Sunday generally failed). In some areas, Jewish congregations experimented with architectural styles so that synagogues came to look like churches from the outside. Even their interiors began to reflect Christian styles, with pews facing the bema or platform where cantor and rabbi stood rather than the more traditional arrangement of men gathered around a bema in the center of the room and women consigned to a gallery. Also, as with many groups that were adding to the American religious mosaic, Reform Jews looked to print media, especially newspapers, to promote their ideas and link together those who shared their commitment to making Jewish practice reflective of contemporary Western culture rather than the ancient Near Eastern past. Isaac Mayer Wise, for example, beginning in 1854, edited two such papers, one published in English (the *American Israelite*) and one in German (*Die Deborah*).

Reform represented a sincere endeavor to emphasize those aspects of Jewish belief and practice that were timeless, but in many ways it downplayed what was distinctive about the Jewish heritage. Given centuries of forced exclusion from the mainstream of society in Europe, confinement to ghettoes or Jewish neighborhoods, and denial of rights of citizenship, almost always at the hands of governments led by Christians, western European Jews moved quickly to adapt to the larger culture when Enlightenment currents lifted some of those encumbrances. Beneath the surface operated an unconscious hope that by abandoning the trappings of religious practice that set them apart from their former persecutors, modern Jews could blend into the larger culture and minimize what might enflame prejudice in the future. The First Amendment's provisions regarding free exercise of religion and prohibition of a national religious establishment seemed to assure that similar recriminations would

The nature of Reform Judaism

- Reform reflected the Enlightenment emphasis on reason
- It questioned whether some beliefs and practices were so tied to the past that they were irrelevant to the modern world
- Reform tried to find what was foundational or enduring in Jewish life and thought
- Critics thought Reform leaders abandoned too much of the religious tradition that sustained Judaism
- Reform did allow Jewish people to assimilate more quickly into an American culture dominated by Christianity

not occur in the U.S. Reform would thus spur more rapid and thorough acculturation in America. Unfortunately, Reform did not eliminate bias or anti-Semitism from American life, even if such lacked government sanction. But in the antebellum period, the ideas associated with Reform not only dominated Jewish life in the United States, they also insured that Judaism added yet another thread to the fabric of American religious life.

Ethnicity's impact on American religion

In the broadest sense, ethnicity has to do with the distinctive character and cultural mores of a people, usually with language, region or nation, race, and sense of identity as key ingredients. These represent artificial constructions in one sense because they are simply convenient ways to classify and talk about the varieties of peoples and cultures that have emerged and often exist side by side. The hundreds of Native American tribal societies and the throngs of immigrants coming from many different nations and cultures that comprise the American peoples mean that ethnicity is a vital feature of American religion and another way to understand why religious diversity in the United States is so rich and expansive. Ethnic dimensions undergird virtually every form of religion in America. For example, even though it is common to talk about "Lutherans" as one strand of Protestant Christianity in the United States, in the background are German Lutherans, Swedish Lutherans, Finnish Lutherans, Norwegian Lutherans, and many others. All illuminate the religious heritage stemming from Martin Luther, but each has distinctive ways of being Lutheran and identifying with that larger Lutheran tradition. In this case, often it had to do primarily with language and place of origin, as Lutheran congregations formed to serve immigrants speaking the same language or coming from the same place, to provide support while they took on an American identity.

American Catholicism and American Judaism also highlight the multifaceted ways ethnicity plays into religious identity. English Catholics provided the core for Roman Catholicism in the U.S., but a significant French component came when Catholic leaders recruited priests to come from France to assist a growing Catholic community in the early republic (not to mention the French and also Cajun ethnic presence in Louisiana and the Spanish presence elsewhere). In time, immigration added German Catholic and, especially, Irish Catholic components. At heart, Roman Catholicism claimed to be a universal church that was the same everywhere. For centuries the use of Latin as the language of the mass or worship demonstrated that sameness. But there were different styles or moods, sometimes different attitudes towards the authority of priests and church officials, and sometimes different ways to celebrate being a Catholic on religious holidays, depending on one's ethnic background. The European parish structure that defined a parish in terms of a given land area did not translate well to the American context. Even in the antebellum period, parishes often came to serve

Catholics who shared the same national, language, or ethnic background. The parish became more than a center for worship and religious practice. It kept alive what was familiar from an "old world" in a new setting as one made adjustments, even one as basic as learning English, in order to be part of American society. One way to think about the parish is to see it as an extended family, with its ministries working like a family reunion to tie together those with kinship ties. That larger function, with its ethnic component, not only made Catholic life in America diverse, it challenged efforts to knit Catholics together in one universal church.

Ethnicity had other facets when it came to American Jewish life. Historically, Judaism's ties to land have to do with God's promise at Sinai to provide those who followed God's ways with a place that would be their own. That "promised land" became a mythic homeland regardless of the actual place or geographic land where Jews lived. At the same time, when governments placed restrictions on Jews just because they were Jews and often violently persecuted them, it was difficult for Jews to develop the emotional ties to place that were part of national identity for other ethnic groups. In some ways, Jewishness itself became an ethnic identity as much as a religious one. Part of what stimulated Reform Judaism in both Germany and the United States was the desire to find some universal basis for Jewish identity. The difficulty, of course, was agreeing about what religious components were integral to Jewish identity. One long-term, but unintended, result is that in the twenty-first century some analysts talk about "secular Jews" or non-religious Jews to describe those who affirm an ethnic Jewish heritage that transcends national backgrounds or geography, but do not engage in specific Jewish religious practices.

Roman Catholicism and Judaism stretched American religion in new directions in the early republic. The interplay of religion and ethnicity that comes into view with these traditions adds yet more depth to that diversity.

Key points you need to know

- Catholics in the early republic relied heavily on support from European Catholics, especially French Sulpicians.
- Immigration, particularly from Ireland, provided the foundation for Catholic growth before the Civil War.
- Some Catholics believed that democracy was incompatible with a strong Catholicism.
- Protestant Americans generally misunderstood the character of Catholicism and were often hostile to its presence.
- Jewish efforts to respond to the modern world led to the Reform movement, which for a time dominated American Judaism.
- Religious identity often reveals close connections to ethnicity.

Discussion questions

1. What contributed to Catholic growth and stability in antebellum America?
2. On what grounds did some Catholics believe democracy was dangerous to Catholicism? On what grounds did other Catholics argue the exact opposite?
3. Why were some Protestants apprehensive of Catholicism? How was that expressed?
4. What roles did women play in allowing Catholicism to flourish in antebellum America?
5. In what ways did Reform Judaism try to rethink Jewish belief and practice to make it reflect conditions of the modern world?
6. What strategies did both American Catholics and American Jews adopt in order to survive in a religious culture dominated by Protestants?
7. How are religion and ethnicity related?
8. What did Catholicism and Judaism add to American religious diversity?

Further reading

Carroll. Michael P. *American Catholics in the Protestant Imagination: Rethinking the Academic Study of Religion*. Baltimore: The Johns Hopkins University Press, 2007.

Gillis, Chester. *Roman Catholicism in America*. New York: Columbia University Press, 1999.

McGreevy, John T. *Catholicism and American Freedom: A History*. New York: W.W. Norton, 2003.

Meyer, Michael A. *Response to Modernity: A History of the Reform Movement in Judaism*. Detroit: Wayne State University Press, 1995.

Sarna, Jonathan D. *American Judaism: A History*. New Haven, CT: Yale University Press, 2004.

9 The impact of civil war and regionalism

In this chapter

This chapter looks first at the impact of the Civil War and sectional division on American religious diversity and how the war itself became a religious event. It then explores how region more generally has spurred its own kind of diversity, using Appalachia, the Southwest, and the areas of Mormon settlement to illustrate developments. The chapter points out how region continued to influence American religious life after the Civil War ended and remains a key factor in religious culture today.

Main topics covered

- How debates over slavery within religious groups and the nation increased regional division
- The splits among several major religious groups along regional lines
- How the end of the Civil War did not end that regional identity
- The continuing development of regional religious styles in other areas such as Appalachia, the Southwest, and places dominated by the Latter-day Saints
- The ongoing role of region in undergirding religious diversity

Debates about slavery spur regional religious consciousness

Although popular perception holds that slavery was the "cause" of the American Civil War, the reality is far more complicated. Many different forces intertwined to create a widening regional difference between the "North" and the "South" in the U.S. As the southern economy became increasingly wedded to cultivation of cotton and tobacco, both of which relied on slave labor, the region remained more agrarian and rural than areas to the north. An expanding network of canals and then railroads in the North provided connections fostering a fledgling industrial economy that gravitated more towards factory villages, towns, and cities. Immigration provided a source for workers in many different fields; immigrants, of course, added to religious diversity as they brought their own religious beliefs and practices with them to the U.S. As public education developed, the greater dispersion of the rural Southern population made it more difficult for schools to succeed. An ongoing hesitation in the South about providing education for African American slaves made the regional educational gap even more pronounced.

Through the first third of the nineteenth century, religious groups served to moderate the effects of this growing regional distinctiveness. Among many evangelical Protestants, for example, emphasis on some inner experience of conversion, reliance on camp meetings and revivals to stir religious interest, and a vision of the nation as a moral example to the world allowed them—regardless of denomination—to feel a strong sense of kinship with one another that more than compensated for economic differences or even disagreements over whether slavery could be morally justified. Even among those who held to lingering Calvinist ideas of predestination and had an aversion to revivals and to efforts of voluntary societies to reform society, a shared religious sensibility fostered bonds that were more powerful than differences that divided. Simply put, Baptists had ties and connections to other Baptists, regardless of region, as did Methodists, New School Presbyterians, Old School Presbyterians, and a host of others.

A few individuals illustrate this linkage across region. Charles Colcock Jones (1804–1863), born in Georgia, received his theological degree from Princeton Theological Seminary in New Jersey, a Presbyterian school, and then served as a pastor, evangelist among slaves, and seminary professor in the South. Methodism's Francis Asbury, who spearheaded organizing the denomination in 1784 in Baltimore, traveled widely in South Carolina and elsewhere in the South, helping plant Methodist class meetings and congregations there. Much of the Baptist presence in the South in the eighteenth century can be traced to Shubal Stearns (1706–1771), who migrated from Massachusetts to North Carolina, and his brother-in-law Daniel Marshall (1706–1784), who left Connecticut and wound up finally in Georgia. In other words, the evangelical spirit, regardless of denomination, transcended region, and the shared religious sensibilities in turn buttressed a sense of identity with the nation and fostered political cohesion.

By the 1830s, though, the ties religion provided were weakening. The American Antislavery Society, a predominantly northern group drawing support from individuals with a variety of religious affiliations, became more aggressive in its efforts to eradicate slavery, rattling even those of a common religious orientation in the South. One of its noted leaders was Theodore Dwight Weld (1803–1895), who had worked with evangelist Charles G. Finney and studied at Lane Theological Seminary in Cincinnati. A religious undercurrent increasingly informed antislavery work, as abolition advocates drew on biblical teaching to condemn the institution of slavery as immoral and sinful. William Lloyd Garrison (1805–1879) gave his antislavery paper,

> ### Garrison links religion and abolition
>
> In a Fourth of July address in 1839 to a Massachusetts antislavery group, abolitionist William Lloyd Garrison highlighted what he saw as the hypocrisy of those who claimed to be Christians yet supported slavery:
>
>> Would to God this [the Fourth of July] were truly what it is not, though lying lips declare it to be—the JUBILEE OF FREEDOM! That jubilee cannot come, so long as one slave is left to grind in his prison-house. It will come only when liberty is proclaimed throughout ALL the land, unto ALL the inhabitants thereof ... Professing to be Christians, yet withholding the Bible, the means of religious instruction, even the knowledge of the alphabet, from a benighted multitude, under terrible penalties!
>
> (From Donald G. Mathews, ed., *Agitation for Freedom: The Abolitionist Movement* (New York: Wiley, 1972), 27)

the *Liberator*, a decidedly religious tone. At the same time, fear of religiously inspired slave revolts in the South remained a constant, especially because the 1831 uprising in Virginia led by Nat Turner (1800–1831) had distinct religious roots. More and more Southern preachers entered the fray, with sermons, pamphlets, and other materials that defended slavery. They abandoned the long-held notion that even if slavery were wrong, it had become an evil necessary to sustaining the Southern economy. Instead they began more shrilly to claim that slavery was ordained by God and therefore a positive good through which Africans could see their presumably savage lives become humanized and civilized. After 1830, the bulk of the most strident pro-slavery literature had clergymen and theologians for authors. As religion fueled both pro-slavery and antislavery endeavors, deeper regional wedges began to appear.

For organized religious bodies, mounting differences linked to slavery led to rupture by the 1840s. Among Methodists, as early as 1808 the General Conference had condemned slavery in principle. For a time, though, the denomination tried to mute the consequences of this position by publishing two versions of its organizational handbook or *Book of Discipline*. One, distributed in the North, contained the resolutions condemning slavery and critical of members who owned slaves; another, intended for use in the South, omitted those sections. Matters began to escalate in the 1830s as antislavery sentiment was growing throughout the North. Although the 1836 Methodist General Conference passed resolutions regarding the evils of slavery, it was also disparaging of the abolitionist movement for enflaming the divisions mounting within the church and the nation. Soon one kind of diversity, that resulting from splinter groups breaking away from a larger denomination, became evident. Some Methodists who were most outspoken in their condemnation of slavery separated from the parent body to form other denominations that remained basically Methodist in their core approach to faith and practice, but were more strongly antislavery than the parent denomination. Among them were the Wesleyan Methodist Church, organized in Michigan in 1841, and the Methodist Wesleyan Connection, emerging in New York over the next two years. Now there were multiple Methodist denominations, very similar to one another except when it came to attitudes toward slavery.

The parent body, though, also soon faced a major rupture. The wife of a Methodist bishop in Georgia inherited slaves who technically then became the bishop's property. The 1844 Methodist General Conference became rancorous when antislavery advocates called for the bishop's dismissal because church policy forbade slave holders from serving as bishops. Northern and Southern delegates recognized that they could not agree on how to deal with the dilemma. So the Southerners at the conference proposed that the denomination divide along regional lines, with a new denomination, the Methodist Episcopal Church, South, being organized the following year. The nation's largest Protestant body was fractured because of slavery; now with two large regional Methodist bodies and a host of smaller ones, the Methodist tradition added to diversity in an unfortunate way.

Similar division followed in 1845 within the largest Baptist body, second only to Methodists in terms of members among American Protestants. There the immediate issue was whether slave owners could serve as officers of various home and foreign mission boards. Some Southerners resented efforts by Baptists from so-called "free" states to make sure no slave holder held such office. They decided to form a new Baptist group. Organized in Augusta, Georgia in 1845, the Southern Baptist Convention at first represented more a coalition of fiercely independent Southern congregations who consented to cooperate with one another on tasks no single congregation could handle appropriately, such as sponsoring missionaries and publishing literature. But it quickly took on all the trappings and vestiges of power that went with the developing denominational structure in the U.S. Once again, diversity came into a denominational family because of internal schism. Once again the issue was slavery.

Although later various Presbyterian groups also splintered along regional lines, some groups did not divide organizationally based on region, even if individual members and congregations often reflected the dominant views held in the larger society—pro-slavery in the South, antislavery or at the very least ambivalent about slavery in the North. Among them were the Roman Catholic Church, which still saw itself as a universal body, and the Episcopal Church. Of course, throughout the nation, scores of local churches did not have ties to a particular denomination. But the splits that occurred presaged the split in the nation at large. Divided churches, historian Clarence C. Goen insisted in a study of religion's role in bringing the nation to the brink of civil war, meant a divided nation.

Others sensitive to the growing sectional conflict turned in an apocalyptic direction. Just as those such as William Miller had looked to signs for the imminent return of

Christ in the 1840s, and revivalists from the time of Jonathan Edwards on sometimes saw upswings of interest in religion as signs of the end, so, too, did some understand the threat of war as another omen that Christ's return was at hand. Sectional division signaled the close of history and impending judgment for the American nation.

The Civil War as a moral and religious event

Divided denominations, coupled with apocalyptic expectation, represent only some of the ways the Civil War is enmeshed with American religious life. In essence, the war itself was a religious event, laden with moral dimensions. It was also a pivotal event, as the American Revolution had been, in transforming the American civil religion, which complicated the fusion of religion and nationalism that helps undergird national identity. Also, the war increased the pace with which industrialization and urbanization gripped the North, while the South found its agrarian economy in ruins, struggling for nearly a century to recover. The end of slavery did come, but at a price—namely the entrenchment of racism and discrimination, especially in the South, but throughout the nation in insidious ways. Yet racism also gave new purpose to African American religious groups and made religious institutions even more central to African American life.

Abraham Lincoln (1809–1865) captured the moral ambiguity of the war in his now well-known second inaugural address, delivered in 1865 when Southern defeat seemed only a matter of time. Never a formal church member, Lincoln nonetheless demonstrated keen religious insight in that speech when he noted that persons on both sides read the same sacred text, the Bible, and sought guidance from the same

> ### Lincoln pinpoints the religious irony of civil war
>
> A famous passage of Lincoln's second inaugural address suggests that the once-dominant religious ethos of the nation had taken on an ironic dimension when the Civil War broke out:
>
> > Both read the same Bible and pray to the same God, and each invokes His aid against the other. It may seem strange that any men should dare to ask a just God's assistance in wringing their bread from the sweat of other men's faces, but let us judge not that we be not judged. The prayers of both could not be answered. That of neither has been answered fully. The Almighty has His own purposes.
> >
> > (Quoted from *Inaugural Addresses of the Presidents of the United States* (Washington: Government Printing Office, 1965), in Conrad Cherry, ed., *God's New Israel: Religious Interpretations of American Destiny*, rev. ed. (Chapel Hill: University of North Carolina Press, 1998), 200)

Figure 9.1 Abraham Lincoln. President Abraham Lincoln, though not a church member, often interpreted the Civil War in highly theological terms (Credit: Portrait of Abraham Lincoln (b/w photo) by American photographer (19th century). Bibliothèque Nationale, Paris, France/ Archives Charmet/ The Bridgeman Art Library. Nationality and copyright status: copyright unknown.)

God through prayer, with each side hoping that such spiritual devotion would bring military victory. Lincoln recognized that these efforts were futile. Both could not receive what they wanted. Instead, he insisted that whatever divine purpose was at work in the conflict remained a mystery. Lincoln also understood that it was useless to try to manipulate God for personal—or regional—gain. It was better, he asserted, and more in keeping with genuine spiritual sensibilities, to seek to bring human actions, even the actions of governments, into harmony with religious principles, not the reverse. Lincoln's assassination just days after Confederate General Robert E. Lee had surrendered to Union forces made Lincoln into a martyr for national unity. He became transformed from a human political leader into a Christ-figure, one whose life was sacrificed for the nation. Lincoln thus became a religious figure, later memorialized in the nation's capital in a structure resembling an ancient temple.

Many Northerners saw victory as a sign of the region's religious virtue, with the abolition of slavery not only an emblem of regional righteousness but a sign that unfettered industrial expansion had divine sanction. With that industrial growth came a growing appreciation for science, sometimes at the expense of religious values. But some were more cautious. Connecticut Congregationalist pastor Horace Bushnell (1802–1876) preached a sermon titled "Our Obligations to the Dead" in which he interpreted the war as a baptism of blood, a ritual of redemption calling both North and South to rekindle commitment to the foundational principles of the nation. But northern Yankees like Bushnell were more inclined to this sort of thinking. For white Southerners, the image of the war as a baptism of blood became more complicated, as white Protestant clergy struggled to craft a regional religious identity that transformed Confederate military figures into religious saints who symbolized the evangelical purity thought to have prevailed in the antebellum South. As a result, there developed a religion of the lost cause, as it has been called, that looked to a mythic past to sustain life. In this view, defeat was God's chastising the chosen people, an effort to recall them to the virtue they had once displayed. But the religion of the lost cause spoke only to the experience of white Southerners, not to that of former slaves.

For Euro-Americans, both northern and southern, the war thus became central to a sense of civil religion, with battlefields transformed into pilgrimage sites and war heroes magnified into exemplars of religious virtue. From the "Battle Hymn of the Republic" for the North and "Dixie" for the white South, songs affirming regional identity took on the qualities of sacred hymns. Protestant denominations that had divided before the war remained divided along regional lines. Religious interpretations of the war and regional civil religion helped perpetuate separate identities. Not until 1939 were northern and southern Methodists able to reunite into a single body; Presbyterian reunion came finally in 1983. Baptists, the other large evangelical body to split into northern and southern bodies, remain in separate denominations even into the twenty-first century.

For African Americans, Lincoln also became heralded as a savior figure, thanks to his issuing the Emancipation Proclamation that ended slavery in those states in rebellion and the Northern victory. But the war hardly became a signal of justice and equality, as racism and discrimination reigned throughout the nation. Those independent African American denominations that had emerged in the North earlier in the nineteenth century moved quickly into the South, recognizing that former slaves were unlikely to want to remain in the same congregations as their former oppressors. Many also launched scores of educational endeavors targeted towards former slaves. They included numerous colleges whose primary aim initially was to train African American clergy. So, too, did numerous mission boards of various northern Protestant groups, with hundreds of women heading south to teach African American children. Some new denominations emerged, further adding to the institutional diversity within American religious life. Among them were the Christian Methodist Episcopal Church, organized in 1870 as the Colored Methodist Episcopal Church and drawing its first adherents from among former slaves who had previously affiliated with the Methodist Episcopal Church, South. Discrimination quickly became the order of the day, and most former slaves found themselves still tied to their old plantations, often now as part of an unjust sharecropping system. The churches took on social, political, and human service functions to meet the needs of a black population that was technically free but still fettered by discrimination.

Freed slaves linked religion and education

After the end of slavery, African American religious institutions blossomed. So, too, did educational efforts among former slaves. Black American leader Booker T. Washington (1856–1915) emphasized that education and religion were closely connected when he wrote:

> Few people who were not right in the midst of the scene can form any exact idea of the intense desire which the people had for education. Few were too young, and none too old, to make the attempt to learn ... The great ambition of the older people was to try to learn to read the Bible before they died. With this end in view, men and women who were fifty or seventy-five years old, would be found in the night schools. Sunday-schools were formed soon after freedom, but the principal book studied in the Sunday School was the spelling-book.
>
> (Quoted in Gunnar Myrdal, *An American Dilemma* (New York: McGraw-Hill, 1964), 2: 883)

The Civil War may have ended legal slavery in the United States, but it did not end regional difference and distinction. If anything, the end of the war solidified distinctive regional identities that became even more magnified as science, technology, and industry continued to transform the North. Nor did the end of slavery create a racially or ethnically inclusive nation. Denominations organized along racial lines kept that component of religious diversity alive. The failure of predominantly Euro-American denominations that experienced regional schism to reunite perpetuated divisions within Protestant groups. Even so, the war serves as only one marker of the ways region was making American religious culture more complex.

Region's impact in larger perspective

Most often one thinks of region in terms of "North" and "South" in the age of the Civil War. But by the middle of the nineteenth century, region was adding to religious diversity in the nation in many different ways. Within the South, for example, the Appalachian area that stretches from northern Alabama through the mountains of Tennessee, Kentucky, the Carolinas, Virginia, and West Virginia was already taking on a distinctive identity that gave a particular tone to its religious culture. Before the end of the 1840s, areas as diverse as Texas and Oregon had become part of the U.S., adding other regional considerations to the mix. Then, shortly after the Latter-day Saints migrated to the area around the Great Salt Lake, war between the U.S. and Mexico brought much of the Southwest, including the Utah Territory, into the nation, and a decade before the Civil War erupted, California had became a state. These areas illuminate the ties between region and religion as much as the sectional division between North and South, albeit in different ways.

Appalachia remains a region within a region. That is, much of what is distinctive about mountain culture and its religious heritage flourishes within but separate from the larger religious culture of the South. Geography and topography are keys to that distinctiveness. Euro-Americans made their way into Appalachia as they pushed westward through the mountains. Although many kept migrating westward, first into what is today Tennessee and Kentucky, some remained in the mountains. Unlike much of the rest of the South, the mountain region was not well suited to cultivation of tobacco, cotton, or much else. The terrain itself worked against thriving agricultural development. At the same time, it was not easy for people—and then for goods and products—to make their way through a mountainous area. When roads and then railroads began to appear, most tried to go around the mountains rather than through them. So the mountains became somewhat isolated, creating a region of its own where contact with the larger culture was sporadic and less interactive than was the case for other areas.

Although Appalachia reveals the denominational diversity that marks the American nation, the character of the region has left a distinctive imprint. Much of Appalachian Protestantism, regardless of the theological heritage of the particular church, exhibits a profound appreciation of visible holiness. Some of that reflects the Holiness Movement whose currents cascaded through the larger culture in the nineteenth century with its emphasis on assuring that all of life reflect the holy nature of God that Christians believed Christ revealed. In Appalachia, that holiness joined with a deep and abiding relationship to the land and nature, in part because the temper of the land for so long shaped daily life in the mountains, to create a regional religious style. In essence, that relationship between holiness and nature infused Appalachian holiness with a keen sense of the supernatural, of the reality of a power beyond human control that could impact the course of life. An appreciation for herbal remedies, which in one sense come from the land, illustrates one way of living in harmony with the land and the supernatural power behind it; in the twenty-first century the increasing awareness of holistic medicine highlights an approach long known in the mountains.

So, too, in the early twentieth century, when a few mountain people understood one passage in the New Testament Gospel of Mark to enjoin them to handle serpents as a sign of faith and holiness, they drew on what they often encountered through living in a dynamic affinity with the natural world around them. Serpents were not natural enemies, but emblems of the power of life and death often encountered in daily life in the mountains. In faith, one could access supernatural power superior even to that of a serpent, demonstrated by handling serpents as an act of religious devotion.

In recent times, phenomena like interstate highways and mass communications have challenged traditional mountain culture by bringing its people into more sustained

Figure 9.2 Appalachian serpent handling. In the heart of the Appalachian Mountains, some Holiness Christians handle serpents as a sign of their faith

The biblical basis for handling serpents

Holiness people in Appalachia live both close to the land and close to the Bible, particularly the King James Version. When some sought to demonstrate their commitment to faith and holiness, they did so by handling poisonous serpents as an act of worship. They believed the Bible commanded them to do so because of the words found in Mark 16: 17–18 (King James Version):

> And these signs shall follow them that believe; In my name shall they cast out devils; they shall speak with new tongues;

> They shall take up serpents; and if they drink any deadly thing, it shall not hurt them; they shall lay hands on the sick, and they shall recover.

Even today in the mountains, churches that identify themselves with the words "signs following" are likely to take this passage as the foundation for their distinctive religious practice.

contact with those for whom mountain life seems a window into a simpler past. Yet for the people of Appalachia, the region itself resounds with echoes of supernatural power and goodness. Ties to the land, to holiness, and to a realm beyond remain strong.

The character of the land also helped shape areas of the Southwest, particularly where the Latter-day Saints followed Brigham Young in the 1840s. Plains and seeming wilderness offered different challenges to them than the mountains did to the people of Appalachia. But the "Mormon belt" which gradually expanded from Utah through Nevada and into Idaho and surrounding areas required as much diligence to render it suitable to support a growing population as did the mountains of Appalachia. It, too, became a region with an aura of its own, not only claiming a majority of the population, but infusing the culture with a Mormon presence through institutions such as Brigham Young University and the many church-sponsored social welfare centers. Some areas remain relatively self-contained even today, allowing for some difference within the larger Mormon tradition. For example, although for more than a century the Latter-day Saints have repudiated the practice of polygamy, some small offshoot groups still believe it is the way ordained by God. There are places within the region where those who represent these strains within Mormonism continue to live, with the practice often overlooked or not really seen by others unless there is some particular incident that calls attention to the community. Region makes this diversity possible.

Various Native American tribal cultures, along with earlier colonial Spanish Catholic missions, dotted much of the rest of the Southwest, from Texas westward. But by the time that Texas entered the Union and war with Mexico brought much of the rest of this area into the U.S., the Catholic presence was rather muted. Nonetheless, there remained vestiges of a Hispanic Catholicism, sometimes intertwined with Native American religious cultures, which endured, stamping the area with a unique style and augmenting the nation's religious culture. In this region and on into California, which became a state in 1850, Americans and other immigrants drawn to the area—spurred especially by reports of the discovery of gold deposits in California and the move to build a transcontinental railroad—found themselves in a region where religious institutions were few and far between. Unlike colonial New England, where Puritanism had dominated, or places where the Church of England had early exercised hegemony, there was no "established" or even quasi-established religion that lingered and sometimes functioned as a foil against which other "minority" groups struggled to find their niche. Rather, when this region became American territory, the heritage of separation of church and state, of a religious marketplace where all groups were theoretically equal and their leaders could seek to persuade people of their validity, was a given. For some smaller religious groups with particular ethnic roots, such as Hutterites and Mennonites, the expanse of space in the Great Plains offered land to locate new religious communities where a religious style could become a total way of life.

Given this ethos, diversity was integral to the religious life of the region at the outset of the area's becoming part of the United States. Other factors also contributed. The boldness and daring required to endure a difficult and long move across the continent meant that some migrants to the West possessed extraordinarily free spirits and inquiring personalities. Many were what that age called "free thinkers," who were suspicious of any formal religious doctrine or creed and open to radical experimentation when it came to religion. Their early presence has left an enduring substratum to the culture of the region, particularly in the Pacific Northwest. Even in the twenty-first century, residents of that region report the lowest rate of formal affiliation with organized religious groups of any in the nation, a sign that free thinking remains central to the common life of the people.

Other dimensions of diversity come into view because of immigration across the Pacific from Asia. By 1882, when federal legislation first excluded immigration from China, more than 60,000 Chinese Americans were living in California, subject to many of the same expressions of hostility and prejudice that had come to the Irish decades earlier when they arrived in large numbers in Eastern port cities. Restrictions on Japanese immigration, much of it coming via Hawaii, came in 1907. Yet when laws banned Chinese immigration, some expressions of Buddhism had already planted themselves on American soil. Many of them were eclectic in approach and family-oriented in practice, reflecting popular practice in China that fused strands of Mahayana Buddhism with traditional Chinese religious ways associated with Confucianism and Taoism. Because of the tight immigration policy, Buddhist religious life remained confined to areas where the small Chinese-American communities survived. In the later nineteenth century, representatives from other Asian lands and religions had opportunity to increase American awareness of the spiritual heritage of the Orient at a venue such as the Chicago World's Parliament of Religions, held in 1893. But their primary audience was composed of American urban intellectuals, rather than those for whom these religious paths echoed the cultures of their ancestral lands. Nonetheless, the Asian presence, particularly in the Far West, added yet another dimension to American religious diversity.

Further north, in the Alaska territory added to the United States in 1867, the oldest Russian Orthodox churches in North America had their beginnings a century earlier. The story of Eastern Christianity's addition to American religious diversity, however, is more intertwined with the immigration that mushroomed between the close of the Civil War and the outbreak of World War I. But its roots are tied to region, to the islands along the coast of Alaska.

Other facets of religion and region

The sectional differences and the religious splits accompanying them that led to the American Civil War in the mid-nineteenth century may represent the most common way of thinking about region. Yet from Appalachia to California and other parts of the Southwest, attentiveness to land and space—to regional particularity—creates yet another lens through which to view religious diversity. With North and South, much of the regional variation had ties not only to religion, but to economic and political differences. With other areas, especially with Appalachia, conditions stemming from life in the mountains and relative isolation from other regions gave the religious culture a distinctive cast, regardless of denominational or institutional difference.

Further west, styles among Native American tribal peoples different from those encountered decades earlier along the Atlantic coast, along with an undercoating of colonial Spanish Catholicism, laid foundations for other expressions of regional religious diversity. Trickles of immigration from Asia and the westward movement of people as different from each other as Mormons and Mennonites fostered yet other faces of the variety of religious options. Because most of these groups wound up doing rather well in their new surroundings, they indicated that the nation could harbor almost any kind of religious expression and still flourish as a nation. There are, however, some episodes of violent conflict between Mormons and government authorities in a story that is as much political as religious, and growing angst about Asian immigrants led in time to highly restrictive and sometimes exclusionary government policies. The "Mormon belt" in time emerged as a distinct region, and Chinese Americans planted Buddhism and traditional Chinese religious approaches on American soil. Diversity reflected regional life as much as it stemmed from differences in belief and practice. What made it all feasible was the long-standing heritage captured in the First Amendment to the U.S. Constitution, which prohibited Congress from establishing a national religion or from restricting the free exercise of religion.

Two generations ago, historian Sidney Mead suggested that the keys to understanding the contours of American religious life after the arrival of Europeans were found in an unusual sense of time and space. He argued that, when compared with Europe, for example, Americans lacked the sense of past time that stretched back centuries and centuries. They thus had a bold spirit that fueled experimentation and fostered the formation of new groups. But they also encountered over time a vast space, much of a continent, where people were free to move away from others to follow their own spiritual pursuits. This sense of space works in other ways as well. It is what buttresses the whole idea of region and religious identity that develops in tandem with a particular region. So space and region continue to nurture and support religious diversity in American life.

Key points you need to know

- Divisions among Protestant denominations over slavery weakened the bonds that helped hold the nation together.
- The Civil War was not just political, economic, or military; it had significant religious and moral implications.
- Efforts to understand the war drew on religious images that helped sustain distinctive regional identities.
- African American churches took on many roles besides being simply religious institutions to respond to the needs of former slaves.
- Other areas, from Appalachia to the Southwest and Far West, also demonstrate particular regional features with consequences for religion.
- Region remains a key ingredient in fashioning American religious life.

Discussion questions

1. How did denominational divisions contribute to the sectional conflict that led to the American Civil War?
2. In what ways did the Civil War become a religious event?
3. How did religious interpretations of the Civil War help sustain regional identity after the war ended?
4. In what ways and why does Appalachia demonstrate the persistence of a regional religious character?
5. What contributes to the regional religious culture of areas such as California and the Southwest?
6. On balance, how are region and religion linked in the United States? How has region added to the story of religious diversity?

Further reading

Frankiel, Sandra Sizer. *California's Spiritual Frontiers: Religious Alternatives to Anglo-Protestantism, 1850–1910.* Berkeley: University of California Press, 1988.

Goen, C.C. *Broken Churches, Broken Nation: Denominational Schisms and the Coming of the Civil War.* Macon, GA: Mercer University Press, 1985.

McCauley, Deborah Vansau. *Appalachian Mountain Religion: A History.* Urbana: University of Illinois Press, 1995.

Mead, Sidney E. "The American People: Their Space, Time and Religion." *Journal of Religion* 34 (October 1954): 244–55.

Miller, Randall M., Harry S. Stout, and Charles Reagan Wilson, eds. *Religion and the American Civil War.* New York: Oxford University Press, 1998.

Moorhead, James H. *American Apocalypse: Yankee Protestants and the Civil War.* New Haven: Yale University Press, 1978.

Noll, Mark A. *The Civil War as a Theological Crisis.* Chapel Hill: University of North Carolina Press, 2006.

Silk, Mark, gen. ed. *Religion by Region.* 9 vols. Walnut Creek, CA: AltaMira, 2004– . Each volume covers a specific region and has an individual editor in addition to Silk.

Stout, Harry S. *Upon the Altar of the Nation: A Moral History of the Civil War.* New York: Viking, 2006.

10 Immigrants, industries, and cities

In this chapter

This chapter probes the major wave of immigration to the U.S. between the Civil War and World War I, along with the impact of rapid industrialization and urbanization on religious life. In particular, it examines the stunning growth of Roman Catholicism, Judaism, and Eastern Orthodoxy as well as shifts in African American religion. The chapter looks at diverse religious responses to these social changes, concluding with discussion of interaction of religious and social forces, changing gender roles in religious life, and the continuing importance of ethnicity in sustaining religious diversity.

Main topics covered

- The stunning increase in immigration after the Civil War
- New sources of immigrants and their religious cultures
- Challenges to American Catholicism resulting from immigration
- New currents within American Jewish life
- The growth of Eastern Orthodox Christianity in America
- Changing roles for African American religious groups
- How Protestants responded to the growth of cities and industry
- Different religious approaches to social change
- New roles for women in American religious life

The United States becomes an urban, industrial nation

Two of the most stunning developments in American life in the half century after the Civil War came with the growth of cities and the growth of business and industry. The first transformed the country from a rural to an urban nation by the time of the 1920 national census and the second signaled a parallel move from an agricultural economy to an industrial one. Between the 1860 census and the 1890 census, several cities in the

Northeast tripled in population; New York City, for example, grew from just under 1.1 million to more than 3.4 million people. More striking, though, are growth rates for cities in the Midwest. Chicago, with fewer than 100 people when it was still Fort Dearborn in 1830, by 1900 counted more than 1.6 million, making it the fifth-largest city globally.

The urbanization of America not only reflected the movement of thousands from farms and villages to larger cities, but it also demonstrated the impact of immigration after the close of the Civil War. Again, numbers suggest the magnitude of the story. In the half century after sectional military conflict ended, around 25 million immigrants arrived on American shores, with the vast majority crowding the growing cities and providing a cheap labor supply that in turn propelled the brisk growth of industry. Estimates suggest, for example, that 80 percent of all persons living in the New York City metropolitan area in 1890 were either immigrants or the children of recently arrived immigrants.

In this era, what a later generation called urban planning was unknown. Also as yet unknown, for the most part, were social welfare programs administered by government agencies. Also, assertions that government should regulate business and industry—even in terms of safety conditions in the workplace, minimum age for employment, or maximum hours for work—were controversial at best. The prevailing philosophy insisted that all depended on the individual. Among the results was the birth of the tenement, a style of apartment building that crammed several families into a few rooms with shared kitchens and, especially, often ill-equipped shared toilet

Urban growth transforms America

Josiah Strong, executive secretary of the interdenominational Evangelical Alliance, in his book *Our Country* (1885) had a telling subtitle: *Its Possible Future and Its Present Crisis*. Strong used emerging social science data to examine changes underway, but believed that the new immigration, urbanization, and industrialization could undermine Protestant visions for the nation. Here he uses statistics to sketch the impact of urban growth:

> The city is the nerve center of our civilization. It is also the storm center. The fact, therefore, that it is growing much more rapidly than the whole population is full of significance. In 1790 one-thirtieth of the population of the United States lived in cities of 8,000 individuals and over; in 1800 one twenty-fifth; in 1810, and also in 1820, one-twentieth; in 1830, one-sixteenth; in 1840, one-twelfth; in 1850, one-eighth; in 1860, one-sixth; in 1870, a little over one-fifth; and in 1880, 22.5 percent, or nearly one-fourth. From 1790 to 1880 the whole population increased twelve fold, the urban population eighty-six fold.
> (Josiah Strong, *Our Country*, edited by Jurgen Herbst (Cambridge, MA: Belknap Press of Harvard University Press, 1963), 271–72)

facilities. In turn, the tenement brought the city slum, for housing could not keep pace with the influx of millions into the cities. Another concern centered on public health, for poor housing, poor working conditions, and poor sanitation combined to make American cities potential breeding grounds for disease. The factory smokestack was quickly replacing the barn silo as the symbol of the American economy, just as the ghetto tenement supplanted the farmhouse as a place of residence.

These demographic changes also had significant implications for American religious culture and for enriching the diversity that lay at its foundation. Those implications come into view from a variety of perspectives. First, already existing religious groups had to rethink how they organized and operated in this new urban, industrial context. Second, many of the social welfare efforts that today seem part of the government's domain fell to religious groups. Who else would look after the poor and homeless? Third, immigration brought new religious orientations into the mix. Some of that reflected a vital shift in the sources of immigration. In the years before the Civil War, the vast majority of European immigrants to the United States looked to countries or regions of northern and western Europe as places of origin. Even though there were ethnic, religious, and cultural differences among them, broad common patterns transcended the differences. After the Civil War, the bulk of immigrants came from southern, central, and eastern Europe, where religious styles were different even within the same religious tradition, cultural patterns reflected different ethnic heritages, and social histories provided rather different senses of the past. In a word, Polish Catholic immigrants might seem as removed from Irish American Catholics who were part of the famine generation as they were from Methodist evangelicals or Scots-Irish Presbyterians, and Jewish immigrants who survived pogroms or active persecution in Russia seemed as unlike Reform Jews in Charleston or Cincinnati as they did Episcopalians in New York or Quakers in Philadelphia. And the bulk of the immigrants who arrived during these decades were Roman Catholic, Jewish, or Eastern Orthodox.

Understanding how immigration, urbanization, industrialization, and religion are all connected together and how the overall story adds more layers to the diversity that characterizes American religious life comes into sharper focus through examination of what transpired among some particular religious traditions. Four examples will provide illustration: the response of American Catholicism, the challenges confronting American Judaism, the growth of various Eastern Orthodox bodies, and the adaptation of African American religious groups to this rapidly changing cultural context.

Immigrants and in-migrants reshape traditions

How immigration shaped American Catholicism comes quickly into view when one looks once more at numbers. Historians of American Catholicism emphasize that every decade between 1880 and 1920 more than one million Catholic immigrants came to the U.S. That rate of immigration, along with natural propagation, swelled the total of Catholic adherents from just over 6.25 million in 1880 to close to 16.4 million forty years later. During that time, the overall U.S. population, according to census figures, grew from just under 76 million to just under 92 million. In other words, Catholics alone accounted for over 60 percent of the total growth in the nation's population in the years immediately following the Civil War.

Institutionally, the church moved quickly to accommodate this enormous influx, but many challenges ensued. Quite naturally, immigrants from one area tended to cluster in the same neighborhood when arriving in America. There they could hear languages that were familiar, share the vicissitudes of adjusting to a new culture with others who would understand, and also celebrate the ethnic and cultural ties to a homeland that remained part of individual and group identity. Consequently, the idea of the Catholic parish as encompassing a geographic area, with all the faithful in that area part of it, gave way to parishes organized along ethnic or national lines—even if Latin remained the language of the mass in them all. Sometimes priests accompanied immigrants, continuing to serve people with whom they could communicate. Together they adjusted to a new political and cultural environment. Many of these Catholic parishes were the nation's first "megachurches" (although that term was not used until the later twentieth century); as immigrant communities grew, a single parish might welcome upwards of 3,000 at mass on a given Sunday morning—most, if not all of whom walked to worship because they lived in the neighborhood.

Soon immigrant communities vied for living space in the nation's cities. In places like Chicago and New York, for example, it was not unusual to find several large churches all within a few blocks of each other, each serving a different immigrant community—Polish, Croatian, Slovak, Bohemian, Hungarian, Lithuanian, and more. These "national" churches—as other immigrant churches and in time many Jewish synagogues—took on multiple functions. They assisted new arrivals in finding housing, struggled to help parishioners gain employment, offered help in learning English, and engaged in a host of other activities that were not specifically religious, but responses to the immediate needs of a burgeoning immigrant population.

Immigrant children posed other challenges. Public schools even in the larger cities were ill equipped to take in thousands more students each year, especially when those students spoke faltering English. As well, Protestant assumptions had so long undergirded public school curricula that Catholic leaders were wary of sending Catholic immigrant children to those schools lest they be subtly—or even directly—weaned away from their Catholic faith. By 1884, when the Third Plenary Council called on every parish to have its own school within two years, four out of ten parishes already had primary schools. Even if the larger goal never became a reality, Catholic parochial schools became vital to sustaining the church and allowing Catholic immigrants to make the transition to a new homeland. Women religious or nuns who immigrated frequently provided many of the instructional staff (at relatively modest cost) in parish schools serving people from their own native lands; they could speak the native language and at the same time provide instruction in subjects necessary for success in the new American environment. Catholic higher education received a boost in 1889 when, thanks to a donation from a wealthy laywoman, the Catholic University of America opened its doors in the nation's capital, although it did not enroll its first undergraduates until 1905. Many other historically Catholic colleges and universities either trace their origins to this era of massive immigration or expanded considerably by adding professional schools and other programs during this same era. For example, the University of Scranton, in a heavily Catholic area of northeastern Pennsylvania, began in 1888, while Fordham University in New York City, although founded in 1841 as Irish immigration skyrocketed, added a law school in 1905.

Alongside the schools, many parishes produced newspapers and other periodical literature. This material proved vital to introducing immigrants to American life in a way they could understand and appreciate. So, too, parishes became centers of ethnic celebration, with regional custom fused onto things Catholic. Indeed that particular fusion helps explain why even Italian Americans, long the least churched among Catholic immigrants, gradually came into parishes in higher numbers than in the Italian peninsula. Another mechanism to spur commitment came with parish revivals, an adaptation of the popular Protestant practice, but in this case a preaching effort over several weeks designed not so much to secure new converts as to deepen the faith of those already Catholic.

This rich diversity within Catholicism produced some stress. The move to organize "national" parishes that would link together congregations serving the same immigrant

An Italian immigrant talks about the church

Julian Miranda, who came to the U.S. from Italy as a child, later recalled the ambivalence that Italian Americans had about the church as an institution:

> On the topic of the church, it must be remembered that Southern Italian men were not so church scrupulous as the women although they were Catholic. I think no one should mistake their non-church attendance for a lack of belief in the Roman Catholic faith. The seeming lack of scrupulosity in Italians should not delude anybody about their lack of commitment to Christianity and its central ideas. I think there is a great paradox, and a great ambivalence there.

(In Salvatore J. LaGumina, ed., *The Immigrants Speak: Italian Americans Tell Their Story* (New York: Center for Immigration Studies, 1979), 131, quoted in Edwin S. Gaustad and Mark A. Noll, eds., *A Documentary History of Religion in America since 1877*, 3rd ed. (Grand Rapids, MI: Eerdmans, 2003), 20) communities into something like separate denominations within the Roman Catholic Church eroded the image of Catholicism as a universal faith. Church leaders successfully quashed such efforts. More problematic was Rome's fear of and ultimate condemnation of "Americanism" that reflected a misunderstanding of the dynamic of church–state relations in the United States. For a time, American Catholic leaders, largely following James Cardinal Gibbons (1834–1921), devoted as much time to assuring church authorities in Rome of the health of the American church and the loyalty of the immigrant millions as to ministering to the needs of the people through parishes, schools, papers, and other endeavors.

Other internal differences complicated the story. In many cities, the "national" parishes formed to serve particular ethnic communities meant that several large churches formed within a few blocks of each other. Since each served a different ethnic constituency, it was awkward to see the church as one unified entity. In other areas, what was in theory a parish serving a geographical area might have virtually all its congregants from one ethnic tradition, since immigrants from that tradition dominated the neighborhood. In this case, to outsiders, Catholicism became associated with a particular ethnic community. Once again, it was hard to see the church's claim to be a universal body that was everywhere the same.

As well, some Catholic immigrants came from areas of Europe that had a distinctive worship life that varied from the standard Latin mass. Some Ukrainian immigrants, for example, adhered to a different liturgy, known as the Eastern Rite. Although faithful Catholics who looked to the pope as a spiritual leader, Eastern Rite Catholics in some cases also had married male priests. Catholic leaders in the U.S., hoping to have a unified church in the midst of a larger culture influenced by Protestant Christianity, sometimes tried to avoid recognizing married Eastern Rite priests. They also frequently tried to impose the Roman Latin mass on Eastern Rite congregations. Hence, even within immigrant Catholicism, there was diversity, and there were times when diversity brought tension.

But that tension was minimal compared to the ways Catholic growth stirred outbursts of anti-Catholicism. Some Protestants evidenced strong prejudice against the new immigrants, demonstrating that legal guarantees of free exercise of religion came with a price. In many communities, conflict over support for schools caused much division. Nationally, much of the anti-Catholic sentiment represented the age-old fear of what was "other" and "different"—in this case the ethnic and cultural styles of southern, central, and eastern Europe. Protestant spokesperson Josiah Strong, in his book *Our Country* (1885), deftly appraised the challenges to urban and national life resulting from the upsurge in immigration, but called for Protestants to try to convert immigrants to Christianity, even the millions who were Roman Catholic Christians. For Strong, an American identity was wedded to a Protestant identity, regardless of the Protestant denomination. It took generations for Catholics to defuse that irrational hostility. But their sheer numbers meant that the additional faces they gave to American religious life were here to stay.

American Judaism also grew by leaps and bounds between the Civil War and World War I. Although the total numbers were well below Catholic figures, the proportional increase was stunning. Estimates suggest that the American Jewish population increased from around 250,000 in 1880 to around 3 million by the time World War I began. As with Roman Catholics, the great immigration of Jews brought its own variety and challenges. Those who came from eastern Europe were less likely than earlier Jewish immigrants to identify with a place of origin, thanks largely to pogroms and other violent moves to contain and restrain the Jewish population. For them, as noted earlier, the ethnic and the religious merged to create a cultural identity of its own. Like other immigrant communities, Jewish Americans clustered in the cities in neighborhoods where there were systems of support and signs of the familiar. Among the more famous was New York's Lower East Side, a ghetto area with a flourishing Jewish immigrant culture.

The history of confinement to European ghettos or to farming villages known as shtetls meant that stricter religious practice and tradition shaped Jewish life for these immigrants. Isolation from the larger culture facilitated maintenance of strong religious observance, although many were illiterate and knew only a life of poverty. With no binding national allegiance or language, Yiddish emerged as something of a uniting force, but it had scores of dialects. For German Jews who embraced Reform after coming to America, these fellow Jews seemed something of an embarrassment.

Once in the United States, eastern European Jews responded to their new environment in diverse ways. Some found strength to survive by keeping to strict religious observance; they coalesced into the movement called Orthodox Judaism because it sought to adhere to traditions passed down over generations. Others reveled in their new freedom, abandoning religious practice and channeling the passion and energy once directed to religion into various social movements, from labor unions to radical politics. For them, Jewishness was more an ethnic than a religious identity, especially given the lack of a single national homeland. Yet others saw release from ghetto and shtetl as a call to reclaim the land promised to Moses in ancient times, a Jewish homeland where Torah and nation would merge; Zionism or the call for a Jewish state added another strain to Jewish diversity.

Some wanting to retain a Jewish religious identity believed Orthodoxy too confining and Reform too willing to abandon essentials. When Romanian-born Solomon Schechter (1847–1915) in 1902 left his teaching post at London's University College to become president of the struggling Jewish Theological Seminary in New York City, this last approach, known as Conservative Judaism, found a strong leader. In essence a middle ground, Conservative Judaism attempted to remain faithful to age-old tradition, but with greater flexibility than Orthodoxy in interpreting how. So, for example, Conservative synagogues might not separate the faithful by gender as was Orthodox practice and they might offer part of the service in English and part in the traditional Hebrew.

Figure 10.1 Jewish Theological Seminary (front entrance). The Jewish Theological Seminary in New York City became a bulwark of the distinctively American movement called Conservative Judaism (© The Jewish Theological Seminary.)

With financial support from the small, but better-established Jewish community, newer arrivals set up a range of social institutions, from hospitals to newspapers to welfare agencies, that helped immigrants find jobs and homes. Part of the stimulus for doing so came from the same forces that propelled Catholic immigrants to establish parochial schools, namely the language and cultural ties that fostered community and comfort in an alien culture. These institutions nourished Jewish identity, whether understood in religious or in ethnic terms, in a social setting where little buttressed such an identity and much undermined it. Some responded to a perceived residual, insidious anti-Semitism. Eastern European Jews were, to many American Protestants, a greater threat than were Catholics. Jewish hospitals, for example, assured that Jews received medical care, should other hospitals refuse them entry.

Adding to the religious diversity marking this wave of immigration was Eastern Orthodox Christianity. Eastern Christianity's roots lie in distinctive approaches to belief, practice, and church organization, developing by the sixth century; more formal division came in 1054. Imbued with a mystical aura, looking to icons as windows into the spiritual realm, and seeing scripture alive with allegory, the Eastern strand of Christianity had interacted with Greek, Slavic, and Russian cultures, absorbing much of their mood. Recruited to labor in mines and steel mills in eastern cities such as Pittsburgh and also in places such as the copper mines of Utah, Orthodox Christians—mostly Greek, Syrian, and Armenian—joined their spiritual cousins who had earlier come from Russia to Alaska and the west coast, bringing a cluster of ethnic denominations that augmented the diversity within American Christianity.

Yet even within the Orthodox tradition there was considerable variety. Once again, ethnicity is critical, for frequently Orthodox bodies had organized along national or ethnic lines in Europe. That distinction held as immigration increased their numbers in the U.S., with several different Orthodox denominations, as Americans called them, staking a claim to this strand of the larger Christian tradition. Many remained wary of the ways ethnic communities other than their own gave Orthodox expression distinctive cultural twists.

A significant internal migration brought thousands of African Americans from the rural South to the urban, industrial North, beginning in the 1890s. So extensive was this shift that it became known as the Great Migration. It received a boost when the fledgling automobile industry got underway just before World War I. Jobs on automotive assembly lines attracted African Americans trapped in poverty by a discriminatory sharecropping system. Many of these in-migrants found northern African American congregations formal and staid, compared with the style of the rural South. There were also socio-economic class differences and often a disparity in educational levels between the middle-class members of northern congregations and those who believed working in northern industries would bring them out of poverty.

The religious dimensions of this migration are multifaceted, yet difficult to pin down. Many African Americans from the rural South formed small independent congregations around dynamic preachers, rather than affiliating with churches identified with African American or other denominations. Hundreds of such "storefront" churches appeared, each drawing on the more affective, enthusiastic style familiar to the rural South to provide some sense of order and comfort to those attending. So these congregations functioned as immigrant parishes did for Catholics; they tried to adapt to a new environment what was familiar and what had provided life with meaning, realizing that changes would accompany adjustment to the urban ethos. Of course, in some areas of the South, black Catholics continued to have a vital presence, more so in areas such as Louisiana, where historically a Catholic presence had been strong.

More complex were ways gender made a difference. As the older African American denominations seemed to cater more to those who were not recent in-migrants, they also became more inclined to echo the gender roles prevailing in the larger culture. Thus, black denominations looked almost exclusively to men to serve as pastors, even if women had once been effective itinerant evangelists. Garnering support for missionary and educational work also became increasingly the domain of women. But among some of the independent congregations made up primarily of those who had moved from the rural South, women could still be found preaching and engaging in pastoral activity. Yet women may have accounted for an even larger proportion of African American congregations than they did among white congregations. But for them, the racism that cascaded through all American life served frequently to limit their opportunities for leadership in either church or society. Few were welcomed into the ranks of those calling for woman suffrage, and few were found in social reform movements such as the Prohibition endeavor.

Diverse Protestant responses to an urbanizing nation

Immigration enriched American religious life not only by adding to the ranks of groups like the Eastern Orthodox, but also by adding to the ethnic mix within Roman Catholicism and Judaism. In the latter case, it also led to the emergence of new expressions of an old tradition in the form of Conservative Judaism. At the same time, the various Protestant bodies also confronted the challenges of rapid urbanization and industrialization, and the responses were also diverse and varied.

Among the evangelically inclined, many looked to groups like the Young Men's Christian Association (YMCA), which had roots in England. First organized in Boston in 1851, the YMCA built residences to house young men who came to the cities looking for work in the new industries and businesses. It also offered activities from Bible study to recreational opportunities as a way to assure that these men were not lured into temptation but remained faithful to their moral and religious heritage. Not all men came under the influence of groups like the YMCA. City missions offered temporary accommodations and such for men whose profligate ways resulted in their being homeless or perhaps victims of alcohol abuse.

Movements such as the YMCA and city missions received support from a revamped urban revivalism that updated the techniques and message stretching back to frontier camp meetings and the earlier urban revivals of Charles G. Finney. The premier revivalist of the later nineteenth century was former shoe salesman Dwight L. Moody (1837–1899), a tireless backer of the YMCA, who added to the appeal of revival meetings by including lively singing of popular hymns led by his associate, Ira D. Sankey (1840–1908). Sankey, from a Methodist background, also had strong connections with the YMCA. The two took their brand of urban revivalism to England, receiving much acclaim. Moody looked like a successful businessman of the era as he preached a simple message of redemption and reasoned with his audience to abandon lives ruined by sin and temptation. Moody understood that responding to a call for conversion would not assure a fresh direction in life. So he founded schools for men and women, a Bible institute to train church workers, and a host of other ancillary activities to provide support.

Far more flamboyant was a one-time professional baseball player who became the leading urban evangelist in the early twentieth century, Billy Sunday (1862–1935). He too had connections with city missions and the YMCA. Sunday in many ways became the stereotype of the "hellfire and brimstone" preacher, punctuating sermons with theatrical displays and using colloquial language that he thought appealed to working men more than a staid, polished style. He singled out working men's use and

Figure 10.2
Dwight Moody. One-time shoe salesman Dwight Moody was the nation's premier urban revivalist in the years just after the Civil War (Courtesy of the Moody Bible Institute.)

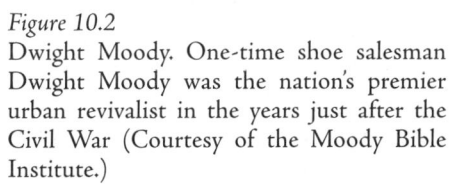

Figure 10.3
Billy Sunday. Former baseball player Billy Sunday thrilled audiences with his theatrical style of revival preaching early in the twentieth century (Courtesy the Ames Historical Society.)

possible abuse of alcohol as one of the major forces infecting urban life. Like Moody, Sunday idealized an image of American life before immigration, urbanization, and industrialization had transformed the nation, sometimes creating a mythic, romanticized past when religious values seemed more central to common life. The diversity accompanying a new age was unsettling, for it revealed that there were many sets of common values in the nation.

Some new religious movements appeared which, like Moody and Sunday, saw individual conversion as the key to improving life in the cities, promoting successful careers for workers, and securing stable family life. Among them was the Salvation Army, founded in Britain in the 1860s when conditions in London's slums stirred William Booth (1829–1912) to action. Salvation Army work in the U.S. began in 1880, and was eventually spearheaded by Booth's daughter Evangeline (1865–1950). Targeting city dwellers overlooked by other denominations, the Army provided job training, some basic education, short-term housing, meals for the hungry, and a range of other programs that all were combined with a religious message urging conversion.

Some congregations in existing denominations became known as "institutional churches" not because they were organized as institutions but because they expanded the scope of what they did to meet the needs of urban residents. Many, for example, added

148 *Immigrants, industries, and cities*

Figure 10.4 Evangeline Booth. Evangeline Booth, a leader of the Salvation Army, assured that women had key roles in this religious movement (Courtesy the Library of Congress.)

buildings with rooms rented at low cost to immigrants. Some built gymnasiums and other recreational facilities to provide a safe environment where workers could spend leisure time. Many offered what today would be called "continuing education" opportunities in areas other than the expected Bible study or devotional experience. These added vocational training for men to what a later age called home economics for women, programs designed to fit people for productive lives in an urban setting. Some organized "settlement houses" in slum or ghetto areas to bring these ministries directly to the people, rather than waiting for them to come to the churches. Women staffed many of the settlement houses and kindred ministries and provided strong leadership within groups like the Salvation Army. Social ministries spawned by urbanization and industrialization created new venues for women to engage in endeavors outside the traditional "woman's sphere" of the Victorian home. In the more rural South, women also entered the arena of social change, leading the struggle to end the practice of lynching.

Others found all these approaches wanting, for they presumed that hope for a better life rested solely with individual initiative. Some believed that systemic problems thwarted individuals who remained powerless to change unsafe working conditions, improve wages, end slum housing conditions, or even make basic necessities such as access to electricity affordable. Consequently, there emerged what became known as a "Social Gospel" movement. At its center were figures such as the Baptist Walter Rauschenbusch (1861–1918) and Congregationalist Washington Gladden (1836–1918). Rauschenbusch, while pastor of a German Baptist congregation in New York City, observed the helplessness of his parishioners at the hands of industrial magnates eager to amass fortunes in part by paying low wages and requiring long working hours. Similar conditions awakened Gladden while a pastor in the industrial town of North Adams, Massachusetts.

At heart, the Social Gospel called for reform of the institutions that controlled workers' lives, from business to government; Social Gospel advocates recognized that calls for individual salvation made little sense to workers struggling to provide for their families, those trapped by the system. Drawing on the message of justice found in the ancient Hebrew prophets and the social teachings of Jesus, Rauschenbusch made a classic case for a Christianity with a social message in his 1907 book *Christianity and the Social Crisis*. Social reform needed to precede and thus pave the way for individual regeneration. In many cases, Social Gospel leaders supported the growing labor union movement as one means to alleviate the situation of workers. Not all calling for social reform were Protestants. The Catholic theologian John A. Ryan (1869–1945) was drawn into reform efforts after seeing the ethical implications of the new industrial order portrayed in a papal encyclical called *Rerum novarum*. In *A Living Wage* (1906), Ryan insisted that workers had an inherent right to a just wage, one to meet basic needs, because of their inherent human dignity.

Many Social Gospel ideals became part of the Progressive movement in politics early in the twentieth century. Their enduring impact on diverse denominations came as more and more Protestant bodies began to adopt statements of social principles, such as the "social creed" approved by the Methodist Episcopal Church's General Conference in 1908. The movement also spurred diverse denominations to engage in cooperative efforts, at first to alleviate some of the suffering that accompanied urban

What is Social Christianity?

Walter Rauschenbusch, one of the key figures of the Social Gospel movement, attempted to describe Social Christianity in a popular study book that he wrote for use by college students:

> The development of what is called "Social Christianity" or "the social gospel," is a fusion between the new understanding created by the social sciences, and the teachings and moral ideals of Christianity. This combination was inevitable; it has already registered social effects of the highest importance; if it can win the active minds of the present generation of college students, it will swing a part of the enormous organized forces of the Christian Church to bear on the social tasks of our American communities, and that will help to create the nobler America which we see by faith.
>
> (Walter Rauschenbusch, *The Social Principles of Jesus* (New York: Association Press, 1916), 196)

industrialization, but then on a more permanent basis when several came together in 1908 to form the Federal Council of Churches. In retrospect, it seems as if Protestants found as many different ways to relate to the emerging urban world as there were different Protestant groups.

Ethnicity, gender, and reform in urban America

Immigration, urbanization, and industrialization added layers of complexity to religious diversity in America. The shift from a northern and western European base for immigration to southern, central, and eastern Europe wove countless new ethnic subcultures into the fabric of society. American Catholicism, especially, found its destiny inextricably tied to ethnicity. In many cases, the distinctive religious qualities of a particular ethnic group emerged first in the American context, as parishes became centers not only for religious affairs, but also for sustaining cultural patterns and an identity linked to what was familiar. In other words, what distinguished Polish Catholicism from, for example, Italian Catholicism became clearer in America, where ethnicity and religious style assumed a fresh importance. The unique feature of Italian American Catholicism—that lively, festive approach—developed on the American side of the Atlantic. So, too, other ethnic communities developed their distinctive auras. For Catholics, parish schools, a religious press, and other periodicals became ways to preserve an identity tied to another place while making the transition to a new identity in a new place.

Much the same held for Jewish immigrants, but with some differences. Lacking the firm identification with place in Europe, many of the millions of Jews who came to the United States between the Civil War and World War I came to regard Jewishness itself as an expression of ethnicity as much as, if not more than, an expression of religious belief and practice. The new environment added to the internal diversity within Judaism, for strands that coalesced into Orthodox Judaism and Conservative Judaism developed as alternatives to the Reform Judaism that dominated American Jewish life. Ethnicity likewise shaped the story of Eastern Orthodox Christian immigrants. Ethnic identity also took on fresh dimensions among African Americans who migrated from the rural South to the urban North.

American Protestantism in its predominantly Caucasian expressions remained incredibly diverse as it moved to deal with the challenges of immigration, urbanization, and industrialization. Some denominations dealt more directly with immigrant constituencies; Lutherans, for example, remained divided into many diverse denominations reflecting the ethnic backgrounds of their members until well into the twentieth century. More evangelically inclined Protestants sought to rescue individuals from the ravages of urban life, offering redemption along with assistance, often through a revamped form of urban revivalism. Some groups that affirmed this approach, such as the Salvation Army, began their ministries during the later nineteenth century and thus added to diversity as new denominations. Other shades of diversity emerged when individuals from a variety of groups sought to reform social structures, attempting to transform the foundations of the social order according to biblical principles of justice; their gospel had a social message as well as one of personal salvation. New agencies, from settlement houses and city missions to the Federal Council of Churches, added to diversity in another way. Many of them drew support from individuals from a variety of denominations or from several denominations. This diversity, then, came not so much in the formation of new religious groups as in cooperative organizations and agencies devoted to meeting the needs of urban working-class families.

Much of the success of all these efforts came from the labors of women. Thousands of Roman Catholic nuns worked with immigrant communities in the cities, especially by providing the staff for parochial schools and other parish ministries. Among African Americans, sometimes women emerged as charismatic preachers in storefront churches attended by recent migrants from the rural South. For other Protestants, denominational and cooperative efforts to respond to the conditions of life among the urban working class offered opportunities for women to engage in activities that drew them from the home into service work that sought to make life better for millions. Although there were a handful of women evangelists among Protestants in the later nineteenth century, most groups other than ones like the Salvation Army shied away from women in positions of formal leadership, even if they depended on women to staff social service ministries.

If a common thread runs through the many tiers of diversity in American religious life as the nineteenth century gave way to the twentieth, it is an optimism that, no matter how great, American religion could face any challenge presented by the arrival of millions of immigrants

Women in the Salvation Army

In an 1899 report about the work of the Salvation Army in the United States, Frederick Booth-Tucker singled out the prominent role played by women, known within the Army as Hallelujah Lassies:

> In no religious or secular organization is there so free a hand allowed to women as in The Salvation Army, and to this fact is undoubtedly due a large measure of its success. The Hallelujah Lass has from the earliest days of the movement proved herself its Joan of Arc. Into the heart of slumdom she has carried the banner of salvation, and if her bonnet has become an equally familiar sight in the offices of our merchant princes, it is only that she may plead the claims of the poor and champion their cause.

(Frederick St. George de Lautour Booth-Tucker, *The Salvation Army in America: Selected Reports, 1899–1903* (New York: Arno Press, 1972), quoted in Edwin S. Gaustad and Mark A. Noll, eds., *A Documentary History of Religion in America since 1877*, 3rd ed. (Grand Rapids, MI: Eerdmans, 2003), 171) and by the transformation of the nation from a rural, agrarian society to an urban, industrial one. Social institutions could be reformed. Immigrants could be housed and trained for jobs, jobs that would pay a living wage. Simply put, the nation had the resources and the abilities to take on all the challenges. Diversity was a boon, for it meant that many different approaches would be tried. Eden, not Armageddon, would be the realized goal. What none expected was the devastation that would come with World War I. That dashed all grand hopes against the rocks.

> **Key points you need to know**
> - Between the Civil War and the end of World War I, the United States became an urban nation.
> - New immigration swelled the ranks of American Catholicism, Judaism, and Eastern Orthodox Christianity.
> - Migration to Northern cities added diversity to African American religious life.
> - Many Protestants thought immigration, urbanization, and industrialization would destroy the nation.
> - Some Protestants sought to address new social problems through revivalism and an approach that stressed individual initiative.
> - The Social Gospel represented a different approach that looked to changes within social structures, based on religious and ethical principles, to create a better society.
> - Women played major roles in helping American religious groups relate to the new conditions that came with immigration, urbanization, and industrialization.
> - This major wave of immigration strengthened the ties between ethnicity and religion in American culture.

Discussion questions

1. How did immigration after the Civil War affect American religious life? How did it add to religious diversity?
2. What new currents emerged within American Judaism because of immigration after the Civil War?
3. What characterized the different approaches to responding to social problems among American Protestants in the late nineteenth and early twentieth centuries?
4. How did urbanization and industrialization transform American religious life?
5. What role did women play in how religious groups responded to the challenges of immigration, urbanization, and industrialization?

6. What new facets of diversity came to light because of urbanization and industrialization?
7. How did immigration between the Civil War and World War I cement the ties between religion and ethnicity in American life?

Further reading

Curtis, Susan. *Consuming Faith: The Social Gospel and Modern American Culture*. Baltimore: The Johns Hopkins University Press, 1991.

Erickson, John H. *Orthodox Christians in America: A Short History*. New York: Oxford University Press, 1999.

Lindley, Susan Hill. *"You Have Stept Out of Your Place": A History of Women and Religion in America*. Louisville, KY: Westminster John Knox, 1996.

Magnuson, Norris. *Salvation in the Slums: Evangelical Social Work, 1865–1920*. Rev. ed. Grand Rapids, MI: Baker Book House, 1990.

Raphael, Marc I. *Profiles in American Judaism: The Reform, Conservative, Orthodox, and Reconstructionist Traditions in Historical Perspective*. San Francisco: Harper and Row, 1988.

Sernett, Milton. *Bound for the Promised Land: African American Religion and the Great Migration*. Durham, NC: Duke University Press, 1997.

Shaughnessey, Gerald. *Has the Immigrant Kept the Faith?* Reprint, New York: Arno Press, 1969.

Winston, Diane H. *Red-Hot and Righteous: The Urban Religion of the Salvation Army*. Cambridge, MA: Harvard University Press, 1999.

11 Other dimensions of urbanizing America

In this chapter

This chapter examines how the missionary movement and the World's Parliament of Religions added global dimensions to American religious diversity. Then it probes issues of gender, in terms of both the role of women and the religiosity of men. Other aspects of diversity come to light when looking at developments among Native Americans, ranging from missionary efforts to the emergence of new religious movements among tribal peoples. Finally, the chapter discusses how a search for relief from the conditions of urban life through rural retreats, Bible conferences, and adaptations of the camp meeting influenced religious life and increased its variety.

Main topics covered

- The ways interest in world missions spurred diversity
- The World's Parliament of Religions
- How changing gender roles continued to impact religion
- Ways men expressed religiosity that diverged from how women expressed religiosity
- New expressions emerging within Native American tribal religious cultures
- The changing nature of camp meetings
- How fresh fascination with the Bible became linked to desires to retreat from city life

American religions encounter world religions

The upsurge in immigration in the later nineteenth century bringing millions of Roman Catholics, Eastern Orthodox Christians, and Jews to America was only one force prompting Americans to become aware of different cultures and different ways of being religious. The years between the Civil War and World War I also witnessed

Figure 11.1 John R. Mott. He was a key figure in the early international missions and ecumenical movement

a dramatic increase of interest in world missions. Much of that interest came to life through some of the same forces that propelled American evangelical Protestants to organize city missions, settlement houses, and other agencies that sought to respond to the problems accompanying rapid urbanization.

The evangelist Dwight L. Moody, an untiring supporter of various home mission enterprises and especially of the YMCA, became a key player in stimulating what that age called foreign missions. Through Moody's influence, religious revivals began to spread among some of the nation's leading colleges and universities in the 1880s, where branches of the YMCA helped stimulate religious fervor. By 1890 several hundred collegiate YMCA groups flourished, as did the cognate organization for women, the Young Women's Christian Association (YWCA). Using the YMCA/YWCA network, Moody organized a conference at his Mount Hermon School in Massachusetts aimed at encouraging collegiate men and women to commit themselves to serve as missionaries carrying the Protestant evangelical gospel—without regard to denomination—to nations overseas, particularly lands in Asia that had long fascinated Americans. More than 2,000 attended Moody's second conference in 1887. This response convinced John R. Mott (1865–1955), who had a Methodist background and spearheaded YMCA work on the campus of Cornell University, to organize the Student Volunteer Movement (SVM) in 1888.

In retrospect it is clear that much of this work was designed to nurture the religious zeal of students and thus almost a form of home missionary work. The SVM and then the Laymen's Missionary Movement, organized first in Presbyterian circles in 1906, did recruit some individuals to serve as missionaries. The rationale was complex, but linked to American imperialism and to fears that the new immigration undermined the presumed Protestant Anglo-Saxon character of American society. Efforts to evangelize the world within one generation reflected a desire to impose evangelical Protestant ways on people whose cultures and religious heritages were not only extraordinarily diverse, but also very different from what white Protestant Americans knew. In this sense there was an eschatological or apocalyptic undertone to the movement; taking the Christian message throughout the world would hasten the arrival of the kingdom of God on earth.

Enthusiasm for global missions also represented a desire to Americanize and Protestantize the world, so that when immigrants came to the United States they would already fit the mold that white evangelical leaders thought carried divine approval. Then, too, it allowed Protestant leaders to avoid dealing directly with some of the more pressing problems facing the nation as it became more diverse in terms of both the ethnic backgrounds of its people and their religious styles. Converting the so-called "heathen" who happened to have a religion different from any form of Protestant Christianity deflected attention from other concerns which were beginning to reveal a growing intellectual diversity within American religion that ignored denominational boundaries, one with roots in ideas associated with evolutionary theory and new methods for studying the biblical text.

Missionary activity did not always result in what was intended. On the one hand, as with those drawn to missionary work during the antebellum evangelical awakening, this generation of missionaries gradually came to recognize that foreign cultures and their religions had integrity of their own. Some women missionaries became loath to return to the United States, for they enjoyed positions of religious leadership and social respect in mission work denied them in the U.S. Missionaries also came to realize that humans in every culture and of every religion wrestled with the same dilemmas of trying to make sense out of their experiences in life, particularly experiences such as suffering and death that seemed to lack much meaning.

One unintended byproduct of the missionary movement was the birth of a field of study, first in Germany and England, known as comparative religion. At its center was German-born Friedrich Max Müller (1823–1900), whose interest in Sanskrit and connections between language and belief systems in ancient India led in 1868 to his becoming the first professor of comparative theology at Oxford University. Max Müller also served as the initial editor of a major publishing project that brought together sacred texts of world religions—Hinduism, Buddhism, Confucianism, Taoism, Jainism, Sikhism, Zoroastrianism, Islam—in English, making them accessible to millions. What was once alien and exotic, almost always seen as "other," became humanized and more real. Slowly, Americans, particularly through university study, found their religious horizons expanding and a new expression of diversity in their midst.

What made religions whose primary home was in other lands even more alive came when a World's Parliament of Religions convened as part of a world's fair held in Chicago to celebrate the 400th anniversary of Christopher Columbus's first voyage of discovery. The idea of bringing together representatives from various world religions came in part from a Swedenborgian who headed the exposition's committee on auxiliary meetings. Individuals with ties to the Free Religious Association or to Unitarians and Universalists did much of the organizing. Although Protestant Christians dominated the planning committee, it included a rabbi and a Catholic priest. Max Müller expressed great support for the undertaking, but had to decline an invitation to attend. The goal of the seventeen-day parliament was to emphasize that all religions shared a universal vision. Even though Christian speakers made just over three-fourths of the 194 presentations at the parliament, planners invited representatives from such religions as Hinduism, Buddhism, Jainism, Shintoism, Zoroastrianism, Confucianism, Taoism, and Islam, along with numerous Christians and Jews. The interfaith atmosphere became clear at the opening session on 11 September 1893, when the Roman Catholic James Cardinal Gibbons led the thousands assembled in reciting the Lord's Prayer.

The parliament aroused considerable controversy. Dwight L. Moody, for example, voiced strident opposition. He and many others felt the gathering dangerous. They believed that the presence of non-Christians talking about their own faith and practice meant that organizers did not believe that Christianity was superior to all other religions. Opponents feared that speakers could too easily lure people into thinking that religions such as Hinduism or Islam also contained truth. At the same time, though, there is little doubt that some organizers had hoped that the parliament would provide the opportunity to persuade non-Christians of the superiority of Christianity to their own beliefs and practices, resulting in their conversion.

Christians—and Protestant Christians at that—dominated the formal sessions, but the hit of the parliament was a young man from India, a disciple of the Hindu thinker Sri Ramakrishna. Swami Vivekananda (1863–1902), born Narendranath Dutta, dazzled the audience with both his charismatic speaking style and his appearance. Sporting a turban, Vivekananda exuded an exotic authority. He also stunned listeners when he spoke persuasively about a universal religion. By that, Vivekananda did not mean that he hoped the scores of diverse religions that existed would somehow merge into one. Rather, based on his Hindu heritage, he described a religious consciousness within all humans that could be awakened. That consciousness was universal, and the same universal spirit could stir it to life anywhere. Vivekananda affirmed religious diversity, but in a far more expansive a way than most Americans, even those coming to terms with the range of ethnic expressions of Catholicism, a host of Protestant denominations, and a variety of other groups in the nation's cities. The diversity he affirmed resulted from the variety of ways this universal spirit awakened the religious consciousness in different people, usually in ways that reflected their own cultural and ethnic heritage. There might be one spirit, but there were diverse expressions of that spirit. In this approach, his understanding was thoroughly grounded in Hindu thought.

> ### Looking toward a universal religious impulse
> At the Chicago World's Parliament of Religions, a Hindu speaker described what he meant by a single, universal divine reality behind all religion. Note how his notion takes in both female and male:
>
>> He is everywhere the pure and formless one. The Almighty and the All-merciful. "Thou art our father, thou art our mother; thou art our beloved friend; thou art the source of all strength; give us strength. Thou art he that bearest the burdens of the universe: help me bear the little burden of this life."
>>
>> (Quoted from John H. Barrows, ed., *The World's Parliament of Religions* (Chicago: The Parliament Publishing Co., 1893), vol. 2, in *A Documentary History of Religion in America since 1877*, 3rd ed., edited by Edwin S. Gaustad and Mark A. Noll (Grand Rapids, MI: Eerdmans, 2003), 72–73)

Vivekananda remained in the United States for around two years, establishing in several cities centers organized around principles of the Hindu teaching of Vedanta that is based on the sacred texts called the Upanishads. He also advocated—and may well have introduced to America—the practice of yoga. Part of the appeal of his Vedanta Society was its non-exclusive nature. That is, one could attend lectures sponsored by the Vedanta Society and remain affiliated with another religious group or congregation. Its thrust was thus primarily intellectual, for it promoted a hybrid understanding in which those interested could combine beliefs and practices from a variety of sources into a personal style. Few Indian Americans came into its orbit.

The fascination with things Hindu that Vivekananda sparked also gave a boost to other religious alternatives already existing in the United States, but still very much on the margins of religious life. Among them was Theosophy or the Theosophical Society, founded in 1875 by the Russian immigrant Madame Helena Petrovna Blavatsky (1831–1891). She insisted that her teachings had roots in ancient Tibetan Buddhist wisdom, but when Annie Wood Besant (1847–1933), the estranged wife of an evangelical Anglican priest, became head of the Theosophical Society after Blavatsky's death, several Hindu ideas were added to the core. Besant caused a stir at the 1893 World's Parliament, for by then she, too, affirmed that there was a single universal religious consciousness within every person.

The World's Parliament, while hoping to show commonalities among religions, really demonstrated how diverse religious expression actually was, particularly when one expanded the scope to include traditions that had long flourished outside the United States. For a time, it promoted a mood of toleration and acceptance, leading some to think that, through mutual understanding, global harmony would result even if the manifestations of religion remained diverse. The comparative study of religion, already a going concern, received quite a boost, as now many more wanted to understand other religions on their own terms, recognizing that, if diversity remained, at the bottom were shared questions and concerns. The parliament also left its imprint on the global missionary movement, for in its wake missionaries became more accepting of the indigenous cultures and their accompanying religious expressions than before. In its own way, the World's Parliament of Religions stimulated religious diversity on an even broader scale.

Gender issues add new dimensions to American religion

In the later years of the nineteenth century, gender issues had their own far-reaching influence in American religious life. It was not only that women religious or nuns provided many of the personnel that allowed a burgeoning immigrant Roman Catholicism to flourish. Nor was it simply that women found opportunities to engage in significant social service through settlement houses and other such endeavors. In retrospect, a gender divide sustained diverse religious worlds throughout the entire culture. It was a divide, however, that often ignored the even deeper rupture in American culture and religion stemming from racial discrimination. Gender issues were, in a sense, the luxury of white Americans.

Chapter 6 noted that seeds of the gender divide were planted in the antebellum period when, in areas of the nation where factory villages appeared, the family ceased to function as an economic unit in which everyone—men and women, adults and children—contributed to provide life's necessities. The separation of paid work from the home increasingly made the home the sphere of women and the world of work outside the home the domain of men. Also, changes in childrearing patterns and even in the religious nurture of children followed. Primary responsibility for both became part of the domestic sphere where women held sway. The acceptance of different gender roles and responsibilities meant, for example, that alongside the Holiness revivals associated with Phoebe Palmer in the years just before the Civil War there was also a businessmen's revival aimed at strengthening the religious commitment of white Protestant men. Also, because women continued to outnumber men as church members, especially among evangelical Protestants, clergy—though almost always male—spent so much time with women in the course of their work that the ministry itself became a feminized vocation.

These trends, coupled with those idealizing the "true woman" as being spiritually inclined, became even more entrenched following the Civil War, especially where white Protestant women were concerned. For Catholic immigrant women, many of whom were part of the labor force, the "true woman" model bore little resemblance to their lived reality. The same was true for African American women, who experienced not only discrimination based on race in the larger culture but also increasingly a discrimination based on gender within the black churches.

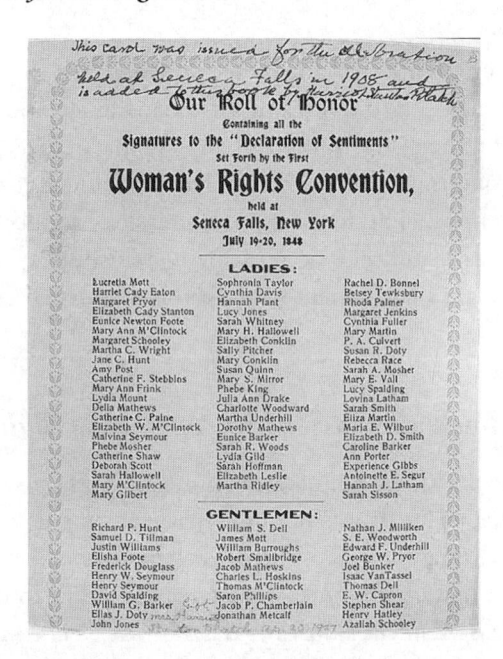

Figure 11.2 Seneca Falls convention. Early feminist Elizabeth Cady Stanton organized a convention at Seneca Falls, New York, that called for full equal rights for women. Stanton also produced a version of scripture called *The Woman's Bible* that reflected her own rationalist views (Courtesy of the Library of Congress.)

Reaction to the trends that dominated white Protestant culture came from both women and men. Elizabeth Cady Stanton (1815–1902), for example, as early as the 1840s, recognized that not only religious institutions, but American society at large denied basic rights to women, the most basic of which was the right to vote. After organizing a convention in 1848 in Seneca Falls, New York in the heart of the burned-over district, where calls for women's rights dominated discussion, she not only continued her efforts to call for woman suffrage, which did not come until nearly two decades after her death, but also launched efforts to transform American Protestant religious institutions so that women would no longer have a second-class status within them. Stanton thought that the churches perpetuated a form of slavery when it came to the status of women, a posture reinforced by blind adherence to scriptural passages thought to call for the submission of women to men. Possessed of a keen intellect, Stanton tackled the biblical text itself, near the end of her life producing the *Woman's Bible* that eliminated passages denigrating women and offering commentary that highlighted women's spiritual capacity.

Methodist-bred Frances Willard (1839–1898) took a different approach. A strong advocate for increased educational opportunities for women, Willard, who lived in Evanston, Illinois, on the edge of Chicago, observed at first hand some of the challenges that urbanization and industrialization brought to American families. At first, she was consumed by a conviction that excessive use of alcohol by working men was destroying

> ### Women claim their place as religious leaders
>
> Methodist Frances Willard, after being denied a seat as an elected delegate to her church's General Conference, began more stridently to address issues of gender. She issued the following call to action in her 1888 presidential address to the WCTU:
>
> > By a strange and grievous paradox, the Church of Christ, although first to recognize and nurture woman's spiritual powers, is one of the most difficult centers to reach with the sense of justice toward her, under the improved conditions of her present development and opportunity ... *Woman, like man, should be freely permitted to do whatever she can do well*.
> >
> > (Frances Willard, "President's Annual Address," *Minutes* (Chicago: Women's Christian Temperance Union, 1888), 41, as quoted in *In Our Own Voices: Four Generations of American Women's Religious Writing*, edited by Rosemary Radford Ruether and Rosemary Skinner Keller (San Francisco: HarperSanFrancisco, 1995), 229)

the American family; men who spent their wages on alcoholic beverages abused their wives, failed to provide adequately for their families, forced poverty-stricken women into prostitution, and offered bad examples of moral behavior. Willard's reputation stems primarily from her work in organizing and then leading the Women's Christian Temperance Union, an agency whose work paved the way for the national experiment with Prohibition in the early twentieth century. Willard also came to believe that temperance, woman suffrage, and the denial of ordination to the ranks of professional ministry were all intertwined. Women voters could use their influence to control the liquor industry and thus enhance family life, which would in turn acknowledge household leadership by women. On the religious front, Willard knew there were far more women than men in the nation's churches; to her, ordaining women as pastors was simply logical. A dynamic speaker, Willard attracted substantial audiences, but also aroused much opposition, even among religious leaders who saw their own prerogatives threatened.

Although most groups refused to ordain them, Protestant women had some opportunities to serve as itinerant evangelists. Among the more well-known is Maria Woodworth-Etter (1844–1924), who began her ministry with a series of revivals in the Midwest in the 1880s. Their success, resulting in large part from her extraordinary speaking ability, led to invitations to hold evangelistic campaigns in major cities throughout the country. Never conventional in her views, Woodworth-Etter pioneered the divine healing that later became more central to Pentecostal expressions of Christianity, although, in her case, lawsuits claimed her healing ministry was a form of practicing medicine without a license. Nonetheless, she laid the groundwork for the ministry of female evangelists in the twentieth century.

Figure 11.3 Maria Woodworth-Etter. Although usually denied roles as pastors, scores of women such as Maria Woodworth-Etter, pictured here, became well-known itinerant evangelists (Courtesy of Flower Pentecostal Heritage Center.)

American Jewish women were also rethinking their roles in religious and public life. The experience of immigration was especially challenging to Jewish women. Even though Jewish life in eastern Europe had been restrictive and women were generally on the periphery of religious activity such as study of the Torah, the role of the wife and mother remained something of a constant. Immigrant conditions often added a pernicious poverty to social dislocation. Jewish women took menial jobs in developing industry, such as doing piece work at home in the expanding garment industry, in order to support their families; some were drawn into labor activism and radical political activity. With the organization of the National Council of Jewish Women in 1891, drawing mostly from among Reform women, and then the Jewish Women's Congress, held in conjunction with the World's Parliament of Religions, calls resounded to rethink the traditional role of women in Jewish life, provide increased educational opportunities, and end the notion that Jewish women were inferior to Jewish men. None wanted to abandon the role of women within domestic Jewish life, but most wanted to expand it.

Matters of gender addressed not only concerns for the role and status of women in American religious life. As America became more urban and industrial, popular perception held that men were absenting themselves from organized religion in ever greater numbers. Among Catholic immigrants, women indeed seemed more likely to engage in church activities, at least during the time of adjustment to a new environment. But by the early twentieth century, Protestant leaders were decrying the absence of men in the churches, noting that more men belonged to fraternal orders and lodges such as the Masons and the Odd Fellows than to churches. For working men, who often lacked the power to control the conditions under which they labored, the workplace itself was by no means a setting celebrating their human dignity. As cultural patterns made the home the sphere of women, working men often felt that they had little control over domestic space as well. For millions, at least until the time of the Great Depression, fraternal orders and lodges became "men's sphere" or space where men associated primarily with other men. Religious leaders often looked askance, for they knew that lodges held ceremonies akin to religious rites (often using religious language and images) and therefore functioned to provide a sense of order and meaning for their members that pastors and preachers believed was the role of the churches. Many of the lodges reinforced other cultural patterns, restricting membership on the grounds of race or ethnicity. Most excluded Roman Catholics and African Americans, even if they were also fellow Christians.

Catholic authorities were also wary of secret societies that were Protestant-based, fearing that participation in them which the church did not control might lure Catholic men away from the faith. But the anti-Catholic posture of many fraternal orders in 1882 stirred Michael J. McGiveny, a young priest in New Haven, Connecticut, to organize a parallel for Catholic men known as the Knights of Columbus. African American men looked to Prince Hall masonic lodges for the same sort of fraternal fellowship fused with religious overtones. Estimates suggest that, by the beginning of the twentieth century, around 40 percent of all American men were lodge members, a figure much larger than the percentage who were members of an organized religious group.

Figure 11.4 Masonic symbol. Fraternal orders like the Masons, whose symbol is shown here, attracted millions of men, some of whom found organized religion too feminized.

In both Britain and the United States, the two leading industrial nations of the time, a "muscular Christianity" recasting the Protestant Christian message in terms designed to appeal to men as men attempted to counter trends that saw women as the bulwark of organized religion and exemplars of genuine spirituality. Social Gospel advocates such as Walter Rauschenbusch portrayed Jesus as a social activist in order to convince men that social service was appropriate for men as well as for women. Evangelist Billy Sunday, as noted before, held services for "men only" and became noted for his use of a crass colloquial style that he believed attracted men. When some New England Protestants early in the twentieth century realized that there were 3 million more females than males in white Protestant churches in America, they organized a program to draw men into the churches and into social service. Called the Men and Religion Forward Movement, this endeavor involved coordinated efforts in 1911–1912 in cities and towns across the nation to involve men in a series of meetings that would in turn engage them in both religious activity and social service work. Some gatherings promoted world missions. But the main thrust was social service at home, predicated on the assumption that a more contemplative spirituality appealed to women but not to men, but one that involved action and service did. A short-lived increase in the number of men in the nation's Protestant churches ensued, but much of the impetus stimulated by the Men and Religion Forward Movement fizzled out with the outbreak of World War I.

Concerns based on gender thus illustrate another vein of diversity. Simply put, women continued to sustain most of the work of organized religion, but were denied opportunities for formal leadership. Little in organized religion recognized the spiritual identity of women as women, even as society increasingly regarded women as more religious than men and made the home not only women's sphere but also the center for religious nurture. Men, especially working men in the nation's cities, continued to spurn membership in organized religion, looking to auxiliary institutions such as fraternal orders and lodges to provide some of the framework of meaning for life that religious institutions thought their particular task. Men and women, regardless of any specific religious label, went about the business of being religious in different ways. Gender thus added yet another layer of diversity within American religion.

New currents among Native American tribal religions

As the American nation spanned the continent, Native American religious life witnessed its own expressions of diversity. The consignment of Southeastern tribes to reservations in Oklahoma by no means ended interaction with the larger culture, which remained hostile to Native Americans and insensitive to the dynamics of tribal life. Federal policies continued to deprive Native Americans of access to ancestral lands, extending wherever possible the reservation system that eroded the heart of tribal life. Gradually some religious communities came to regard Native Americans as subjects for conversion, organizing missions on the reservations and other efforts to bring indigenous peoples into the orbit of Christianity. Conversion became equated with "civilizing" native peoples, just as it became identified with "Americanizing" immigrants—all of whom had some sort of religious identity. Among some Native American peoples in the Southwest and West, the heritage stretching back to Spanish colonial missions left an imprint, with a residue of Christianity tacked on to tribal custom and practice.

The deep cultural dislocation that resulted from national expansion and official policy stimulated efforts to revitalize tribal life, even if the resulting religious expressions diverged from traditional ways by incorporating ideas drawn from Christianity. Among the earliest is a form of millennialism that emerged in the Pacific Northwest in the teachings of a Wanapum prophet named Smohalla (c.1815–c.1895). Educated at Catholic mission schools, Smohalla experienced numerous visions, as did other Native American shamans. By the 1850s, he urged his people to become Dreamers who renounced Euro-American ways and restored traditional ones—but with a twist. Smohalla added a millennialist aspect, insisting that if Native Americans returned to tradition, at some future moment, they could vanquish the Euro-American invaders. This idea enabled Native Americans to adapt to the presence of aliens in their midst, seeing them as a temporary menace whose future defeat was assured; American governmental authorities saw inherent danger in the movement, similar to how earlier generations found links between slave religiosity and possible rebellion. The result was also similar; officials, supported by military threats, quashed the Dreamers.

Better known are movements that came among native peoples in the Southwest, centering around the Ghost Dance, the first traces of which appear around 1850. A prophet known as Wodziwub (c.1844–c.1873) called on the Paviotso in Nevada to engage in a ritual dance that triggered a corporate ecstatic experience transporting dancers to a realm of supernatural power. Caught up in ritual frenzy, dancers called upon this power to demolish the Euro-American invaders encroaching on their ancestral lands. Apparent failure led most to abandon the dance, but its message remained with Tavibo (c.1835–?). Thanks to him, by 1870 the blend of future hope and restoration of tribal integrity basic to the Ghost Dance had spread among numerous Plains tribes from Nevada north to the Dakotas. Its major manifestation revolved around a Paiute named Wovoka (c.1856–1932), who may have been Tavibo's son.

Wovoka (also known as Jack Wilson) had visionary experiences that reveal how native ideas intertwined with Christian ones. He claimed to have entered heaven itself, where God instructed him to return to his people with a message of mutual love, high moral conduct, and the practice of the Ghost Dance. Interplay with Christian notions also comes through in the expectation that those who were moral and faithfully practiced the dance would spend eternity in paradise, one with no Euro-Americans present. There is also an eschatological dynamic to the Ghost Dance in that those who practiced it would help restore tribal life to its ideal, one that this time would endure beyond chronological time and extend into eternity.

> ### Wovoka encounters God
>
> Leading to the rebirth of the Ghost Dance in the late 1880s were visions reported by Wovoka, whose roots were in the Paiute people. In the winter of 1888–89, up in the mountains, Wovoka reported:
>
> > When the sun died, I went up to heaven and saw God and all the people who had died a long time ago. God told me to come back and tell my people they must be good and love one another, and not fight, or steal, or lie. He gave me this dance to give my people.
> >
> > (Quoted in James Mooney, *The Ghost-Dance Religion and the Sioux Outbreak of 1890*, edited by Anthony F.C. Wallace (Chicago: University of Chicago Press, 1965), 2)

Wovoka's understanding spread among many tribal groups in the late 1880s. But when the Lakota Sioux, recently forced by government policy to cede more land, turned the Ghost Dance into a form of militant resistance, brutal suppression followed, climaxing in the massacre at Wounded Knee in 1890. Regardless of that brutality, the Ghost Dance illustrates ways in which diversity penetrated Native American religious life through the fusion of Christian and indigenous beliefs that resulted in a new form of religious expression.

The melding of ideas from different sources pushed Native American religious cultures in another direction when Apache groups, perhaps as early as the 1870s, began to combine ritual practices more common among Mexican tribal peoples with Christian notions. Here the practice concerns the ritual ingestion of peyote, classified by the federal government as a hallucinogenic substance but regarded by some Native Americans as a sacramental medicine whose ritual use brought entry into a realm of supernatural power. Adapting traditional sweat lodge purification rites, peyotists identified this supernatural power with Jesus Christ and the God of Christianity. For them, this sacrament involves not only ingestion of peyote, but also prayers to Jesus. This movement, as a distinctly religious phenomenon, owes much of its formulation to the Comanche Quannah Parker (c.1840s–1911), and it took structure in Oklahoma in 1918 when it received incorporation as the Native American Church. Over the years, as peyote became a federally controlled substance, court cases attempted to restrict or prohibit its ritual use within the Native American Church, but by the late 1990s federal legislation protected its religious use within the church after earlier laws had been found unconstitutional.

In revitalization efforts that ranged from to the Ghost Dance to the Native American Church, diversity penetrated Native American religious life as it did the rest of the nation. In most cases, these shifts reflected the ways in which the fusion of

Figure 11.4 Ghost Dance of the Sioux Indians. The Ghost Dance was a revitalization movement with a decidedly apocalyptic dimension, provoking such fear among governmental authorities that they brutally suppressed it (Courtesy of the Library of Congress.)

tribal ways with aspects of Christianity gave birth to new religious movements even as governmental policy and reservation life continued to eat away at the core of Native American tribal life.

Bible conferences and summer retreats offer relief from urban life

Different faces of diversity come into focus when looking at how city dwellers revamped the old frontier camp meeting to provide some respite from the strains of city life. The transformation of the camp meeting from an evangelical technique to secure converts to a way to nurture believers in their faith also reflected the continuing inroads of the Holiness Movement in American Protestantism, the emergence of the Sunday school to complement religious instruction in the Victorian home, and an ongoing passion among Protestant Christians to understand the Bible.

In areas where urbanization and industrialization altered the character of life, summer retreats that adapted the models of camp meetings began to flourish. Some associations built large auditoriums for preaching services and cognate activities, while encouraging people to take up residence, perhaps in cottages used just during the summer months or in structures that combined frame and tent construction. During the summer season, camp grounds along lakeshores or the ocean became sacred space. Services launching the camp season consecrated the grounds, signaling their transformation into sacred space; those marking its end returned them to ordinary space. Women and children might spend the summer in these temporary quarters; husbands and fathers joined them on weekends. Such religious centers, forerunners of beach and summer resorts, reflected a shift in focus from that of earlier camp meetings. Frontier camp meetings emerged in part because of a lack of organized religious institutions to serve the people; a primary goal was securing converts to religious faith. By the later nineteenth century, churches abounded in the cities, and those seeking respite from the stress of urban life were often already among the faithful. Hence the focus shifted to nurture and spiritual growth.

Some summer associations had strong ties to the Holiness Movement, particularly those inclined towards Methodist ways. In 1867, for example, under the leadership of the Methodist John Inskip (1816–1884), the National Camp Meeting Association for the Promotion of Holiness formed after a particularly successful summer event in Vineland, New Jersey. The evangelist Dwight L. Moody, although never identified with the movement, largely endorsed its efforts to promote sanctification or holiness among evangelical Protestant Christians.

Many summer centers also offered training for those, particularly women, who taught in the Sunday schools being added to the programs of many urban churches. Such endeavors needed both trained teachers and curriculum materials. To meet those needs, in 1874 Methodist bishop John H. Vincent organized a training program for Sunday school teachers at Lake Chautauqua in New York, that developed into a summer institute with a wide-ranging program dealing with topics of religious interest; he also spearheaded development of standardized materials that teachers could use in instruction. Dwight Moody also became involved, forming the Moody Bible Institute in Chicago in 1886 to train lay workers to serve in local congregations. These various educational enterprises helped strengthen the growing identity of many white Protestants as middle class, for they added a semblance of the knowledge and learning associated with the middle class to much Protestant practice.

Other summer conferences, many of which also had links to Moody, concentrated on Bible study. The best-known picked up interpretations of scripture developed by John Nelson Darby (1800–1882), founder of a small British Protestant movement called the Plymouth Brethren. Darby traveled widely in both the U.S. and Canada, promoting the view known as premillennial dispensationalism. That perspective believed that scripture showed how God revealed a single truth to humanity but in different ways in different time periods or dispensations. All led to the anticipated Second Coming of Christ that would launch the millennium or thousand-year period before the final struggle between cosmic forces of good and evil. Dispensationalists also popularized the idea of the Rapture, a miraculous event in which faithful believers would be whisked up into the heavens when the millennium began. Darby insisted that the present, the church age, was the final one before Christ's return. Like the millennialist expectation associated with William Miller decades earlier, this surge of interest in biblical prophecy stirred many to correlate current events with scripture. Many saw urbanization, industrialization, and immigration as signs that the end was

Defining dispensationalism

C.I. Scofield, whose reference edition of the King James Version of the Bible popularized premillennial dispensationalism, summarized the principles of that theology in another work when he wrote:

> The Scriptures divide time, by which is meant the entire period from the creation of Adam to the "new heaven and a new earth" of Rev. 21: 1, into seven unequal periods, called, usually, "dispensations" (Eph. 3: 2), although these periods are also called "ages" (Eph. 2: 7) and "days"—as, "day of the Lord," etc.
>
> These periods are marked off in Scripture by some change in God's method of dealing with mankind, or a portion of mankind, in respect of the two questions of sin and man's responsibility. Each of the Dispensations may be regarded as a new test of the natural man, and each ends in judgment—marking his utter failure.
>
> Five of these Dispensations, or periods of time, have been fulfilled; we are living in the sixth, probably toward its close, and have before us the seventh, and last—the millennium.
>
> (C.I. Scofield, *Rightly Dividing the Word of Truth (2 Timothy 2: 15)*, 2nd ed. (Philadelphia: Philadelphia School of the Bible, 1923), as quoted in *A Documentary History of Religion in America since 1877*, 3rd ed., edited by Edwin S. Gaustad and Mark A. Noll (Grand Rapids, MI: Eerdmans, 2003), 288)

near. Dispensationalist teaching made deep inroads into many strands of American Protestantism with the publication in 1909 of a reference Bible prepared by Cyrus I. Scofield (1843–1921) which used its ideas as the basis for its guide to studying scripture. It also came to dominate schools like Moody Bible Institute which sent graduates to work in local congregations.

In these various enterprises, diversity takes on a different character. The later Holiness Movement associated with summer camp meeting associations spawned the formation of several new Protestant denominations, such as the Christian and Missionary Alliance and the Pilgrim Holiness Church. It thus advanced the diversity reflected in the sheer variety of religious groups, but it also added to the various ways American Protestants understood the dynamics of the religious life. More emphasis became placed on teaching, nurture, and instruction, making growth in religious consciousness one way of affirming faith, alongside more ecstatic conversion experiences. Some summer centers, such as Chautauqua, attracted people from many religious backgrounds, even if there was one denomination that propelled them. When

Other dimensions of urbanizing America

Bible conferences organized around dispensationalism became fashionable, another aspect of diversity appeared, for now there were diverse ways to look at and interpret the Bible itself. But soon many of these diverse dimensions of religious expression in American life would bring controversy.

> **Key points you need to know**
> - The missionary movement spurred an interest in other religions, stirring some new dimensions of pluralism.
> - It also sparked a new field of study, comparative religion, based on the idea that all religions wrestled with the same questions and issues.
> - The World's Parliament of Religions, held in Chicago in 1893, brought much popular attention to religions such as Hinduism, Buddhism, and Islam, thereby promoting a broader pluralism.
> - Women also began questioning the traditional roles assigned to them in all religions that flourished in the U.S., using gender to paint another dimension of diversity onto the canvas of American religious life.
> - Working men sometimes found spiritual outlets in fraternal orders and lodges, seen by religious leaders as competing with the churches, and were drawn to an activist faith manifested in service more than in membership in religious institutions.
> - Centuries of interaction between Native American religious styles and those of their Euro-American conquerors led to movements that sought to revitalize or reinvigorate tribal life.
> - Two of the more well-known examples of this interaction are the Ghost Dance and the Native American Church.
> - Others feeling displaced by change resulting from immigration, industrialization, and urbanization revamped the frontier camp meetings into summer institutes and vacation ventures.
> - Some used summer conferences for intensive Bible study, drawing on the theories associated with premillennial dispensationalism.
> - World religions, gender, Native American movements, and new approaches to both the camp meeting and Bible study illustrated wide-ranging aspects of American religious diversity.

Discussion questions

1. In what ways did the growing missionary movement expand the religious horizons of Americans?

2. How did the World's Parliament of Religions bring new diversity to American religious life?
3. What did differences in gender roles and stereotypes contribute to American religious culture as the U.S. became more urban and industrial?
4. How and why did the lodge and fraternal order movement take on a religious dimension for American men?
5. What new diversity came to Native American religious life through movements like the Ghost Dance and the Native American Church?
7. How do ideas associated with apocalypticism add to our understanding of both Native American and white Protestant life during this era?
6. How did a passion to understand the Bible and a desire to have respite from the stress of urban life change American religion?

Further reading

Hittman, Michael. *Wovoka and the Ghost Dance*. Edited by Don Lynch. Expanded ed. Lincoln: University of Nebraska Press, 1997.

Hutchison, William R. *Errand to the World: American Protestant Thought and Foreign Missions*. Chicago: University of Chicago Press, 1993.

Kern, Kathi. *Mrs. Stanton's Bible*. Ithaca, NY: Cornell University Press, 2002.

Lippy, Charles H. *Do Real Men Pray? Images of the Christian Man and Male Spirituality in White Protestant America*. Knoxville: University of Tennessee Press, 2005.

Robert, Dana Lee, ed. *Converting Colonialism: Vision and Realities in Mission History, 1706–1914*. Grand Rapids, MI: Eerdmans, 2008.

Seager, Richard H., ed. *The Dawn of Religious Pluralism: Voices from the World's Parliament of Religions*. LaSalle, IL: Open Court, 1993.

Weber, Timothy P. *Living in the Shadow of the Second Coming: American Premillennialism, 1875–1982*, rev. ed. Grand Rapids. MI: Zondervan Academie Books, 1983.

12 Modernity brings more change

In this chapter

This chapter explores currents of thought and religious developments associated with, and sometimes reacting to, modernity. They include interest in Darwin's theory of evolution, the idea of Social Darwinism, critical methods of interpreting the Bible, and the belief that science and scientific method would one day replace religion as the source of meaning in life. The chapter also looks at the clash between these diverse modern viewpoints and more traditional ways of thinking that led to fundamentalism and to the fundamentalist–modernist controversy in the 1920s. The chapter also looks at the nature and character of Pentecostalism as it emerged as a distinct movement in American culture

Main topics covered

- The nature of Darwin's theory of evolution and how it caused controversy in American religious life
- The development of modern approaches to studying the Bible built on critical method
- How and why fundamentalism developed as a response to many of these ideas
- The clash between "fundamentalists" and "modernists" that came to a peak in the 1920s
- The religious implications of Social Darwinism
- The Gospel of Wealth and its ties to modern life
- Alternate schools of thought like humanism that some thought would replace traditional religion
- The emergence of Pentecostalism and Pentecostal denominations
- How Pentecostalism's emphasis on ecstatic religious experience added to American religious life

New intellectual approaches challenge traditional thought

Those attracted to premillennial dispensationalism as the best way to expose the real meaning of scripture were not the only ones looking to fresh approaches for studying the Bible. Nor were those enthralled by diverse new religions and by the way the field of comparative religion widened horizons the only ones discussing new ways of understanding the nature and role of religion in human culture. Some other strategies resulted in very different conclusions and helped spur even greater intellectual diversity within American religious life.

Even before the Civil War, for example, geologists raised questions about whether the biblical creation narratives in the book of Genesis were plausible historical and scientific accounts of the origin of the world and human life. Some of their concern recalled a dating scheme proposed by the Irish archbishop James Ussher (1581–1656) that claimed creation occurred in 4004 B.C.E. This date meant that, by the middle of the nineteenth century, the earth was only around 5,850 years old. The dilemma came when geologists dated strata in the earth as much older, concluding that the development of the physical earth was a more gradual process extending over a much longer period of time.

The notion of gradual development or evolution took a different form when the Englishman Charles Darwin (1809–1882) published his groundbreaking *The Origin of Species* in 1859. Darwin posited that all species of living things had evolved from earlier, rather different forms. Traits that enhanced chances for survival guided that evolutionary development; those traits that did not slowly disappeared, as did some species. Over long periods, a living entity gradually evolved into something almost totally different from its original form, although imprints of its development remained. When Darwin's book appeared, the U.S. was on the brink of Civil War, and few had the time or inclination to take serious note of it. Circumstances had changed when Darwin published *The Descent of Man* in 1871, extending his theory to include human life. Even then, Darwin's theories had wider currency in European universities, but slowly they began to have an impact on American thought, at first largely through individuals who pursued their education at European universities.

Americans studying abroad were also among the first to absorb both comparative religion and newer methods for analyzing and understanding sacred texts such as the Bible. Those methods reflected a historical-critical approach. In this context, criticism denotes sustained, careful analysis. Aware that no original manuscripts of any part of the Bible were known to have survived, scholars had long used the tools of textual criticism to try to determine what the original wording might have been. They compared all the surviving manuscripts then available as well as earlier translations. Other critical techniques involved attempting to find out as much as possible about the original audience to whom a particular book of the Bible was directed, about the author and the author's background, and about the social and religious context in which the author and audience

Figure 12.1 Charles Darwin. Charles Darwin developed the theory of evolution that religious fundamentalists thought denied the biblical story of creation (© Popperfoto/Getty Images.)

lived. Advocates of these methods knew that similar procedures were already enriching study of other literature, but their application to sacred texts like the Bible was new. They hoped that by uncovering as much as might be known about historical context, they would better understand the meaning of the text. Biblical scholars also recognized that the Bible was not a single uniform text but contained many different literary forms or genres—poetry and gospels, historical narratives and stories, and many more—that required different strategies for understanding their deepest meaning.

Use of these methods seemed a modern, scientific way to analyze any religious writing and thus a parallel to advances in society resulting from scientific inquiry, industrial development, and even theories like Darwin's evolutionary scheme. In Europe and then in the U.S., historical-critical method, comparative religion, and a host of other newer intellectual forces joined together to create what some called modern thought or modernism. Others called it liberal thought because faith and belief were freed or liberated from distortions or misunderstandings developing over the centuries. Many of these currents informed the thinking of the Social Gospel that emerged in response to the conditions intensified by rapid industrialization and urbanization. Some American scientists applauded the newer approaches, finding them a bridge between traditional faith and scientific knowledge. Asa Gray (1810–1888), a distinguished Harvard University botanist born in the heart of the antebellum burned-over district in New York, insisted, for example, that evolutionary theory represented how God controlled the design of the world and continued to work in it.

How historical-critical method views the Bible

For those drawn to historical-critical method as the best way to understand scripture, the Bible was not:
- a textbook for studying ancient history
- a book of science
- only one kind of literature
- a work where all parts were equally valuable.

At the same time, for these scholars, the Bible was:
- a library of different kinds of books
- in each part addressed to a specific audience
- always reflective of its culture and context
- an invitation to faith.

Other thinkers felt differently. Charles Hodge (1797–1878), a stalwart Presbyterian and professor at Princeton Theological Seminary, thought Darwin's theory denied the biblical creation account and left no place for divine providence working in all human affairs. His colleague, Benjamin Breckinridge Warfield (1851–1921), was more concerned that historical-critical method undercut Christian affirmation of the Bible as the inspired Word of God and thus not a set of documents that could or should be analyzed like other writing. He was among the first to talk about the inerrancy of the Bible, although he meant something rather different than those who used the word a century later. For Warfield, inerrancy meant that the Bible was without error if interpreted and understood as the individual inspired writers intended. Of course, being certain of the original intention was another problem. Those who attacked evolutionary theory and critical method had many of the same fears as those troubled by comparative religion. All of them seemed to whittle away at the notion that Christianity possessed the only ultimate truth and that the Bible had unique status as the sole text through which God communicated that truth to humans. Regardless, the inroads made by these intellectual currents highlight the growing diversity in Protestant thinking that cut across denominational lines.

One episode brings that diversity into sharp relief. In 1891, Charles A. Briggs (1841–1913), an Old Testament professor at Union Theological Seminary in New York City, gave an inaugural address when he took up a new professorship at the school. Having studied in Germany, Briggs advocated the use of historical-critical method. He had also come to see religious development, both in history and in individual experience, as a process of evolutionary growth. Although he insisted these convictions were compatible with faith and belief, Briggs wound up being charged with heresy by some fellow Presbyterians who concluded that such views demolished faith. Especially troubling to them was Briggs's rejection of the notion of inspiration and inerrancy advanced by another Presbyterian, Benjamin B. Warfield. Finally, the Presbyterian General Assembly in 1893 returned a guilty verdict, revoked Briggs's ordination credentials, and censured the seminary for allowing Briggs to continue on its faculty. Consequently, Union Seminary severed its Presbyterian connections, becoming an independent school committed to academic freedom and the use of modern research methods; Briggs in turn became a priest in the Episcopal Church in 1899, while continuing to teach at Union. This episode and others like it illustrate the growing intellectual differences within American Protestantism and represent an approach sometimes called evangelical or Protestant liberalism, and occasionally evangelical modernism. The variety of labels used to describe various positions itself indicates something of the range of approaches to belief that was becoming available.

In time, modern methods and ways of thinking found acceptance among many denominations and among many theological schools. In the early twentieth century, for example, the Divinity School at the recently established University of Chicago became a major center for modernist thought. One of its leading faculty members, Shailer Mathews (1863–1941), saw theological ideas, such as the doctrine of God, developing in an evolutionary pattern and concluded that gradually those whom science influenced would increasingly cast doctrine and creed in scientific terms. The school of thought associated with this position became known as scientific modernism.

Those who still feared that such currents damaged religious faith and would ultimately corrode all of Christianity became convinced that more aggressive action was needed to thwart modernism's growing influence. The result added another layer of diversity to religious thought with the emergence of fundamentalism, a movement still prominent in the American religious mosaic a century later.

Fundamentalism's impact on American Protestantism

Several forces coalesced in American Protestantism in the early twentieth century to crystallize the fears of those worried about historical-critical method, Darwinism, comparative religion, and changes resulting from urbanization, immigration, and industrialization. One was the vitality of an urban revivalism, now centered on Billy Sunday, which resisted tampering with social structures and sought to change culture through the conversion of individuals. Another was ongoing fascination with premillennial dispensationalism, which presumed the Bible was a historical, scientific document and expected that Christ would soon return in bodily form to launch a thousand years that would culminate in the final conflict between good and evil. Its advocates found historical-critical method particularly threatening because it assumed scripture's meaning was more myth and symbol than hard fact. A third strand centered around the "Princeton theology" of Charles Hodge and B.B. Warfield that looked askance at Darwinian theory and exalted the Bible as the inspired Word of God, inerrant in its "original autographs" or original form, and traced its roots back to the earlier fascination with Scottish Common Sense Realism. Yet another captured reservations about comparative religion and historical-critical method because they seemed to undermine the superiority and finality of Christianity among world religions by finding kernels of truth in many belief systems. At heart, the common denominator in all these fears was the way new approaches looked to reason and scientific ways of analysis, raising questions about claims grounded in revelation and God's miraculous action in history.

A concerted response to modernism, sometimes a catch-all phrase for all of these threats, emerged first among those associated with Moody Bible Institute in Chicago and the Moody Church there. Reuben A. Torrey (1856–1928), head of the institute, helped the church's pastor recruit several theologians to write a series of twelve pamphlets defending what they believed to be basic truths under attack. Published between 1910 and 1915, the pamphlets were called simply *The Fundamentals*. The reaction to modernism now had a name derived from that title, fundamentalism. In the popular mind, fundamentalism became associated with five basic ideas, all of which promoted revelation and miracle over reason and science. One was the miraculous birth of Jesus to a virgin. Another was proof of his divinity, grounded in miracles reported in the Bible that were taken as historical facts. A third emphasized an interpretation of the significance of Jesus's crucifixion called "substitutionary atonement" or the idea that Jesus's death miraculously compensated for humanity's sins—at least the sins of those who believed. Miracle also trumped reason in the resurrection of Jesus, taken as an actual physical, historical event; parallel was another miraculous assertion grounded in premillennial dispensationalism, namely that at a future moment Jesus, in a physical body, would return to earth. The final idea was to regard the Bible as the inspired, inerrant Word of God, accurate as a work of science and history as well as of faith.

At first, fundamentalists brought their perspective to bear most directly in Baptist and Presbyterian circles in the North, stamping both groups with such diversity that conflict between fundamentalists and modernists became inevitable. The fundamentalist stance gained credibility when William Jennings Bryan (1860–1925), a one-time presidential candidate and respected political populist who was also an extraordinarily dynamic speaker, endorsed its basic postulates. But some inclined towards modernism soon reacted themselves. They feared that fundamentalism, if it became the norm, would stir prejudice against modernists and quash intellectual diversity.

Two examples illustrate the passion prevailing on both sides. One concerns a preacher, Harry Emerson Fosdick (1878–1969), who, like Bryan, was a compelling orator. In 1922, while serving as visiting pastor at New York City's First Presbyterian Church, Fosdick preached a powerful but controversial sermon entitled, "Shall the Fundamentalists Win?" The title question was rhetorical; Fosdick was appalled at the inroads fundamentalism had made and called for its speedy defeat. He soon found himself in a swirl of controversy, with some calling for a heresy trial to strip him of his

> ### How early fundamentalists understood inspiration
>
> Archibald Alexander Hodge and Benjamin Breckinridge Warfield, both professors at Princeton Theological Seminary, wrote an article on biblical inspiration for the *Princeton Review* in 1881. Their ideas informed fundamentalism's understanding of inspiration. They claimed that:
>
>> The word Inspiration as applied to the Holy Scriptures, has gradually acquired a specific technical meaning, independent of its etymology ... Christian scholars have come to see that this divine element, which penetrates and glorifies Scripture at every point, has entered and become incorporated with it in various ways, natural, supernatural, and gracious, through long courses of providential leading, as well as by direct suggestion, through the spontaneous action of the souls of the sacred writers, as well as by controlling influence from without ...
>>
>> The doctrine of Inspiration, in its essence and, consequently, in all its forms, presupposes a supernatural revelation and a supernatural providential guidance, entering and determining the genesis of Scripture from the beginning ...
>>
>> The writers of this article are sincerely convinced of the perfect soundness of the great Catholic doctrine of Biblical Inspiration, *i.e.*, that the Scriptures not only contain, but ARE THE WORD OF GOD, and hence that all their elements and all their affirmations are absolutely errorless, and binding the faith and obedience of men.
>
> (Archibald A. Hodge and Benjamin B. Warfield, "Inspiration," *Presbyterian Review* 2 (1881), in H. Shelton Smith, Robert T. Handy, and Lefferts A. Loetscher, *American Christianity: An Historical Interpretation with Representative Documents*, vol. 2 (New York: Charles Scribner's Sons, 1963), 325, 330, 331)

pastoral credentials. That did not happen. John D. Rockefeller, Jr. (1874–1960), whose father founded Standard Oil, helped finance the building of the Riverside Church in New York City so Fosdick would have a pulpit. That church remains an icon of interracial and interdenominational liberal Protestantism.

The other episode occurred in Dayton, Tennessee in 1925. A group of local merchants hoping to bring fame and fortune to the area worked with the American Civil Liberties Union to challenge a Tennessee statute banning the teaching of Darwin's theory of evolution in the state's public schools. When John Scopes (1900–1970), a substitute biology teacher, agreed to participate in a test case, the stage was set for a landmark clash between not only science and religion, but also with everything associated with both modernism and liberalism. William Jennings Bryan came to Dayton to advise the prosecution, while the ACLU brought in an equally famous attorney, Clarence Darrow (1857–1938), to assist the defense. Darrow made fundamentalism seem anachronistic, a throwback to earlier times, when he pummeled Bryan with questions on the witness stand. Although the court found Scopes guilty, media representatives covering the event mistakenly believed the trial sounded the death knell for fundamentalism.

The clash between fundamentalists and modernists splintered the fundamentalist movement. Some drew on premillennial dispensationalism to see the ascendancy of liberal modernism as a sign that only a righteous remnant would survive the end of the present age and be prepared for the Second Coming of Christ. Many retreated from the public sphere, but a host of publishing companies, the popularity of the Scofield Reference Bible, schools like Moody Bible Institute, and other agencies kept an underground fundamentalist network alive and well, waiting for time to vindicate their cause.

Other intellectual currents bring more variety in belief

Not everyone influenced by new methods and theories wound up identifying with either the fundamentalist or modernist camps. There were other ways that Darwinian ideas and a growing interest in scientific approaches added to the intellectual diversity within American religious life, particularly in Protestant circles. One of those expanded on Darwin's idea of natural selection by applying it to society. The notion of Social Darwinism received articulation in the work of British economic theorist Herbert Spencer (1820–1903), who coined the phrase "survival of the fittest" seven years before Darwin published *Origin of Species*. He contended simply that economic success (survival) came to those who had the innate skills and abilities required (the fittest). Spencer endorsed laissez-faire capitalism, for regulation of business interfered with natural processes by which the fittest rose to the top. In the U.S., one of the most vocal proponents of Social Darwinism was the one-time Episcopal priest William Graham Sumner (1840–1910), who became a sociology professor at Yale. For Spencer and Sumner, poverty came to individuals unfit to survive in society; it was a natural way to prune society of its weakest elements. Social Darwinists regarded the growing gap between the rich and the poor in urbanizing, industrializing America as confirming that those with superior abilities prospered, while those who lacked ability or even moral character did not. In other words, those who struggled to support families on low wages and who lived in slums had only themselves to blame for their condition.

Parallel to these ideas came another strand of thought called the Gospel of Wealth. A bit more humane than Social Darwinism, the Gospel of Wealth presumed that the rich, often industrial magnates reaping large fortunes, owed their status to God's will as much as to their own abilities. One key proponent of this idea was Scottish-born Presbyterian Andrew Carnegie (1835–1919), who amassed a fortune in the rapidly growing steel industry. A "self-made" man, Carnegie illustrated the idea of the survival of the fittest in his own life, calling for free competition in business that involved paying workers low wages to assure his own survival and economic gain. He added a different twist, however. Reflecting his Presbyterian theological heritage, Carnegie believed that God had granted him wealth for a purpose. He must act as a steward of those resources, using them not just for personal glory but also for enhancing the common good. So the Gospel of Wealth, taking its designation from the title of a pamphlet Carnegie wrote in 1889, summoned those blessed with abundance to engage in philanthropy. Carnegie, for example, gave millions of dollars to build public libraries in towns across the country, convinced that access to books would spur the poor to engage in self-improvement, to pull themselves up by their own bootstraps.

One popular manifestation of ideas bringing together Social Darwinism and the Gospel of Wealth came from Russell Conwell (1843–1925), a lawyer and newspaperman who became a Baptist pastor and then president of Temple University in Philadelphia. Conwell saw the inequities stemming from unregulated capitalism through his work with laborers associated with the YMCA. His fame rests largely on a lecture he delivered countless times, published first in 1890 with the title "Acres of Diamonds: How Men and Women May Become Rich." It, too, was an exhortation to self-help, to look quite literally in one's backyard where there might be hidden "acres of diamonds" that the diligent worker would uncover.

People such as Carnegie and Conwell intertwined capitalist success with religious belief, knowing that success in business and industry relied on new methods, technological advances, and scientific ways of thinking and doing things. By the early years of the twentieth century, others began to look to science and technology as ultimately replacing religion altogether; they believed that the use of reason required for scientific advancement would ultimately eliminate the need for religious faith based on revelation, and at the same time yield what religion promised, namely human happiness in an ideal world here and now.

One such current that added to the intellectual diversity within American religion developed around pragmatism, a term first used by the philosopher Charles Sanders Peirce (1839–1914). Pragmatism emphasized the results of religious belief more than its content. Among its more strident advocates was the Harvard professor whose work helped give birth to the discipline of psychology, William James (1842–1910). James was keenly interested in religious experience and launched an effort to analyze it through case studies of hundreds of individuals. Although most of James's subjects came from a Protestant background, he discerned some rather different types of personalities. He concluded that how individuals experienced and understood religion reflected the structure of their personalities as much as it did any presumed truth identified with religious teaching. He claimed that the value of any religious belief rested in what it did for the individual in terms of bringing meaning to life and producing happiness and well-being. For James, as for other pragmatists, the "truth" of a belief rested in this function, not in any claims a particular belief might assert about God or any other doctrine. Pragmatism elevated the function of religious belief to a place of prime importance, insisting that the content of belief evolved to reflect changing circumstances.

Pragmatism's approach sometimes became intertwined with other psychological understandings as psychology gained ground as a behavioral science. Central was the influence of Sigmund Freud (1856–1939), born in what is now the Czech Republic, whose ideas formed the basis for psychoanalysis. Freud, a Jew by background, had little use for traditional religious belief, seeing most such views as projections or extensions of human wishes and desires. His understanding, along with pragmatism, had an impact on another seminal thinker, John Dewey (1859–1952), who was also for a time associated with the scientific modernists at the University of Chicago. Remembered most for adapting evolutionary theories to the learning process and thereby revolutionizing American education, Dewey represented another way that a progressive scientific approach enriched the intellectual diversity in American religion. Dewey thought that religious institutions had a pragmatic value in teaching morals and providing a sense of community, but that religious beliefs—especially those about a supernatural realm—would disappear as they evolved according to scientific principles. Like the pragmatists, his end goal was human happiness, sometimes equated with self-fulfillment. In other words, the aim of belief was to discover one's potential as a human being in the present. Consequently his views picked up the label of

The humanist alternative

The "Humanist Manifesto" listed fifteen points which signers believed to offer a scientific and modern religion that would replace older forms of religion, affirm evolutionary theory, and promote human happiness. Among them were:
- *First:* Religious humanists regard the universe as self-existing and not created.
- *Second:* Humanism believes that man is a part of nature and that he has emerged as the result of a continuous process ...
- *Seventh:* Religion consists of those actions, purposes, and experiences which are humanly significant ...
- *Eighth:* Religious humanism considers the complete realization of human personality to be the end of man's life and seeks its development and fulfillment in the here and now.

(From "A Humanist Manifesto," *The New Humanist* 6 (May–June 1933), as excerpted in H. Shelton Smith, Robert T. Handy, and Lefferts A. Loetscher, *American Christianity: An Historical Interpretation with Representative Documents*, vol. 2 (New York: Charles Scribner's Sons, 1963), 251, 252)

humanism, a term with a long history, but here denoting human self-expression and achievement apart from belief in a supernatural God. Dewey was a signer of the first "Humanist Manifesto" (1933), which posited humanism as a new religion that would replace all forms of supernatural theism in time.

A related, but somewhat different, blend of philosophical and psychological insights in an alternative to traditional religious thinking came in the work of Horace M. Kallen (1881–1974). A rabbi's son, Kallen, like James and Dewey, cast aside traditional belief and practice, but in doing so helped many American Jews reconcile their religious heritage with modern life. Kallen, as Dewey, talked about self-realization and fulfillment as keys to happiness, but also understood that social conditions often inhibited the quest for happiness. He used some traditional religious concepts to describe the forces that thwarted human self-realization, condemning them as evil. Kallen was also committed to social action, to ridding the world of evils such as war and injustice, in order to improve the quality of life. Consequently, he worked with the American Jewish Congress, founded as World War I came to a close, to advance the civil rights of European Jews whose lives had been severely disrupted by the war. Always strongly opposed to anti-Semitism, the congress became an advocate for the civil rights of any minority group and a supporter of the nation of Israel. It still echoes what Kallen believed, namely that liberty was essential to self-realization, not just for American Jewish immigrants, but for all humanity.

Pentecostal stirrings enrich religious life

Fundamentalism and modernism had their greatest effect within Protestant denominations that enjoyed positions of broad influence in American life, demonstrating that there were many different approaches to being a mainline Protestant, besides the differences in denominational labels. So, also, Social Darwinism, pragmatism, and new insights from psychology left their strongest imprint on Protestantism, bringing a wide range of ways to think about intellectual matters. Yet in the midst of the swirl of forces behind all of these emerged another stream that remains a vital force within American religious life. As with other movements that add to religious diversity and a growing, though sometimes conflicted pluralism, Pentecostalism—the name usually given to this movement—represents the confluence of many factors.

One chapter of this story begins at an independent Bible school in Topeka, Kansas, founded by Charles Fox Parham (1873–1929). Some students there had particular concern for the account in the Christian New Testament recorded in the book of Acts, chapter two, describing what happened to Jesus' disciples as they gathered in a private room in Jerusalem during the Jewish festival of Pentecost. That festival attracted thousands of tourists who spoke many different languages. According to the account, the Holy Spirit enabled the disciples to speak in these different languages. This phenomenon is called "speaking in tongues" or glossolalia. Those who spoke in other languages believed the Holy Spirit granted them the gift or power to do so. Much of

> ### The biblical basis for Pentecostal experience
>
> Early Pentecostals believed that the same Spirit that came on Jesus' disciples on the Day of Pentecost could empower them with spiritual gifts, based on this passage from the New Testament book of Acts:
>
> > And when the day of Pentecost was fully come, they were all with one accord and in one place.
> >
> > And suddenly there came a sound from heaven as of a rushing mighty wind, and it filled all the house where they were sitting.
> >
> > And there appeared unto them cloven tongues like as of fire, and it sat upon each of them.
> >
> > And they were all filled with the Holy Ghost, and began to speak with other tongues, as the Spirit gave them utterance.
> >
> > (Acts 2: 1–4, King James Version)

the Christian tradition restricted such miraculous gifts to the age of the apostles and did not expect them later. Parham's students in Topeka felt otherwise. They found nothing in the biblical text that limited such spiritual gifts to an ancient time. Finally, on New Year's Day 1901, Agnes Ozman (1870–1937) received the gift of speaking in tongues. Skeptical at first, Parham soon embraced the idea, equating such spiritual gifts with a "second baptism" that followed the traditional baptism which used water to anoint individuals. This second baptism was a baptism of fire. Like the experience of many Native American shamans, glossolalia is a form of ecstatic experience when for a time another power seizes control of one and manifests itself. The Pentecostal style also echoes the sense of divine invasion in individual lives marking conversions at frontier camp meetings a century earlier.

Parham relocated to Houston, Texas, where a young African American, William J. Seymour (1870–1922), came under his influence. Experiencing much discrimination because of race, in 1906 Seymour left Houston for Los Angeles, then as now a city of extraordinary ethnic diversity. His preaching led to a major religious revival centered in a small mission on Azusa Street. The Azusa Street revival, a formative event in American Pentecostalism, broke many boundaries. Not only did it shatter ideas of what it meant to be religious, but also it was interracial and welcomed both women and men into this new realm of spiritual power. The revival's spontaneity led even critics to regard it as an extraordinary sign of divine presence. Thousands came by train and by other means to witness this miraculous event as word of it spread throughout the country.

Many who came to Azusa Street carried the Pentecostal message with them when they returned home. Consequently, the Pentecostal fervor eventuated in several new denominations, all of which saw this baptism of the Spirit or baptism of fire as a mark of authentic religious experience. When Pentecostal denominations formed, however, patterns of racial division marking American life intruded. Although the revival in Los Angeles was multiracial, the denominations tended to be either Euro-American or African American in their constituency. Hence the Assemblies of God, organized in 1914 in Hot Springs, Arkansas, were predominantly white, while the Church of God in Christ, which became a Pentecostal body in 1907 after its founder, Charles H. Mason (1866–1961), visited the Azusa Street revival, remained predominantly African American.

Independently of Parham's school and Azusa Street, similar stirrings occurred in North Carolina, some in the area around Dunn, a town in the central part of the state. Also as early as 1886 religious seekers associated with Ambrose Jessup Tomlinson (1865–1943), an itinerant evangelist in the mountains of east Tennessee and western North Carolina, resolved to reclaim the heart of New Testament Christianity. Like Parham, Tomlinson was influenced by Holiness thinking, but this passion for reliving the ways of the New Testament church also echoed earlier Restorationism. Ten years later, Tomlinson's group sensed a powerful presence of the Spirit. Then, gathering in a private home in January 1906 at Camp Creek, North Carolina, they signed a statement of faith that gave birth to another strand of the diverse Pentecostal movement. Called simply the Church of God, signers pledged to hold only to biblical teaching in matters of faith and practice. For them, that included spiritual gifts—not just glossolalia or speaking in tongues, but also divine healing, since they were convinced that rebirth brought both spiritual and physical wholeness. The Church of God made Cleveland, Tennessee, its headquarters, but soon it too experienced internal division, with Tomlinson leading a group that formed the Church of God of Prophecy.

In one sense, Pentecostalism by its nature lends itself to diverse expression and division, for by definition the spiritual power at its heart cannot easily and readily be controlled. An ongoing issue—and one reason why centuries ago church leaders tried to claim that spiritual gifts were limited to the apostolic age—is determining whether any individual claim to experience the Spirit is genuine and authentic, not just a sham.

Key points you need to know

- New ways of studying the Bible using historical-critical method added another strain of intellectual diversity to American religion.
- Darwin's theory of evolution had significant implications for religion, both for those who saw it as how God worked and for those who believed it undermined religious faith.

- Perceived attacks on the Bible led some thinkers to develop new ideas of inspiration and inerrancy.
- Fundamentalism emerged in part to combat the inroads of modernism by stressing revelation and miracle.
- Gaps between fundamentalists and modernists led to episodes like the Scopes Trial and heresy charges brought against some seminary professors.
- Social Darwinism and the Gospel of Wealth allowed some Protestant Americans to see economic success as a sign of moral righteousness,
- Pragmatism emphasized the function or practical value of faith and de-emphasized the content of doctrine and belief.
- Humanism developed as a radical alternative to bring religious belief into closer harmony with science and reason.
- Pentecostalism arose as a fresh expression of ecstatic religious experience, stabilizing in a cluster of new denominations.

Thus, in quite a different way from fundamentalism, modernism, pragmatism, and other intellectual forces, Pentecostalism added yet one more layer to the diversity of American religion.

Discussion questions

1. What characterizes historical-critical method as a way to study the Bible? Why was it controversial?
2. How did Darwin's theories challenge traditional religious thinking?
3. What forces combined to make "modernism" a threat for some?
4. How did fundamentalism represent a coming together of many diverse currents? What gave it credibility?
5. In what ways did fundamentalism try to counter modernism?
6. How did the Briggs heresy episode and the Scopes Trial illuminate the clash between fundamentalism and modernism?
7. How did Social Darwinism and the Gospel of Wealth affect American religion?
8. What did pragmatism contribute to the growing intellectual diversity in American religion?
9. What was religious humanism? What made it attractive as an alternative to traditional religion?
10. Why did Pentecostalism come about? How does it reflect and yet differ from other expressions of ecstatic religion in America?

Further reading

Hofstadter, Richard. *Social Darwinism in American Thought*. Philadelphia: University of Pennsylvania Press, 1944.

Hutchison, William R. *The Modernist Impulse in American Protestantism*. Cambridge, MA: Harvard University Press, 1976.

Marsden, George M. *Fundamentalism and American Culture: The Shaping of Twentieth-Century Evangelicalism, 1870–1925*. New York: Oxford University Press, 1980.

Synan, Vinson. *The Holiness-Pentecostal Tradition: Charismatic Movements in the Twentieth Century*. Grand Rapids, MI: Eerdmans, 1997.

Turner, James. *Without God, Without Creed: The Origins of Unbelief in America*. Baltimore: The Johns Hopkins University Press, 1985.

13 Reaction and retreat

In this chapter

This chapter explores some of the reactions to the increasing diversity in American religious life in the early twentieth century. Desires to retreat from the transformations resulting from massive immigration, urbanization, and industrialization prompted many of them. One centers on the movement for national Prohibition. Another looks at changes in immigration laws intended to assure that a more western European, Protestant heritage would retain its historic cultural dominance in the U.S. The chapter will also look at reactions, both racial and religious, associated with the rise of the Ku Klux Klan and outbreaks of both anti-Semitism and anti-Catholicism. The final section will examine a very different form of diversity, namely a paradoxical response issuing from advances in communication that came with the introduction of both radio and film and also from trends in popular religious literature.

Main topics covered

- How and why Prohibition seemed a viable way to deal with some of the problems of urban life
- The role of women and the undertone of racial and religious prejudice in the Prohibition movement
- Restrictions placed on immigration following World War I that sought to reverse the trends in place since the close of the Civil War
- How a variety of fears and passions generated sometimes very overt and sometimes very subtle religious intolerance directed primarily towards American Catholics and Jews
- Religious dimensions of racial intolerance, with the Ku Klux Klan and episodes of lynching
- The ways changes in American culture, ranging from the increased use of the automobile to the media revolution accompanying radio and film, challenged American religion

- Why some thought that these new media would spur a decline in the influence of religion on American life
- The way some popular religious writing reflected the emerging world of business and the impact of religious changes

Prohibition as social reform and as a reaction to diversity

Frances Willard and her Women's Christian Temperance Union represented only one aspect of a larger story that led to the national experiment with Prohibition. Willard, as noted earlier, led a crusade that fused calls for granting full rights to women in both church and society, protecting traditional family life in an urban context, and improving the conditions in which laborers worked. In one sense, Prohibition signaled one way in which women could work for social change that would enhance their own status and deal with issues of particular importance for American women, while at the same presumably improving the quality of life for all Americans by raising the standards of socially acceptable behavior. In another sense, the movement to end the sale and consumption of alcoholic beverages in the United States echoed earlier efforts at social reform, particularly the difficult struggle to bring an end to slavery. Like the earlier antislavery movement, for example, advocates of Prohibition increasingly recognized that individual reform would not resolve the dilemma; the government must intervene to assure that Americans remained morally upright. There was also an underside to this endeavor. Many who advocated Prohibition were convinced that African Americans, so recently released from slavery, and the newer immigrants from southern, central, and eastern Europe (most of whom were Roman Catholic and Jewish) were more likely to drink to excess and, when inebriated, engage in immoral behavior as they lost any sense of responsibility or self-respect. Most of this fear stemmed from prejudice and lack of understanding of cultural and religious styles in which moderate use of alcohol was part of ordinary practice, not suspect or taboo.

Seen in this vein, the Prohibition movement has racial and religious overtones that go well beyond there being religious leaders, like Willard, propelling the endeavor. Restriction of access to alcoholic beverages became one way to subjugate and control African Americans once they were no longer under the control of slave owners and masters. It was also a way to compel newer immigrants to take up Protestant ways of living and to impose on them standards of behavior perceived to be appropriate to the U.S. and thus better than what prevailed elsewhere. Hence the move to ban the manufacture, sale, and consumption of alcoholic beverages became a way to "Americanize" immigrants in the sense of impressing on them the superiority of white evangelical Protestant modes of behavior. At the same time, the Prohibition movement gained momentum because of a broad cultural angst that swept through American society during and immediately after World War I. The perception in much of Europe, the Middle East, and North America that a world that was familiar had vanished because of the unsettledness and political turmoil accompanying the war came into sharp focus when one also took account of events such as the Bolshevik Revolution in Russia and the war bringing independence to Ireland. Calls for Prohibition captured that frustration and also a hope of returning to an idealized past that had never been as tranquil in reality as it was in memory.

Willard and the WCTU opted primarily for moral persuasion as a technique to get individuals to forsake consumption of alcoholic beverages. The WCTU mobilized thousands of women who took up the cause not just of temperance or moderation, but of total abstinence. Many dedicated their children to the cause even as infants, placing a white ribbon on them as a token of the mother's pledge to rear children, especially sons, who would forsake alcohol. Other religious leaders and groups that relied largely on an evangelical Protestant base were more political. The American Anti-Saloon League, for example, was clearly oriented towards political action, seeking at first to pressure state legislatures to ban alcohol and then looking to Congress to impose nation-wide Prohibition. From the start, evangelical Protestants dominated its ranks. Especially prominent was southern Methodist bishop James Cannon (1864–1944), named to the league's executive committee in 1902. Known as the "Dry Messiah," Cannon was instrumental in lobbying the Virginia state legislature to adopt Prohibition in 1914 and became the most prominent Prohibition advocate lobbying the U.S. Congress to do the same. Others joined the crusade. Popular revivalist Billy Sunday delivered a sermon condemning beverage alcohol well-known for its dramatic effect many times in different evangelistic campaigns, often advertising the subject in advance because it was sure to draw a large audience. Even some Roman Catholic leaders joined the effort through

Billy Sunday attacks the saloon

In a sermon preached many times called "Get on the Water Wagon," Protestant revivalist Billy Sunday railed against the saloon in a call for Prohibition:

> The saloon is a coward. It is a thief, it is not an ordinary court defender that steals your money, but it robs you of manhood and leaves you in rags and takes away your friends, and it robs your family. It impoverishes your children and it brings insanity and suicide. It will take the shirt off your back and it will steal the coffin from a dead child and yank the last crust of bread out of the hand of a starving child; it will take the last bucket of coal out of your cellar, and the last cent out of your pocket, and will send you home bleary-eyed and staggering to your wife and children ... It is the dirtiest, most low-down, damnable business that ever crawled out of the pit of Hell.

(From Billy Sunday, "Get on the Water Wagon," in Lyle W. Dorsett, *Billy Sunday and the Redemption of Urban America* (Grand Rapids, MI: Eerdmans, 1991), 194) groups such as the Catholic Prohibition League and the Catholic Total Abstinence Union of America. Support for Prohibition was one way for them to dispel lingering fears that Catholics were not good Americans and that Catholic immigrants were more prone to engage in behavior thought unacceptable by evangelical Protestants.

Adoption of the Eighteenth Amendment to the U.S. Constitution in 1919, which banned the manufacture, sale and transportation of any intoxicating beverage in the U.S. once enabling legislation (the Volstead Act) was passed, brought a sense of victory. Voices extolling moral reform were jubilant. Yet, in retrospect, the national experiment with Prohibition was anything but a victory. It spurred the expansion of an underground criminal network that supplied Americans with alcoholic beverages. Many Protestant Americans in the ranks of the political and economic elite openly ignored the ban, buttressing the notion that the real intent was not moral reform but social control of a population in which racial, religious, and ethnic diversity had challenged the dominance of Anglo-Protestants increasingly desperate to retain power. Prohibition and its failure signaled that many forms of pluralism had arrived in the U.S. and ultimately could not be quashed.

Growing intolerance reflects fears of a pluralistic culture

Other currents in the first decades of the twentieth century reveal that a backlash was mounting against the pluralism that had become more obvious since the end of the Civil War. Some was direct and overt, but much of it was subtle and a matter of innuendo. Most targeted the growing Catholic population and the much smaller, but also growing, Jewish population. Immigrants or those of the first and second generation born in the U.S. accounted for much of the constituency of both traditions. They bore the brunt of the outbreaks of intolerance and bias.

Directed against both as part of the post-war "return to normalcy" was legislation passed by Congress in 1924 that for the first time placed large-scale restrictions on immigration. Earlier laws had primarily singled out persons from various parts of Asia, especially China and Japan, for exclusion. Now the law was more expansive. It placed a quota on the total number of immigrants who could enter the U.S. in any given year, but with a twist. It also limited the number from any individual country who could immigrate each year. Figures of foreign-born and foreign stock from the 1890 census provided the basis for the latter figure. By using that census, the resulting quotas favored areas of northern and western Europe, while discriminating against those from southern, central, and eastern Europe who by 1890 constituted the bulk of new immigrants. In other words, the law intentionally sought to preserve an Anglo-Saxon/Teutonic ethnic dominance in American society and to bolster the societal influence of evangelical Protestants.

Some of the fear prompting this restrictive legislation went beyond the newer trends in immigration. With the demise of the Austro-Hungarian Empire as a result of world war and the unsettledness in Russia in the wake of the Leninist overthrow of the tsarist regime, some expected that a flood of immigrants would want to come to America, bringing with them radical political ideas, strange cultural mores, and a religious style that was anything but evangelical Protestant. Talk of a "Red Scare" and consequent anarchy joined with a dread of presumed immigrant atheism to buttress calls for halting or at least greatly limiting immigration. Although Congress made some adjustments in subsequent years, the quotas put in place in 1924 governed U.S. immigration policy for more than forty years. Not until 1965 did Congress approve a complete overhaul, in a move that would have great significance for religious pluralism and diversity.

Anti-Semitic discrimination had one of its most notorious expressions just before the outbreak of World War I when, in 1913, Leo Frank, president of the Atlanta B'nai B'rith, was accused of murdering a young Christian female worker at the pencil factory where he was a manager. Found guilty in a trial that was little more than a farce, Frank was sentenced to death. Before the execution date arrived, however, a mob broke into the jail and lynched Frank. The episode fueled a growing backlash against Jewish Americans, becoming one of the formative events leading to the resurgence of the Ku Klux Klan.

When the British government promulgated the Balfour Declaration in 1917 and then assumed control of Palestine as a protectorate after World War I, the stage was set both for more internal differences within American Judaism and for fresh outbursts of anti-Semitism. The Balfour Declaration prompted a surge of Zionism, or moves to establish a national state in Palestine under Jewish control. Jews had not exercised political control of the area, the "promised land" of ancient Hebrew conviction, since the days of Alexander the Great, except for one brief interlude. Expectations of a new Jewish state, however, caused some division within American Jewish circles. Some, particularly among the most Orthodox, believed that divine messianic intervention alone would restore Palestine to Jewish authority; pressuring the British government under its new mandate to create an independent Jewish state was human intervention in the affairs of God. Others, of course, thought differently. But from then until the independence of Israel became reality in 1948, Zionism was a key component of American Jewish life and a matter of controversy within American Jewish communities.

In the 1920s, when Zionist activity began to percolate after the war ended, many Christian Americans looked askance at what they thought was unusually strong Jewish power in political and economic life. In many areas, they perceived threats to their own influence within the larger culture. Elite colleges and universities began imposing quotas, often never made public, to restrict the number of Jewish students who could enroll, although attendance at state colleges and universities had already made higher education a reality for a larger proportion of the American Jewish population than any other. As well-educated Jews moved upwards in positions of responsibility in the

> ### Anti-Semitism surges after World War I
> Noted historian John Higham (1920–2003) highlighted the way "the seeds of a new movement against Jews were to be found in the 100 per cent Americanism of the war years." He traced some of the prejudice to the perception that many of "the more wealthy and prominent Jews were of German background. Certain 100 per centers, therefore, applied to the Jews the suspicion of all things foreign." Especially important, Higham noted, was the feeling that there was "German-Jewish influence in high places" in the government. Higham quoted a Texas businessman of the time who ranted that "The government ... seems to be permeated with the atmosphere of different kinds of Jews."
> (Quotes from John Higham, *Strangers in the Land: Patterns of American Nativism, 1860–1925* (New York: Atheneum, 1969), 278–79)

workforce and sought to enjoy the trappings that went with their professions, country clubs and other such associations began to limit or restrict Jewish membership, just as they did African American membership. Neighborhood homeowners' associations adopted exclusionary covenants to minimize the possibility of "undesirable" people buying homes there; undesirable often included Jews, African Americans, and other "foreign" elements. Not until the 1950s were many of these jettisoned, and then often only because of court intervention.

The most insidious anti-Semitic backlash came when automobile magnate Henry Ford (1863–1947) urged a Michigan newspaper to print a series of essays attacking presumed "Jewish influence" in American life, an influence believed to be destroying the purity of Anglo-Saxon culture. Ford also bankrolled the publication of a spurious treatise, the *Protocols of the Elders of Zion*, which trumpeted the existence of a growing and increasingly powerful Jewish conspiracy to take over the global economy and thus to control international political life. At the close of the decade, when the stock market crash signaled the plunge into the Great Depression, those taken by such arguments insisted that Jews were responsible for the disaster. Such undercurrents of anti-Semitism were in their own way acknowledgment that Judaism in whatever form it took had become integral to American religion pluralism. It would hardly be worth the effort to launch irrational attacks against a group that was truly of no account. Anti-Semitism cast a pall on American religious pluralism until well after the close of World War II. When Americans became aware of the near-destruction of European Jewish life during the Holocaust, they gradually abandoned most overt anti-Semitism, in part because a more dangerous threat had appeared in the form of "godless" communism.

American Catholics, struggling with the ethnic diversity within the church, also confronted hostility. When the U.S. joined the allied cause in World War I, many expected there would be a fresh suspicion of Catholics because of their ethnic backgrounds. Many German Americans, for example, were practicing Catholics; the skeptical presumed they would undermine the American war effort and encourage treasonous support of the enemy. This fear extended as well, for example, to Protestants of German stock, especially among the Missouri Synod Lutherans. But the suspicion also came to Catholics from other nations and ethnic clusters, particularly if ancestral ties linked American Catholics to military foes. The Catholic leadership dispelled much of this suspicion, at least for the moment, when in 1917 the National Catholic War Council formed. Organized to mobilize Catholic support for the allied cause, ranging from recruiting Catholic chaplains to serve the troops, to cooperative ventures with groups like the Salvation Army to offer humanitarian assistance, the council symbolized the genuine patriotism of American Catholics. Additionally, Catholics who served in the armed forces did much to allay fears that Catholics were not loyal citizens because of their allegiance to the pope, whose political power in Europe had disintegrated following the unification of Italy a generation earlier.

Such endeavors did not eliminate anti-Catholic attitudes, however. Just as anti-Semitism mushroomed during the 1920s, anti-Catholicism was always just beneath the surface, especially among those who mourned the loss of Protestant hegemony in American life. The most telling episode came in 1928 when a Roman Catholic, Governor Al Smith of New York, became the Democratic candidate for president. Generally in areas of the country with proportionally smaller Catholic populations, attacks on Smith because of his religion added a sinister note to the campaign. So, too, did his association with New York, because New York City was the major entry point for immigrants—whom these same people perceived as dangerous—and probably the most ethnically and religiously pluralistic metropolitan area in the nation. When the Democratic Party also supported repeal of Prohibition, negative feelings escalated, turning the presidential campaign of 1928 into one of the last large-scale anti-Catholic events in American common life. Yet, as was the case with the outburst of anti-Semitism, this irrational hostility obliquely represented a cultural awareness that an ethnically diverse Catholicism had left an indelible imprint on American religious pluralism.

The vision of a reborn Klan

Many of the irrational fears stirred by the increased diversity in American life coalesced in the rebirth of the Ku Klux Klan in 1915. Originally organized in Tennessee in 1866, the Klan had pretty much disappeared by the beginning of the twentieth century, especially as racial segregation became the norm not only in the South, but in much of the nation. But two events came together to revitalize the Klan in 1915. One was the trial and lynching of Leo Frank, which brought together much anxiety about the large-scale immigration underway at the time, along with a strident anti-Semitism.

Figure 13.1 Ku Klux Klan Klansmen marching in 1925. A hybrid of religious and fraternal elements, the Ku Klux Klan came to symbolize the racism that pervaded American religion and culture (© Getty Images.)

The other was the release in 1915 of one of the earliest commercial motion pictures, *Birth of a Nation,* based on two novels, *The Leopard's Spots* (1902) and *The Clansman* (1905), by Thomas Dixon (1864–1946), an ordained Baptist preacher from North Carolina. The Klan also capitalized on the attraction of the fraternal order movement, with its penchant for dramatic ritual and sense of elitism.

Most responsible for the rebirth of the Klan as a quasi-religious fraternal order was William Joseph Simmons (1880–1945), a one-time minister in the Methodist Episcopal Church, South. From its organization at Stone Mountain, Georgia, just outside Atlanta, the Klan spread quickly through the South and the Midwest. Almost all of its constituents were white Protestant men. From their white robes to rituals using the Bible and to making a cross a central symbol, the Klan fused religion with the fears cascading through society not only as a result of the end of slavery, but also as a response to the massive numbers of non-Anglo-Saxon Protestants entering the country each year. Klan parades often featured a ceremony where the Klan would present a prominent local pastor with a Bible to confirm his role as one called to nurture the purity of his flock, in this case by excluding all who were "other" than white from full participation in both church and society.

Although anti-Catholic, anti-Semitic, and anti-immigrant to the core, the Klan garnered its greatest strength in areas where the proportion of the population who were Catholic, Jewish, or recent immigrants was small, but its membership spanned the nation by the mid-1920s. Consequently, in the South especially—though the

> ### "Native, white, Protestant supremacy"
>
> This title quote formed the slogan for the reconstituted Ku Klux Klan. One-time Klan Imperial Wizard Hiram Wesley Evans (1881–1966) expounded on the slogan:
>
>> First in the Klansman's mind is patriotism—America for Americans ... He believes, too, that Americanism can only be achieved if the pioneer stock is kept pure ... The white race must be supreme, not only in America but in the world ... The third of the Klan principles is that Protestantism must be supreme, that Rome shall not rule America ... Protestantism is an essential part of Americanism ... Protestantism contains more than religion. It is the expression in religion of the same spirit of independence, self-reliance and freedom which are the highest achievement of the Nordic race.
>
> (From Hiram Wesley Evans, "Imperial Wizard and Emperor, Knights of the Ku Klux Klan," *North American Review* 223 (March–May 1926), as excerpted in Edwin S. Gaustad and Mark A. Noll, eds., *A Documentary History of Religion in America since 1877*, 3rd ed. (Grand Rapids, MI: Eerdmans, 2003), 257–59)

Klan may have had greater numerical strength elsewhere in the 1920s—the Klan became a religiously based terrorist body that was stridently racist; racist tones also undergirded Klan life in areas where the "Great Migration" had brought hundreds of African Americans to northern cities, especially as the automotive industry developed. Numerous lynchings resulted from alliances between local officials and Klan leaders to overlook the law and due process; of course, many of these local officials were Klan members as well. Accounts report several cases where young African American military veterans returning home from serving in World War I were lynched, even while in uniform, though the actual number of lynchings of veterans or others remains contested. Many Klan rallies trumpeted the anti-Semitism which insisted that a secret alliance of Jewish bankers sought to dominate the world economy, the same kind of absurdity that made its way into the *Protocols of the Elders of Zion*.

Of course, the Klan did not view itself as a nativist, bigoted agency that fused religion and fear in its war against diversity. To the contrary, the Klan believed itself to be a force for moral and social reform, endeavoring to retain the purity of an Anglo-Saxon Protestant culture by assuring that all who were "other" either conform to a single standard of belief and behavior or recognize that they had no rights within the larger society, despite the guarantees of the Constitution. Hence the Klan had its own vision of a unified America, but one that rejected the inroads made by racial, ethnic, and religious diversity.

In order to promote its vision for the nation, the Klan joined with other religious and quasi-religious groups in calling for Prohibition, believing that banning the sale of alcohol was a mechanism to control the social behavior of non-Protestant immigrants and non-white Americans. With five million members by 1925, the Klan for a time was an important political force, a powerful fraternal group, and a significant quasi-religious body. It captured the many pervasive but often undefined fears, often fears of what was unknown or unfamiliar, and provided an outlet, too frequently a violent one, to express those fears. At the same time, though, as with anti-Catholicism and anti-Semitism, when the Klan gathered momentum, pluralism was already too deeply embedded within American religious culture and social life to be displaced. But once again, pluralism came only at a price and with conflict.

Communications media move in new directions

The years after World War I witnessed much reaction to the pluralism that was so evident in American life. But that epoch also moved American religion in new directions as new communications media made their mark throughout the culture. Although some saw these new media—radio and film—as dangers that would further destroy the religious and moral fabric of the nation, they actually added a very different dimension of diversity, for they expanded the ways in which religious leaders and groups could disseminate their message to the people. What compounded the impact of these media was a broader cultural shift that was underway. Industrial growth and technology had increased for millions not only disposable income, but also their time for leisure pursuits, as the standard working pattern shifted from a twelve-hour day six days a week to the more familiar forty-hour work week. In turn, the automobile stimulated a new mobility among those who benefited most from the economic growth of the 1920s. Together, these changes represented challenges to the way American religions went about their business and sought to endow life with meaning for their adherents.

In 1920, Pittsburgh radio station KDKA launched the communications revolution by beginning regular broadcasting. Science had succeeded in transmitting sound and the human voice across the airwaves, bringing them into private homes. Those who saw radio as a threat believed that people would exit the nation's churches and synagogues in large numbers, preferring to stay in the sacred space of their homes and perhaps listen to a religious service on radio. Many thought financial support for organized religion would dwindle. This bleak expectation proved entirely misdirected. Instead, radio became a means by which religion could reach those unable to attend, offer spiritual nurture to the homebound, and perhaps even communicate with those who spurned religion. It was a medium that required new techniques, and those who mastered the medium added to the diversity of how religion in America reaches ordinary people.

By the 1930s, religious people had conquered the new technology. Although most network stations as a public service granted free air time to programs developed by

The growth of religious broadcasting

- The first radio broadcast actually occurred on Christmas Eve, 1906.
- Pittsburgh station KDKA, the first commercial radio station in the U.S., started regular religious broadcasting after just two months on the air.
- By 1925, there were more than 600 radio stations, almost all of them with religious broadcasting.
- Donald Grey Barnhouse, a Philadelphia pastor, in 1928 was the first religious broadcaster who bought network time.
- Among the earliest long-running religious broadcasts on commercial radio was *The Lutheran Hour*, which featured Walter A. Meier preaching weekly, from 1930 until his death in 1950.
- By the fall of 1939, Charles E. Fuller's *Old Fashioned Revival Hour* had a weekly audience of more than 10 million listeners.

mainline Protestant denominations, often working together, air time was available to others who could muster the resources to purchase it. Among the most successful was Charles E. Fuller (1887–1968), an itinerant evangelist and pastor of an independent fundamentalist congregation in Pasadena, California. By 1933, he had left the pastorate to devote full time to his new Gospel Broadcasting Association, which sponsored his radio and revival ministry. Before the end of the decade, his "Old Fashioned Revival Hour" was broadcasting on network radio, becoming radio's single most popular program and reaching more than 10 million listeners each week at its peak. When New Deal initiatives extended electricity to more remote rural areas, such as parts of Appalachia, radio provided opportunities for preachers and congregations, many of them inclined to Holiness and/or Pentecostal approaches, to extend their ministries to thousands who otherwise might not have ready access to religious services. In some cases, religiously based groups launched their own radio stations, although many early ones were short lived because their backers had inadequate financing to sustain them. Moody Bible Institute's WMBI, operating in Chicago, was a stunning exception.

The growth of the film industry also presented challenges. Commercial film, especially, appeared a threat to some religious leaders, not only because of the image of theater professionals as poor examples of proper behavior, but also because of fears that ordinary people would attend movies and other morally suspect entertainment venues rather than participate in activities organized under religious auspices. Religion, however, provided material for many of the more successful early commercial films. The life of Jesus and Christian themes became the focus of some of them. In 1912, an Italian version of the novel *Quo Vadis*, published as a book in 1896 by Polish Nobel Prize winner Henryk Sienkiewicz (1846–1916), became the first commercial "blockbuster" silent film shown across the U.S.; it featured a young Christian heroine in Rome during the time of Nero. One-time Civil War commander and New Mexico governor Lew Wallace (1827–1905) had his fictional *Ben-Hur: A Tale of the Christ* (1880) become another huge success in a silent film version in 1925. Two years later came the first major epic, *King of Kings*, the brainchild of the legendary Cecil B. DeMille. In time, even those most concerned about the moral dangers of film recognized that this medium could also serve religious purposes; separatist fundamentalist Bob Jones University, for example, eventually developed a first-rate course of study in film making.

At the same time, religious bestsellers signaled that print was still a vital form of communication. When Bruce Barton (1886–1967), an advertising executive who had pondered a ministerial career, published his interpretation of Jesus, *The Man Nobody Knows*, in 1925, this portrayal of Jesus as the successful urban business entrepreneur became an American bestseller for two years. It wedded a popular picture of Jesus to urban, industrial America even as it fascinated its audience with a dynamic, very masculine Jesus who was the model for any successful business executive. This executive Jesus wore no denominational or theological label.

Media ventures—whether radio, film, or print—represent new and diverse ways to craft a religious message. More importantly, they present a paradox. On the one hand, they reflect the burgeoning religious diversity in American culture simply because they seek to present a message that crosses over boundaries that distinguish various religious groups. DeMille's Jesus in *King of Kings*, for example, bears no denominational label. The move to find a "least common denominator" becomes significant simply because there are so many individual, distinct understandings associated with different religious groups. On the other hand, by offering up a portrait of Jesus stripped of theological particularity, a portrait that does not reflect the doctrine or teaching of any single religious group, these media endeavors are attempts to harmonize if not minimize differences, to create an overarching religious viewpoint that transcends differences and therefore provides a basis for a common identity. But none would have had power or achieved popular acclaim were there not a dynamic pluralism at the heart of American religious culture. Pluralism made the effort to homogenize belief seem an appropriate way to demonstrate that an overarching unity linked together Protestant Americans from diverse theological and denominational backgrounds.

> ### Key points you need to know
>
> - Prohibition captured many of the fears of different kinds of pluralism and became a religious crusade to reform the nation.
> - First-wave feminism was central to the effort to make Prohibition the law of the land.

- The opening decades of the twentieth century witnessed renewed outbursts of anti-Semitism and anti-Catholicism.
- That hostility demonstrated the depth of religious and ethnic pluralism that characterized the nation and led to laws restricting immigration.
- The Ku Klux Klan, reborn in the early twentieth century, drew from religious sources and operated as a religious movement in its own right.
- The Klan fueled racist, anti-Semitic, anti-Catholic, and anti-immigrant prejudices.
- Advances in technology that made the automobile common and launched new forms of communications media, such as radio and film, brought both controversy and new faces of diversity to American religion.
- Some, however, drew on popular culture to refashion how religion presented itself.

Discussion questions

1. In what ways was Prohibition a religious movement? How did it stir religious prejudice in America?
2. How did the work of the WCTU and the Anti-Saloon League both complement each other and take distinctive approaches?
3. What stirred anti-Semitism in first third of the twentieth century? What forms did it take?
4. How did anti-Catholic sentiment express itself in early twentieth-century America?
5. What was the focus of the reborn Ku Klux Klan?
6. In what ways do anti-Semitism, anti-Catholicism, and the Ku Klux Klan represent a reaction against increasing diversity?
7. What reservations did some religious leaders have about advances in communications technology such as radio and film?
8. Why and how did the religious response to these new media represent a paradox when it came to dealing with currents of religious pluralism in American life?

Further reading

Dinnerstein, Leonard. *Antisemitism in America*. New York: Oxford University Press, 1994.

Erickson, Hal. *Religious Radio and Television in the United States, 1921–1991: The Programs and Personalities*. Jefferson, NC: McFarland, 1992.

Higham, John. *Strangers in the Land: Patterns of American Nativism, 1860–1925.* New York: Atheneum, 1969.

Kobler, John. *Ardent Spirits: The Rise and Fall of Prohibition.* New York: Putnam, 1973.

MacLean, Nancy K. *Behind the Mask of Chivalry: The Making of the Second Ku Klux Klan.* New York: Oxford University Press, 1994.

Massa, Mark S. *Anti-Catholicism in America: The Last Acceptable Prejudice.* New York: Crossroad, 2003.

Newton, Michael. *The Invisible Empire: The Ku Klux Klan in Florida.* Gainesville: University Press of Florida, 2001.

14 Quests for unity amid diversity

In this chapter

This chapter opens with discussion of the impact of the Great Depression and World War II on American religious life. It then examines how, in the years after the war, when "godless communism" became the new enemy, there was a push to find common religious ground, despite the pluralism that existed in the U.S. It considers how the ecumenical movement, or an effort at cooperation among religious groups, and even a new urban revivalism in the post-war years eclipsed the diversity that had become a hallmark of American religion. The final section explores challenges that undermined attempts to create unity or common ground.

Main topics covered

- How the Great Depression and World War II affected American religious life
- New religious images of the nation that emerged during the Cold War era
- The effort to create a veneer of religious unity in American culture
- How the ecumenical movement and post-war religious revival helped emphasize unity
- The way the civil rights movement began to challenge the effort to promote a common identity
- Challenges from other calls for social change, such as second-wave feminism and protests against American military engagement in Southeast Asia
- Ways the idea of an American civil religion sought to buttress a sense of commonality

Depression and another world war complicate religious life

The "return to normalcy" after World War I that sought to limit immigration and thereby deter increasing diversity and pluralism in American religion was short lived.

In October 1929, over a period of several days, the stock market sustained one of the most severe downturns in history. In actuality, the decline was part of a global economic crisis, not just an American one, and the years that followed became known as the Great Depression throughout the industrializing world. The nation had experienced periods of economic depression before, but the duration of the Great Depression and its international dimensions became a defining moment in American life.

With depression and war, immigration plummeted, even with the new quota system in place. For about a decade and a half, there was relatively little change in the trends already in place. Historians who track participation in religious groups suggest that attendance and certainly financial support for religious institutions dropped during the Depression years, largely as a consequence of the challenges cascading through the whole culture. Membership in fraternal orders also began a decline that continues into the twenty-first century. During hard economic times, people simply did not have the financial resources or what today is called disposable income to pay lodge dues and support other fraternal activities. Although some religious leaders had long seen lodges and other fraternal movements as competing with religious groups for the allegiance of American men, regardless of race and ethnicity, the drop in lodge participation did not bring any significant increase in male membership or engagement in religious organizations. Hence the threat some found in fraternal societies was not as real as they imagined, despite the use of religious language and imagery in lodge rituals.

Historians still debate whether there was actually a "religious depression" that paralleled the economic downturn. Most of the evidence suggesting that organized religion faced equally difficult times comes from statistical data and similar measurements. Less money was available for constructing buildings used for religious purposes, for example, or for supporting any kind of religious enterprise. At the same time, however, there is little evidence to suggest that ordinary Americans abandoned religious belief or jettisoned spiritual pursuits, despite the economic challenges. Those who look at material culture and examine such matters as whether homes contain objects of a religious nature—from books and Bibles to wall hangings and other artwork—conclude that people continued to find religion important, if not vital, to sustaining a framework of meaning in life even when it might have been impossible to support a religious group financially, or at least not at the same level as before the Depression set in.

The sobering dimensions of depression spurred new currents in American religious thought that in their own way suggest that diversity was still part of the larger picture, particularly in terms of how theologians and other religious professionals tried to understand what was transpiring in the world around them. One example comes in the thought of Reinhold Niebuhr (1892–1971). After studying at Yale Divinity School, Niebuhr embarked on a career as a pastor in Detroit in 1915, just as the automobile industry began rapid expansion there. Niebuhr had absorbed the optimism of the Social Gospel as a student. But now he saw that movement's enthusiasm as naive.

Individual and collective morality

Reinhold Niebuhr drew stark contrasts between the moral behavior of individuals and any moral behavior exhibited by social institutions, particularly nation-states. He saw that contrast stemming from different principles that guided individual and corporate action:

> From the internal perspective the most moral act is one which is actuated by disinterested motives ... [F]rom the viewpoint of the author of an action, unselfishness must remain the criterion of the highest morality. For only the agent of an action knows to what degree self-seeking corrupts his socially approved actions. Society, on the other hand, makes justice rather than unselfishness its highest moral ideal. Its aim must be to seek equality of opportunity for all life. If this equality and justice cannot be achieved without the assertion of interest against interest, and without restraint upon the self-assertion of those who infringe upon the rights of their neighbors, then society is compelled to sanction self-assertion and restraint.
>
> (Reinhold Niebuhr, *Moral Man and Immoral Society*
> (New York: Charles Scribner's Sons, 1932), 258–59)

World War I shattered hopes of bringing religious ethics and technological advancement together to create the ideal society, as did the lived reality his working-class congregation confronted with long hours, unsafe working conditions, and low wages. Consequently, Niebuhr moved to a theological position that he believed recovered what the Social Gospel overlooked, namely the extent of human greed or what theologians called sin. Evidence came in the growing gap between rich and poor, propelled by unregulated capitalism and industrial expansion. Because Niebuhr thought his assessment more realistic in terms of how human beings actually experienced life, he called his theological approach "Christian realism."

Niebuhr left the pastorate to teach at Union Theological Seminary the year before the stock market crashed. Once the Depression began to set in, he looked to both the government and the religious sector to provide relief. Convinced that the lack of regulation of business and industry was one factor bringing economic collapse, Niebuhr wrote about the need to use ideas associated with socialism, although by no means the form of socialism linked to Marxist thought and Lenin's Russia, to advance the common good. He insisted that although individuals might be capable of moral behavior, nations and societies faced far greater challenges in trying to do what was right and just. If individuals succumbed to temptation and greed when they regarded their own achievements and potential as absolute, societies and nations could never overcome a kind of collective or corporate egotism and self-centeredness. In Niebuhr's

Figure 14.1 Buddhist Churches of America. Some Asian religious groups, such as the Buddhist Churches of America shown here, imitated Christian styles in order to adapt to the larger culture (© Jeffrey Kimoto).

realism, this assessment meant that every human system, even democracy in politics and capitalism in economics, fell short of absolute justice and goodness.

Niebuhr began to offer his critique, which some associated with neo-orthodoxy, just as President Franklin Roosevelt launched the programs popularly called the New Deal that used the government's power and resources to reshape the economic foundation of the U.S. and to begin to lift the nation out of Depression. Not all religious leaders saw government intervention as providing the best tools to deal with the economic crisis. Roman Catholic priest Charles Coughlin (1891–1979), who, like Niebuhr, had once served a parish in Detroit, used his popular radio program not just to highlight social injustice, but in time also to condemn the New Deal for its entanglement with international economic affairs. Coughlin injected an anti-Semitic dimension into his attacks, insisting that New Deal advocates were in league with a presumed Jewish conspiracy to control the international economy.

Coughlin's anti-Semitic rhetoric resounded across the airwaves as Adolf Hitler (1889–1945) and his Nazi party were coming to power in Germany in part because they stirred anti-Semitic fears of a Jewish conspiracy. When war began in Europe in 1939, most Americans recognized that U.S. neutrality, although an ideal, could not be realized for long. After Germany's ally, Japan, bombed American territory in Hawaii in 1941, America entered the global conflict. The war accentuated some strands of religious diversity and also the ongoing uncertainties about diversity that prevailed in certain sectors of society. Japanese Americans were at the center of that anxiety. One of the larger religious communities that served a constituency of primarily Japanese ancestry sought to allay fears by changing its name to the Buddhist Churches of America. Since "church" was a distinctively Christian term, Buddhist Churches of America leaders hoped that their adaptation of the designation would signal both the patriotic loyalty to the U.S. of Japanese Americans and the compatibility of a Buddhist religious style with American ways. The effort was only partially successful, however, as the government moved to relocate Japanese American citizens to internment camps, convinced that they were a threat to American security and the war effort in a way that German Americans and Italian Americans were not. Acceptance of diversity had its limits.

A righteous nation confronts "godless" communism

Americans were barely coming to terms with the extent of Nazi efforts to eliminate the Jewish population of Europe in the Holocaust of World War II when a former ally in the war, the Soviet Union, became the new "enemy" and communism became the major threat to democracy and capitalism in the American mind. Sociologists have long posited that identifying a common enemy or threat, whether real or imagined, works within a culture to mute difference and enhance common identity. An "other" perceived as dangerous makes internal differences seem less important; what binds or unites a people becomes more important. Religion, of course, becomes one of the key elements in promoting that common identity, reinforcing the sense that "we" are both right and righteous and "they" are wrong and evil. That dynamic became a central feature of American life in the first couple of decades after the end of World War II, although at the time it seemed that other forces were also at work.

Several events in the 1950s illuminate this process. None attempted to deny that variety and difference continued to enrich American religious life. There were still hundreds of denominations of Protestants, scores of ethnic Catholic communities, various branches of Judaism, and several expressions of Eastern Orthodox Christianity, along with a host of other alternatives demonstrating that many faces of pluralism continued to define American religion. But there were countervailing trends that sought to demonstrate that, despite that deep and abiding diversity, Americans shared a common moral sensibility based in religious belief.

An early example came in 1953 at the inauguration of World War II war hero Dwight D. Eisenhower as president of the United States. The public knew little at the time about Eisenhower's personal religious views; he did not actually join a church until later. Before beginning his inaugural address on the steps of the nation's Capitol, Eisenhower offered a brief prayer, starting what has since become a routine practice at such events. More important than what Eisenhower said was what the prayer signaled. Having a public figure like the president offer a prayer suggested that Americans as a people were religiously inclined and therefore moral and upright. Nothing in the content of the prayer indicated that Eisenhower would soon identify with a Presbyterian congregation in Washington. It was a simple prayer that linked the American people and their destiny to divine providence, trusting this providence to bless and protect the nation. In the context of the Cold War, however, the prayer had additional force, for it aligned the U.S. with righteousness and reinforced the popular perception that communist regimes were by definition "godless" and atheistic. They were therefore not moral and righteous.

Within two years, Congress passed legislation that added the phrase "under God" to the Pledge of Allegiance to the flag and ordered the words "in God we trust" to appear on all currency; that phrase previously had appeared only on coins. These actions are also efforts to promote a sense of common identity and national unity as well as an image of the United States as a righteous nation. Neither offers a theological statement about the nature of the God in whom Americans presumably trust; one can define or describe God however one chooses. To be specific about matters of doctrine and belief would defeat the purpose intended. Doing so would reveal the degree of diversity and pluralism that marked American religion. In other words, going beyond a generic religious reference would highlight how many different views of God flourished. It would show disagreement, not unity. So long as the overt religious reference remained vague and general, common identity and unity could prevail. But also important is the simple inclusion of such language in setting apart the American nation, especially from "godless" realms where communist ideology prevailed. The words became a subtle signal to differentiate between the different styles that the U.S. and the Soviet Union represented, claiming a moral high ground for the U.S. as a nation "under God" and whose people trusted in God.

In a similar vein, analysts of American religious life in the 1950s began to talk about a shared "Judeo-Christian tradition" that collapsed distinctions not just between American Jews and American Christians, but between the hundreds of different denominations that claimed the label of Christian. It, too, was a mechanism to foster common identity by emphasizing a shared biblical heritage. A similar understanding emerged in a now classic study by Jewish sociologist Will Herberg (1901–1977), who taught at a Protestant theological school (thus exemplifying in his own life and career the push to common ground). In 1955, Herberg published his *Protestant, Catholic, Jew*, in which he argued that, for all practical purposes, most Americans regarded identification with any of these three broad religious traditions as equally legitimate and viable ways to acquire the moral basis for being a good citizen. Although particular beliefs and practices still differed, the three functioned the same way in the public arena. The inference was that simply having a religious label identified with one of those three broad traditions was what mattered, not which one it was. Herberg also described what he called "the religion of the American way of life" oriented around conspicuous consumption, a sort of culture religion that transcended the particularities of belief and practice associated with being Protestant, Catholic, or Jewish. Herberg found problems with this culture religion, particularly because it did not make the same demands for commitment that he found in the biblical background for any "Judeo-Christian" expression.

Asserting a common American religion

Sociologist Will Herberg saw how the push for common ground muted distinctions between diverse religions in America, in his mind often compromising the integrity of each and the prophetic posture of religion:

> Equally dubious from the standpoint of Jewish-Christian faith is that aspect of the present religious situation which makes religion in America so thoroughly American. On the one side this means that no taint of foreignness any longer adheres to the three great American "faiths" ... And all Americans may be thankful for the new spirit of freedom and tolerance in religious life that the emergence of the tripartite system of three great "religions of democracy" has engendered ... But on the other side, the "Americanization" of religion has meant a distinct loss of the sense of religious uniqueness and universality: each of the three "faiths," insofar as the mass of its adherents are concerned tends to regard itself merely as an alternative and variant form of being religious in the American way.
> (Will Herberg, *Protestant, Catholic, Jew: An Essay in American Religious Sociology*, rev. ed. (Garden City, NY: Doubleday Anchor, 1960), 261–62)

Other efforts to promote common identity

Numerous moves in the religious sector also highlight the effort to advance unity and common identity, while still acknowledging the diversity at the heart of American religion. Several of these moves shape what is called the ecumenical movement, a term that denotes being part of a common, single religious "household." In 1950, for example, the Federal Council of Churches, spawned by Social Gospel efforts in the early twentieth century, reorganized as the National Council of Churches in order to promote better cooperation among member bodies. Most of the nation's larger mainline Protestant denominations joined the council, which was affiliated with a global body founded a few years earlier, the World Council of Churches. Recognizing that there were still theological differences, and thus much variation in the particulars of belief and practice among member denominations, the Council and scores of state and local affiliated groups stressed what all had in common, the basics that made all of them Christians. That way, they could work together in response to matters such as human suffering resulting from war, famine, or disease, as well as be more efficient by combining resources when it came to operations such as publishing materials for religious education and nurture. Not all groups joined these endeavors; some held observer status without becoming actual members. Regardless, however, these endeavors sent a signal that the old divisions that had separated American Protestants were less important than what united them. The ecumenical movement thus reinforced the notion of

America as a righteous nation, one where religious values undergirded common life and difference thrived without provoking hostility.

Another prong of the ecumenical movement promoted actual church union among bodies that had historical relationships and common histories. Among groups that had divided over slavery in the decades before the Civil War, both Methodists and Presbyterians ultimately effected some sort of reunion, the Methodists as early as 1939 and the Presbyterians in 1983. Several of the nation's Lutheran bodies came together in the Evangelical Lutheran Church in America, although some, such as the Missouri Synod Lutherans, remained separate. In the case of the Lutherans, earlier divisions were grounded more in ethnicity than in any regional or theological differences. Sometimes groups of a similar theological bent merged, adding to the notion that what people shared superseded what divided them. Two examples are the formation of the United Church of Christ in 1957, which brought together two groups with roots in New England and German immigrant Congregationalism, and the organization four years later of the Unitarian Universalist Association, which combined two of the more liberally inclined religious groups.

At the same time, the hope in the minds of many remained the collapsing of all Protestant denominations into a single body, a hope not yet achieved. In 1960, a prominent Presbyterian leader, Eugene Carson Blake (1906–1985), in a sermon preached in an Episcopal cathedral in San Francisco, called for that kind of ecumenical union. The result was the formation in 1961 of the Consultation on Church Union, renamed Churches Uniting in Christ in 2002. The hope of a single Protestant body remains elusive, but the ecumenical movement has led to many cross-denominational experiments, recognition of the theological integrity of all cooperating bodies, and sometimes allowing pastors ordained in one body to serve congregations affiliated with another.

Some efforts spanned the lines that divided faith traditions. In 1962, at the call of Pope John XXIII, the first worldwide council in nearly a century brought together Roman Catholic leaders in Rome. Known as Vatican II, the council in its sessions from 1962 to 1965 welcomed many Protestant observers and signaled a fresh willingness of Roman Catholic Christians to engage in dialogue and conversation not only with Christians outside the Catholic tradition, but also with persons from other religious traditions. In the U.S., many of the changes instituted by Vatican II, from increasing lay participation in parish operations to use of the vernacular in the celebration of the mass, had profound effects, although in 1968 Pope Paul VI's reaffirmation of the church's traditional ban on the use of artificial means of contraception seemed to some a step back from the more open environment prompted by the council.

Even before the Second Vatican Council began, events in the public sector indicated that the anti-Catholic sentiment that had long been an undercurrent in American religious diversity was fading, perhaps in part because of the felt need in the Cold War era to promote common identity and a facade of unity. The most obvious was

Ecumenism and cooperation

The National Council of Churches, a symbol for the entire ecumenical movement since 1950, captured the spirit behind cooperation among diverse religious groups, suggesting that working together was more effective and efficient than working separately:

> This Council has been constituted by twenty-nine Churches for the glory of God and the well-being of humanity ... It is designed to be an instrument of the Holy Spirit for such ministries of evangelism, education, and relief as are better achieved through Christian cooperation than by the labors of separated groups. It coordinates and continues the work of eight interdenominational agencies ministering in as many fields of Christian usefulness.
>
> (National Council of Churches, *Christian Faith in Action: Commemorative Volume* (New York: National Council of Churches, 1951), 150, quoted in Edwin S. Gaustad and Mark A. Noll, eds., *A Documentary History of Religion in America since 1877*, 3rd ed. (Grand Rapids, MI: Eerdmans, 2003), 510)

the election of Roman Catholic John F. Kennedy as president of the United States in 1960. Kennedy knew that many American Protestants, especially, harbored fears that a Catholic president might be too willing to advance policies that would impose church teaching on all citizens, fears that had surfaced in the 1928 election campaign. Accordingly, in campaign addresses Kennedy made bold assertions of his commitment to separation of church and state and to insist that his personal religious faith would in no way predetermine the policies of his administration. Only what he believed would promote the general welfare would influence his decisions as president. The election was one of the closest in U.S. history in terms of the popular vote, and, looking back, Kennedy's efforts to draw sharp lines between faith and politics seemed a critical factor in his victory.

Other interfaith endeavors that crossed boundaries that usually separated traditions also became more common in the years after World War II. The National Conference of Christians and Jews, founded in 1927 to counter some of the anti-Semitic rhetoric prompted by Henry Ford's financing the publication of the *Protocols of the Elders of Zion*, was one agency whose public visibility increased in the era of the 1960s, when ecumenical cooperation was the order of the day. In one sense, what pushed American Christians and Jews to work together was the devastation of the Holocaust and Hitler's attempts to exterminate the Jewish population of Europe; many Jews and Christians worked together, for example, in the Zionist efforts that led to the creation of Israel as an independent nation in 1948 and encouraged U.S.

Figure 14.2 Billy Graham crusade. Thousands packed arenas such as this to hear Billy Graham, America's premier twentieth-century evangelist (Courtesy of Archives of the Billy Graham Center, Wheaton, Illinois.)

President Harry Truman to recognize Israel as a nation. The ensuing conflict in the Middle East reinforced some of the interfaith ties that had developed as Christians and Jews alike sought to support the Israeli cause. By the 1960s, domestic issues came to the fore to sustain Jewish–Christian cooperation, particularly the civil rights movement which, as we shall see, revealed some of the cracks in the veneer of religious unity that tried to present the U.S. as a righteous nation. In time, shared concerns for social justice superseded the need to combat the anti-Semitism that prompted the council's founding. One result was a change in the name of the organization to the National Council for Community and Justice.

Even a fresh burst of urban-oriented revivalism helped promote the image of an America that was righteous and, although diverse, unified in its moral opposition to "godless" communism. Much of that revivalism centers around Billy Graham (1918–), who gained international renown after a wildly successful evangelistic crusade in 1954 in a Great Britain still struggling to recover from the devastation of World War II. Graham took his finely honed revivalism to New York City's Madison Square Garden in 1957, in a crusade whose duration was extended several times and that closed with a dramatic rally that packed Yankee Stadium. Although Graham was a Southern Baptist by affiliation, he made no overt denominational references in his preaching and calls for conversion. He also sought widespread support from diverse religious groups for his crusades. The Protestant Council of the City of New York, for example, provided much of the backing for the 1957 crusade. At revival meetings, Graham frequently welcomed to the platform religious leaders from many denominations, a clear symbol that unity transcended diversity. Individuals who indicated that they had made a religious commitment in response to Graham's message received referrals to congregations near their residences, without regard to denomination, that were part of the network of churches endorsing the crusade. This muting of denominational distinctiveness promoted in its own way the perception that all denominations were pretty much the same, that whatever divided them was far less important than the common ground they shared. Hence Graham's revivalism reinforced the larger ethos that promoted common identity and unity, even while affirming religious diversity.

Cracks start to erode the veneer of unity

Although much of the religious culture of post-war America looked to unity and thus downplayed the depth of diversity in the nation, by the mid-1950s currents were developing that undermined that spirit of unity and common identity. In 1954, the U.S. Supreme Court, in *Brown v. Board of Education*, declared unconstitutional the practice of maintaining "separate but equal" facilities based on race. The next year, Rosa Parks (1913–2005), an African American, defied local law in Montgomery, Alabama, by refusing to give up her seat on a bus. The boycott of the bus system that followed launched the civil rights movement, a religious revival in its own right, and propelled Martin Luther King, Jr. (1929–1968), then pastor of Montgomery's Dexter Avenue Baptist Church, to the forefront of civil rights activity. Churches had long honed the leadership skills of African Americans pushed to the margins by a racist culture. Churches also provided meeting spaces for rallies calling for an end to legal segregation at every level of American society.

King's Southern Christian Leadership Conference built on visions of a just society rooted in the Social Gospel. But it also drew on tactics of non-violence used effectively by Hindu-inspired Mahatma Gandhi in the struggle for India's independence from Britain. As a pastor and preacher, King peppered his speeches with metaphors and language from the Bible, turning a movement for political and social transformation into a religious crusade. Leaders across the religious spectrum laid aside difference to endorse the call for civil rights. Once again, divisions took a back seat to a larger cause. Rabbis, Catholic priests, Protestant ministers, and seminary students from every religious community joined the movement, with many suffering imprisonment or becoming the victims of violent reaction from those determined to maintain the status quo. The movement reached a symbolic peak in the 1963 March on Washington, which drew hundreds of thousands to the nation's capital in a rally that mirrored a Billy Graham crusade in its intensity and impact.

Ironically, some of those fighting to maintain a segregated society also claimed religious backing for their views. They strained to find biblical support for racial separation, fearing especially that marriage across racial lines would lead to the "dilution"

Martin Luther King fuses religion and civil rights

In his famous "Letter from Birmingham Jail," written while he was incarcerated in that Alabama city in 1963, Martin Luther King, Jr. powerfully demonstrated how he saw the non-violent civil rights social protest as a religious enterprise, as biblical images framed his thinking:

> We will have to repent in this generation not merely for the hateful words and actions of the bad people but for the appalling silence of the good people. Human progress never rolls in on wheels of inevitability; it comes through the tireless efforts of men willing to be co-workers with God ... Now is the time to make real the promise of democracy and transform our pending national elegy into a creative psalm of brotherhood. Now is the time to lift our national policy from the quicksand of racial injustice to the solid rock of human dignity.

(Martin Luther King, Jr., "Letter from Birmingham Jail," in his *Why We Can't Wait* (New York: New American Library, 1964), 86)

of any "pure" racial stock. Hence the civil rights movement also revealed yet another strain of diversity, one that echoed the dynamics at work in the years before the Civil War, when religion became both an agent for social change and an agent to buttress the status quo.

As the civil rights movement grew, it also brought additional religious dynamics to the fore. Some African Americans linked American racism to the Judeo-Christian congregations and groups long dominant and called for African Americans to abandon any allegiance especially to Christianity. To some, a tradition such as Islam seemed more appealing, for Islam had a long history within African religious life. Others saw Christianity as the agent of slavery and called for a separate African society not diluted by white evil; Elijah Muhammad (1897–1975), Malcolm X (1925–1965), and others made the Nation of Islam or Black Muslims a viable alternative to Christianity for many African Americans. With these calls for African Americans to look to other religious options becoming more prominent, the civil rights movement revealed weaknesses in the effort to mute difference in order to cast the U.S. as a righteous nation and bastion of the Judeo-Christian tradition standing united against "godless" communism.

The civil rights movement unleashed a host of other efforts that challenged the status quo, both in society and in religion. Women, for example, looked back at the first wave of feminism that had brought the right to vote and gave support to Prohibition, but realized that much remained undone. By the 1950s there were more sustained calls for the ordination of women to professional ministry. Among the major Protestant bodies, the Methodist Church was among the first to grant ministerial orders to women, beginning in 1956. Over the next two decades many other groups followed suit. American Catholics who had hoped that the Second Vatican Council might end the centuries-old practice of a male-only, celibate priesthood found their hopes dashed, however. But as second-wave feminism created fresh opportunities for women in the larger society, fewer looked to volunteer work within religious groups or even to serving, for example, as nuns in the Catholic tradition.

Native Americans also took up the call for liberation from both governmental policies that ignored the integrity of their indigenous cultures and efforts to "convert" them to other ways of being religious. Among many tribal clusters came a revitalization of ancient traditions, calls for a return to ancestral lands, and an appreciation of the intertwining of human life with the land that was vital to many Native societies. An unintended effect of renewed Native American identity was an increase in the celebration of all sorts of ethnic identities, reminding Americans of how diverse the nation really was.

By the late 1960s, other voices called for recognition of the rights of gay and lesbian citizens, soon joined by the formation of caucuses supporting gay and lesbian members within denominational bodies as well as moves to allow gays and lesbians to seek ordination to professional ministry. These efforts had an impact on American religion. They made sexual identity a matter of spiritual concern, but they also added to the array of religious bodies in the U.S. In 1968, a former Pentecostal pastor, Troy Perry, launched what became the Universal Fellowship of Metropolitan Community Churches, a denomination originally targeted to meet the religious needs of gay, lesbian, bisexual, and transgendered persons. Debates over their inclusion in the ministry of other religious bodies continue into the twenty-first century.

As these movements challenged the status quo, undermined traditional authority, and brought to the surface additional dimensions of diversity, concern mounted over U.S. military engagement in Southeast Asia. Many of the religious leaders who lent their support to the civil rights movement joined the ranks of those who questioned American policy and the destruction occasioned by a jungle-based war whose horrors reached American living rooms via nightly television news. Groups such as Clergy and Laity Concerned about Vietnam once again set aside differences in promoting a common interest, ending the Vietnam conflict.

To some, however, the various liberation movements, from civil rights to second-wave feminism and religiously inspired war protests, reeked of an unpatriotic sensibility and represented the imposition of one moral perspective on the whole nation—something that Prohibition had also done. Those wary of the direction in which American society was heading also pointed to decisions of the U.S. Supreme Court in 1962 and 1963 that ended obligatory devotional prayer and Bible reading in the nation's public schools. While some saw such activities as a breach of the "separation of church and state" and the creation of an unofficial religious establishment, others bemoaned the demise of the religious base of American culture.

In one sense, all these issues raised questions as to how much difference—whether in terms of sexual identity or in debates over public religiosity expressed in a school prayer—the nation could embrace without losing any sense of common ground. One quasi-religious response came in 1967 when a prominent sociologist, Robert Bellah (1927–), called for the revitalization of a shared religious core for the entire culture through the affirmation of what he called an American civil religion. It was a reaction against a diversity that seemed to be becoming divisive and in many ways an affirmation of the mythic American way of life so troublesome to a sociologist like Herberg.

Like the blending of religious and political symbols in the age of American independence, Bellah's proposed civil religion claimed that citizens, regardless of particular religious differences, shared a common belief in a providential God who acted in the events of American history. Prominent among those events were wars that defined or refined American identity. Bellah found in religious allusions in presidential inaugural addresses confirmation of this special relationship between the nation and a providential supreme being. Bellah's approach insisted that individuals could affirm a host of diverse theological beliefs and pluralism could flourish, so long as there remained a basic commitment to core principles such as liberty, justice, and equality.

Bellah was searching for a new common ground, much as those who saw the U.S. as "one nation, under God" in the 1950s. Then the foe was "godless" communism; for Bellah, it was the forces stirring the disintegration of community. In his efforts to craft a single vision for the nation, though, Bellah may have not recognized that his ideal civil religion was not inclusive of all Americans. Critics, for example, wondered whether African Americans whose ancestors were slaves or women who lacked the right to vote until the twentieth century could rejoice in such a rhapsodic, mythic American past. Those for whom the horrors of anti-Catholicism and anti-Semitism were very real also stood on the margins. Because of the depths of diversity and pluralism prevailing within American life, it was doubtful that one formulation of a civil religion could embrace everyone. So the proposal of a civil religion, rather than creating a new unified vision for a single nation, revealed how diversity and pluralism made claiming common ground a challenge—whether in religion or in society. That challenge became a major motif in American life in the decades after World War II.

Key points you need to know

- The Great Depression and efforts to redirect the course of American life after World War I brought diverse religious responses, including the Christian realism of Reinhold Niebuhr.
- Some religious voices condemned the New Deal, while others saw it as a moral response to economic depression.

- During the Cold War, both religious and political leaders tried to emphasize religious unity, despite religious differences.
- The emphasis on unity helped create the image of the U.S. as a righteous nation in contrast to the "godless" communism of the Soviet empire.
- Ecumenical efforts, denominational mergers, and similar endeavors also helped create a veneer of unity and common identity.
- Billy Graham and a revitalized urban revivalism added to efforts to find a moral and religious common ground for the diverse American peoples.
- The civil rights movement, a religious revitalization crusade in one sense, challenged the surface unity that prevailed.
- Other challenges came in the form of different "liberation" movements and protests against American involvement in Southeast Asia.
- These challenges caused some to think that whatever held the diverse American peoples together was in danger of collapsing.
- For American Catholics, Vatican II served as a reminder of both their bonds to a global church and the diversity within that church.
- One effort to recapture a sense of a common religious underpinning for the nation came in efforts to kindle an American civil religion.
- The turmoil of the 1960s revealed that religious pluralism was too deep to be covered with any mask of contrived unity.

Discussion questions

1. What consequences did the Great Depression have for American religious life?
2. How did Reinhold Niebuhr's "Christian realism" try to respond to the social situation of industrial America?
3. Why did some religious leaders support the New Deal? Why did others condemn it?
4. What aspects of religious diversity did World War II accentuate?
5. How did the U.S. position itself as a righteous nation in contrast to "godless" communism?
6. How did Will Herberg's analysis affirm religious diversity but downplay its significance?
7. What is the ecumenical movement? How did it relate to issues of unity and diversity?
8. In what ways did the post-war revivalism of Billy Graham also reflect both religious diversity and the effort to promote common ground?
9. What was the impact of Vatican II on American Catholicism?
10. What challenges did the civil rights movement, second-wave feminism, Vietnam War protests, and related endeavors present to American religious life?

11. How can the civil rights movement be understood as a religious revitalization enterprise?
12. Why did some analysts regard these movements as signs of decay and decline within American society and religion?
13. How did the call for a renewed American civil religion try to deal with this presumed decay and decline?

Further reading

Allitt, Patrick. *Religion in America since 1945: A History*. New York: Columbia University Press, 2003.

Bellah, Robert N. *The Broken Covenant: American Civil Religion in Time of Trial*. San Francisco: HarperSanFrancisco, 1984

——. "Civil Religion in America." *Daedalus* 96, 1 (Winter 1967): 1–21.

Branch, Taylor. *Parting the Waters: America in the King Years, 1954–1963*. New York: Simon and Schuster, 1988.

——. *Pillar of Fire: America in the King Years, 1963–1965*. New York: Simon and Schuster, 1998.

——. *At Canaan's Edge: America in the King Years, 1965–1968*. New York: Simon and Schuster, 2006.

Brown, Charles C. *Niebuhr and His Age: Reinhold Niebuhr's Prophetic Role and Legacy*. Harrisburg, PA: Trinity Press International, 2002.

Chappell, David L. *A Stone of Hope: Prophetic Religion and the Death of Jim Crow*. Chapel Hill: University of North Carolina Press, 2004.

Herberg, Will. *Protestant, Catholic, Jew: An Essay in American Religious Sociology*. Garden City, NY: Doubleday, 1955.

Marsh, Charles. *God's Long Summer: Stories of Faith and Civil Rights*. Princeton, NJ: Princeton University Press, 1997.

Marty, Martin E. *Modern American Religion*, vol. 2: *The Noise of Conflict, 1919–1941*. Chicago: University of Chicago Press, 1991.

15 The "new pluralism" of the later twentieth century

In this chapter

Discussion of some new religious movements taking hold in the U.S. beginning in the 1960s opens the chapter. Of special concern will be why they attracted followers and why some thought they were dangerous. Then attention turns to changes in the immigration laws in 1965 that spurred a "new pluralism" as immigrants from Asia, Africa, the Caribbean, and Latin America brought their religions and religious styles with them. The legal issues raised by this explosion of religious diversity, especially as evidenced by court cases concerned with "separation of church and state," forms the focus for the third section. Finally, the chapter explores the impact of this expanding pluralism on ways Americans worshiped and on personal spirituality.

Main topics covered

- The fascination with new religious movements such as Krishna Consciousness and other Asian forms of religiosity
- What social and religious conditions made these movements appealing, particularly to younger adults
- Why some believed these new movements dangerous and talked of a "cult scare"
- How critics countered the presumed "brainwashing" they felt characterized dangerous cults
- The impact on religion of changes in U.S. immigration law in 1965
- How immigration from Africa, the Caribbean, and Latin America added to religious diversity in the U.S.
- The rapid growth of religions such as Islam, Buddhism, and Hinduism in the U.S. because of "new" immigration
- The ways that new religions complicated legal issues surrounding the separation of church and state

- How and why American religious groups began to experiment with new ways to worship in the later twentieth century
- The surge of interest in personal spirituality, distinct from organized religion, which reflected the new pluralism

New religious movements spark interest and fear

In the midst of antiwar protests and ongoing civil rights agitation in the 1960s, Americans in the nation's cities and on its college campuses also found themselves confronting a host of new religious movements, many with ties to Asia or at least to Asian guru-like leaders. In 1965, for example, His Grace A.C. Bhaktivedanta Swami Prabhupada (1896–1977) arrived in the U.S. Born in Calcutta, India, Prabhupada was a devotee of Krishna, a manifestation of the Hindu deity Vishnu, who believed he had a divine call to bring the truth of Krishna to America. His followers, formally called the International Society for Krishna Consciousness (ISKCON), became known popularly as Hare Krishna, from the first two words of a Sanskrit chant repeated as a devotional act. Those who followed Krishna tended to be younger adults, many of whom found traditional religion bankrupt because of its complicity in racism and its support for American military policy in Asia. Those attracted to ISKCON donned saffron robes, took on Sanskrit names as a sign of their new identity, lived simple, chaste lives in contrast to the presumed license offered by the sexual revolution of the day, burned incense, exchanged the Bible for the Bhagavad Gita, and chanted on street corners throughout the nation. Many severed ties with their biological families, opting to live communally with fellow believers, but separated by gender if unmarried.

Prabhupada was only one of countless Asian religious teachers who found a welcome reception, along with some hostility, in the U.S. For a time, the Guru Maharaj Ji (1957–) and his Divine Light Mission captured public imagination. Many Americans were stunned to see a teenager who offered a seemingly simple way to find truth, with inner serenity coming at times simply from proper touch on the forehead. By far the best-known, however, was the Maharishi Mahesh Yogi (1917–2008), whose Transcendental Meditation (TM) gained much publicity because of the interest of the Beatles, the most popular singing group of the day, in its techniques. Millions of Americans flocked to TM centers where, for a fee, they received a personal mantra or Sanskrit syllable to chant, with the promise that even twenty minutes of chanting twice a day would bring inner peace and contentment. This chanting was rarely audible, but an inner exercise, an understanding that allowed practitioners to meditate almost anywhere.

Among the more controversial new groups was the Holy Spirit Association for the Unification of World Christianity, better known as the Moonies because of the name of the founder, Sun Myung Moon (1920–). Moon drew on aspects of a missionary Presbyterian Christianity in his native Korea, strands of Buddhism, and some features

> ### What Transcendental Meditation promised
>
> Part of the appeal of Transcendental Meditation or TM was its promise of a kind of bliss or sense of contentment that had the potential to connect the individual with a universal power that pervaded all reality. Founder Maharishi Mahesh Yogi described it as the "art of living":
>
> > As the art of making a flower arrangement is to glorify every flower by the beauty and glory of every other flower, in a similar way the art of living is such that every aspect of life is supplemented by the flowers of every other aspect. It is in this way that the transcendental aspect of life supplements the subjective and objective aspects of existence, so that the entire range of subjectivity and objectivity enjoys the absolute strength, intelligence, bliss, and creativity of the eternal Being.
>
> > (Maharishi Mahesh Yogi, *Transcendental Meditation* (1963), first published as *The Science of Being and the Art of Living*, in *The Columbia Documentary History of Religion in America Since 1945*, edited by Paul Harvey and Philip Goff (New York: Columbia University Press, 2005), 438)

of traditional Chinese religion to craft a theology that gave him messianic status as the incarnation of Christ returned to earth. Moon started his movement in Korea in 1954, but after visiting the U.S. in 1965 began to plan for an American presence that mushroomed after he relocated to the U.S. in 1971. Known for its aggressive proselytizing, and ceremonies where hundreds were married to partners selected by Moon, this group startled many Americans because of its unorthodox understanding of family, along with its fusion of things Christian, Buddhist, and Chinese.

Not all groups had an Asian flavor, although many did, largely because the Vietnam era spurred much general intrigue in things Asian. Some drew on the long heritage of communal or utopian living as a basis for a new religious ideal. Even ISKCON formed communes for its followers. Some, such as the Children of God, drew on aspects of the Jewish and Christian traditions, albeit crafted in unorthodox ways, as a basis for a new religious understanding. Rooted more directly in Christianity was the People's Temple, organized by James Warren (Jim) Jones (1931–78), that shocked the world when over 900 members committed mass suicide on Jones's orders at their communitarian settlement in Guyana in 1978.

Critics of these new religious movements and of the scores of others that came and went in the last third of the twentieth century readily called them cults, a term with negative overtones long divorced from its original meaning that had to do with the worship and devotional practices of any religious group. Those upset by these newer movements questioned the apparent total allegiance to founder figures and leaders such as Moon. They insisted that, despite being charismatic, these leaders were manipulating and even "brainwashing" their adherents. Many condemned what seemed extraordinarily aggressive recruitment tactics and efforts to secure financial support from both followers and the public. When many devotees took on new names to signal their new identities or severed contact with biological families and friends, opponents saw other signs of coercion and loss of free will. One result was a booming business in "deprogramming" or psychological efforts to restore former identities and beliefs, often using drastic measures to do so. Some groups faced legal issues; Sun Myung Moon, for example, was convicted of income tax evasion and served a brief prison sentence.

Most of the charges against these groups had no real foundation. Because they drew on Asian ways of being religious, they were different, and that difference provoked fear—just as difference had provoked fear of Catholics and Jews in an earlier era. Some drawn to new religions found their belief systems compelling and saw efforts at recruitment no different than those employed by some Christian groups that eagerly sought converts. Issues of free speech and of separation of church and state added to the swirl of debate over how new religions—or any religion, for that matter—sought to persuade others to join up in a free marketplace. Families who believed their children brainwashed often failed to understand that these children were adults who found traditional religion wanting because of its ties to racism, the Vietnam War, and other expressions of social injustice.

The new immigration and growing religious pluralism

In the midst of the social upheavals of the Sixties and the panic some felt over the fascination younger Americans had with "cults" and various liberation movements, the U.S. Congress authorized significant changes in immigration law, changes that effectively jettisoned the quota system in place since the 1920s. Although U.S. President Lyndon Johnson (1908–1973) declared that the immigration changes would have little effect on the daily lives of most Americans, the results were different. Immigration began to grow significantly in total numbers, such that by the end of the twentieth century the number of immigrants entering the U.S. annually matched or surpassed the number for any year in that last major wave of immigration ending just before World War I.

There were differences, however. Whereas immigrants from southern, central, and eastern Europe comprised the bulk of those who arrived on American shores between the Civil War and World War I, this latest wave saw dramatic increases in the numbers of immigrants coming from Asia, Africa, the Caribbean, Mexico, and other parts of Central and South America. If the earlier wave had assured that Roman Catholicism, Judaism, and Eastern Orthodox Christianity would be integral to the religious pluralism of the U.S., this more recent wave extended the scope of that pluralism in ways no one anticipated. Yet the newer immigrants were doing just what earlier ones had done, namely, bringing their religions and their religious styles from their lands of origin to their new homes in the United States.

Now, for example, alongside American young-adult converts to Asian-based groups like Krishna Consciousness or the Unification Church, there were millions for whom some expression of Hinduism or Buddhism was part of their personal and collective identity. Between 1970 and 2000, the number of Americans identifying themselves as Buddhists increased ten-fold, reaching around 2 million. Buddhist centers or temples were found in most cities by the dawn of the twenty-first century. Many readily escaped notice, however, since most served small, ethnically based communities. Vietnamese Buddhists, Thai Buddhists, Cambodian Buddhists, and countless others often forged associations joining religious identity with ethnic identity. In smaller cities, Buddhists of a particular ethnic origin might gather in a home or use a house or some other structure for meeting space rather than erecting a building readily identified as a temple.

Like earlier immigrant communities that fused religious and ethnic cultures, these groups contributed significantly to the process by which newer immigrants made the transition from one land to another. Most had little to do with Zen centers or other Buddhist institutions that served primarily an American clientele. Similarly, the very small Tibetan American Buddhist population that looks to the prominent Dalai Lama (1935–) as a spiritual leader has little interaction with American devotees. Much of the American fascination with Tibetan Buddhism may stem from the interest of celebrities such as movie star Richard Gere (1949–) in its teachings.

Also, although smaller, the Hindu population grew rapidly in the closing decades of the twentieth century, increasing from around 100,000 in 1970 to just over a million thirty years later. Hindu expression has ties to the Indian subcontinent and an ethnic dimension stretching back centuries. "Hindu" comes from the same root as the word India, and, for hundreds of millions of people, the two are virtually synonymous. In some American towns, the Indian immigrant community has transformed churches once part of other denominations into Hindu temples or places where Indian Americans come not just for prayer and a blessing, but to celebrate cultural festivals that renew their sense of being, shaped and sustained by things Indian. In the U.S., temples often reflect the diverse character of the Indian immigrant community by having statues and other artistic representations of many different Hindu divine representations rather than just one, as might be the case in India. The Gujarat Samaj of East Tennessee in Chattanooga, for example, transformed what had been a Baptist church into a temple that houses statuary depicting several devas or divine beings. Such builds on an idea pervasive in Hindu thought, namely, that there is but one ultimate reality that can take countless forms, since any one form reflects only a small aspect of a divine greatness that exceeds all thought.

Additionally, because temples in the U.S. take on a primary role in the transmission of a cultural and ethnic identity, Indian immigrant men are frequently more engaged in temple life in America than they would be in India. There the barometer of devotion is less what transpires in the temple—even going to a temple to leave an offering

222 *The "new pluralism" of the later twentieth century*

Figure 15.1 Contemporary mosque in the USA. The growing number of mosques, centers for Muslim prayer and worship, illustrates the increasing religious diversity in contemporary America (Courtesy Saudi Aramco World/PADIA.)

and receive a blessing—than what happens in the home, where a shrine or even a room provides a center for prayer.

The growth of Islam in the U.S. is even more striking than the growth of Hinduism and Buddhism. Estimates indicate that, in 1970, the U.S. was home to around 800,000 Muslims, not including those associated with the Nation of Islam or Black Muslims. Thirty years later, there were at least 4 million, with some analysts claiming that the number was much higher, perhaps as high as 5.5 million. Islam, like Judaism and Christianity, has deep roots in the Middle East and shares with those two traditions a strident monotheism or belief that God is One. From its origins in the Arabian Peninsula in the seventh century C.E., Islam has held the Arabic text of the Qur'an sacred and centered its belief and practice around "five pillars" or primary teachings. The first emphasizes monotheistic belief in asserting that there is no God (Allah in Arabic) but God (Allah), with Muhammad as God's final prophet. Other pillars include praying five times daily facing in the direction of Mecca (the city where Muhammad lived when he received the revelation that became the basis for Islam), giving financial support for the mosque (place of prayer) and for the poor, fasting during the daylight hours in the month of Ramadan, and, if at all possible, making a pilgrimage to Mecca to participate in the rituals recalling Muhammad's vision and then his flight from Mecca to Medina.

In Muslim cultures, Islam has as many diverse forms as American Protestant Christianity has denominations. Many have to do with how one relates to Muslim law or guidelines for individual and societal behavior. Like the Torah for the ancient Hebrews, Muslim law intermingles religious and civil matters, for at heart there is no

> ### Muslim immigrants adapt to American life
>
> Historian Patrick Allitt has noted some of the ways the American religious environment has influenced how Muslims approach their religion:
>
> > Mosques, for example, which were built in most cities after 1970, often fell into the Christian pattern of providing collective prayer and schools for children on Sundays, even though Friday at midday was the traditional time for collective prayer ... The imam, or prayer leader, sometimes became ... more like a Protestant pastor, advising and counseling community members and helping them overcome problems with non-Islamic neighbors ...
> >
> > (Patrick Allitt, *Religion in America since 1945: A History* (New York: Columbia University Press, 2003), 202)

divergence between the sacred and the profane. Like Christianity and some strands of Buddhism, Islam historically has sought converts, since the faithful believe that its truth is God's universal, final revelation to humanity. In the U.S., with its tradition of separation of church and state and its post-Enlightenment ethos of distinguishing between the sacred and the secular, implementation of a Muslim culture has been nearly impossible. Many Muslims remain unaffiliated with mosques, even though attendance at Friday prayer services is expected at least of Muslim men, making it difficult to determine accurately just how many Muslims there are. As well, Islam remains a minority tradition about which the majority of Americans are ignorant. Since the attacks on the World Trade Center in New York City in 2001, many U.S. Muslims have muted efforts to persuade others to convert. The lower profile means that outsiders are less likely to be aware of the growing Muslim presence. Since Muslim Americans reflect an array of ethnic and national backgrounds, the delicate intertwining of religion and ethnicity not only enriches how Islam augments religious diversity and pluralism in the U.S., but also complicates analysis of just how various expressions of Islam themselves take root on American soil.

The experience of these traditions as minority religions in a culture long dominated by forms of Christianity and Judaism echoes that of earlier minority movements, yet is profoundly different. It is similar in that, for millions, religious identity is interwoven with ethnic and/or national identity. But because that identity is largely non-European, more subtle forms of discrimination and hostility replaced the overt anti-Catholicism and anti-Semitism of earlier generations. At the same time, many immigrants who have planted the new pluralism have found the American environment a challenge; for example, American patterns of courtship and marriage provide little support for the Hindu practice of arranged marriages, suggesting that in time intermarriage may raise issues about the survival of the tradition in ways that go deeper than the impact of intermarriage on American Judaism. These newer immigrants, especially those from Asia, are less likely than those who came a century earlier from southern, central, and eastern Europe to find themselves in the lower socio-economic brackets, struggling for upward mobility. Their standing in socio-economic terms has made them less willing to accept discrimination and more emphatic about claiming their rightful place among the nation's religions, a place guaranteed by the constitutional provisions prohibiting a religious establishment and assuring "free exercise" of religion.

More significant in terms of both religious and cultural impact than the stunning growth of traditions such as Islam, Buddhism, and Hinduism is the surge in immigration, both legal and undocumented, from Mexico, Central America, South America, and the Caribbean. The tendency to talk about Hispanic or Latino/a immigration as a single entity obscures linguistic and other cultural differences among this largest cluster of "new" immigrants, although the way this immigration has increased religious diversity may be less complicated. Most immigrants entering the U.S. from other lands in the western hemisphere are Christians; the majority identify with Roman Catholicism. Since 1965, when immigration law changed, Hispanic/Latino immigrants and their children born in the U.S. account for more than two-thirds of the growth in the total number of U.S. Catholics. By the early twenty-first century, nearly 40 percent of U.S. Catholics had Hispanic/Latino roots. These numbers alone suggest the enormous impact of Hispanic migration on American Catholicism. If, in earlier eras, thanks to the colonial presence of the Spanish, Hispanic religious influence was concentrated largely in areas such as the southwestern U.S., by the twenty-first century, that influence permeated every part of the country.

How western hemisphere immigrants expressed a Catholic identity is different from that which shaped earlier American Catholicism. Over the centuries, Catholic practice had become intertwined with various Latino cultures whose style was quite removed from the Irish, German, or even southern European Catholicism of earlier generations of immigrants. For example, its worship drew readily on more exuberant song and dance, some reflecting indigenous approaches. Favored saints and festivals emerged from local experience, such as the devotion to Our Lady of Guadalupe that has been central to Mexican Catholic devotion since the sixteenth century. Such devotion continued to inform immigrant piety. Attitudes towards church authority also varied. Because institutional authority in much of Latin America linked church officials to those who exercised what seemed an oppressive political and economic power, many Catholic laity remained suspicious of church authority, if not of all authority. That ambivalence was part of the immigrant experience in the U.S. Also, western hemisphere Catholic immigrants adhered to a stance on social issues such as abortion and homosexuality that, while it often reflected church teaching, was more consistently conservative than views among other American Catholics.

Many of these characteristics also marked western hemisphere Protestant immigrants. Scores of Protestant immigrants found that Pentecostal groups resonated more with their way of being religious than did old-line Protestantism and the traditional denominations. They offered a more lively and dynamic approach to worship and also held more conservative views on social issues.

Additional dimensions of pluralism came to the fore when some immigrants sought to continue religious practices common in their places of origin. Some coming from Caribbean areas, for example, planted Santería on U.S. soil. This tradition fuses aspects of Christianity, African tribal religious expression, and ideas and practices associated with indigenous native religiosity in the Caribbean. The word Santería itself means "way of the saints" and thus reflects the Christian backdrop to the religion. But practices such as the ritual slaughter of chickens have other sources. Some communities attempted to restrict or ban that particular rite; practitioners believed their right to sacrifice chickens to be protected by the First Amendment's "free exercise" clause. Court cases followed. Finally, in 1996 the U.S. Supreme Court recognized Santería as a legitimate religion and its rituals as therefore protected.

At the same time, the presence of undocumented or illegal immigrants complicated the impact of western hemisphere immigration. As persons of Latino/a ethnicity comprised the largest minority ethnic community in the U.S. by the early twenty-first century, surpassing African Americans, many congregations—Catholic and Protestant alike—not only offered worship services in Spanish or some Spanish dialect, but also developed an array of social service programs to assist these new immigrants in adjusting to the American environment and to wrestle with issues ranging from

The impact of Latino immigration

Immigration from Central and South America since 1965 has had at least four significant consequences for American religious culture:

- It is geographically diffuse; that is, it has brought immigrants into every part of the country, not just the region that shares a border with Mexico.
- Its style is decidedly more hybrid and enthusiastic than that of most U.S. Protestants and Catholics.
- Except for views on immigration policy, Latino/a immigrants tend to hold a more conservative position on matters of social and ethical import, such as abortion, than do most other Americans.
- Hispanic immigrants are displacing African Americans in many urban neighborhoods where, historically, African American churches have dominated religious life.

(From Charles H. Lippy, "Religious Pluralism and the Transformation of American Culture," in *Our Diverse Society: Race and Ethnicity—Implications for 21st Century American Society*, edited by David W. Engstrom and Lissette M. Piedra (Washington: NASW Press, 2006), 92–95) arrest and deportation for those who lacked appropriate documentation to accessing social services such as health care, when the immigrant generation, as earlier ones, had faltering knowledge of English and therefore faced challenges in communicating.

A more global dimension ties Latino/a immigration to another trend, namely the higher birth rate in most southern hemisphere countries. Some analysts suggest that, if demographic patterns in place at the dawn of the twenty-first century continue, before 2050 more than half of all the world's Christians (Roman Catholic, Orthodox, Protestant) will live south of the Equator—not just in the western hemisphere, but also in Africa and the Pacific, where a more Pentecostal and charismatic style likewise has had great appeal. If those patterns continue, the more charismatic worship style and more conservative social posture that many Latino/a immigrants bring to the U.S. may soon dominate the Christian tradition around the globe.

The courts wrestle with pluralism

Earlier mention called attention to some of the Supreme Court cases dealing with prayer and Bible reading in the nation's public schools and to efforts to secure recognition of Santería as a legitimate religion. All represented responses to increasing diversity. These cases were only a few of those that reflected the expanding pluralism in American religious life. Others raised legal questions about the efforts of new religions to promote their perspective and gain new adherents. If critics saw those efforts as brainwashing, advocates recognized that freedom of speech, another constitutional guarantee, complicated the matter. One could not silence a new religious movement simply because one did not find its beliefs and practices to one's own liking. One case, for example, involved the International Society for Krishna Consciousness, which insisted that prohibiting members from speaking about their faith on public property violated their right to free speech. In 1981, the Supreme Court concurred, although it mandated that those who sought to trumpet their religious views might be relegated to a specific area within public space so as not to infringe on the rights of others using the same public space.

Some cases forced courts to consider whether particular cultural practices led to a de facto religious establishment in the sense that they favored the beliefs or positions of particular groups at the expense of alternate ones. A cluster of such cases came to the fore as a result of the ambivalence of many Americans regarding U.S. military engagement in Southeast Asia in the 1960s and 1970s. Conscription, popularly known as the draft, required young men to register for military service—unless exempt or otherwise disqualified—until the U.S. armed forces switched to an all-volunteer basis in 1973. Policy provided exemption from combat service for those with staunchly pacifistic religious views. For generations, that meant exemption from combat service required membership in one of the historic "peace" churches that opposed all war (such as the Quakers) or in a religious group that supported individual members who held such views. The increasing pluralism of the 1960s complicated matters when some sought conscientious objector status, as it was called, because of philosophical opposition to war but did not hold membership in any religious group, and also when some sought that designation because of their moral opposition to a particular war, not necessarily all war. Amid much controversy, courts finally dropped the requirement of religious membership for claiming conscientious objector classification (*United States v. Seeger* [1965], *Welsh v. United States* [1970]). But in 1971, in *Gillette v. United States*, the Supreme Court refused to grant legal recognition to what at the time was called "selective" conscientious objection.

Cases primarily in local and state courts raised questions about whether prohibiting business activity on Sunday, the sacred day for most Christian groups, represented unconstitutional endorsement of majority Christian practice. Some Christian groups, such as the Seventh-Day Adventists for whom the Sabbath is from sundown on Friday to sundown on Saturday (as in Judaism), had long suffered discrimination in many communities with strict "blue laws" or regulations governing Sunday business and leisure activity. So, too, many Jewish leaders believed "Sunday closing laws" infringed on their right to free exercise. By the latter decades of the twentieth century, new voices were heard. Muslims, for example, in addition to praying five times daily facing Mecca, hold prayer services in mosques on Fridays. For millions, cultural practices were unfair not just because Sunday received special legal sanction, but also because often, to keep employment, they had to work on days that their own religion held sacred. As recently as 1961, the U.S. Supreme Court in two decisions (*McGowan v. Maryland* and *Two Guys from Harrison-Allentown, Inc. v. McGinley*) upheld the legality of blue laws, claiming historical precedent, not support for Christianity, supported them. The Court further claimed that urging a day of rest each week was beneficial to all citizens, not just Christians. However, in local communities and states across the nation, blue laws began to disappear as pluralism grew. Changes in family work patterns also helped dismantle blue law; because women entered the paid workforce in larger numbers, weekends became times for shopping and family activity that often preempted the notion of a single "day of rest" or worship.

Pluralism provided part of the context for other cases where courts wrestled with implications of the First Amendment. Those who rejected evolutionary theory, for example, tried to use the courts to assure that approaches such as creation science and then intelligent design were taught. Opponents regarded such theories as matters of religious belief and argued that their inclusion in school curricula favored religion in a way that violated the principle of separation of church and state. A federal court in Pennsylvania, for example, ruled in 2005 that intelligent design theory was an article of faith, not science, and therefore could not be taught in schools.

Far more complicated issues followed in the wake of *Roe v. Wade*, the 1973 U.S. Supreme Court decision that struck down scores of state and local ordinances banning abortion in the early months of pregnancy. Although many second-wave feminists applauded the decision as acknowledging a woman's right to choose whether to give birth, opponents quickly raised religious and moral objections. Those who called themselves "pro-life" believed that legalized abortion represented another effort to impose a non-religious stance on all Americans, in the name of freedom and thus encouraged immoral behavior dangerous to the common good of the entire society. A host of religious groups, from the Roman Catholic Church to a variety of conservative Protestant groups, joined forces to oppose legalized abortion. Because religious belief undergirded their attempts to legislate anti-abortion regulations, critics argued that banning abortion or severely restricting it was equivalent to the government's endorsing a particular religious or theological position.

Alongside the controversy over abortion were scores of cases that challenged such practices as posting the Ten Commandments in court houses and public schools, using religious language in city and state mottoes, placing religious displays on public property at holiday times, and even retaining the religious language found in the Pledge of Allegiance and on coins and currency. Some believed these practices acknowledged the religious roots of American society. For them, they were part of the fabric of American life, perhaps part of a civil religion like that discussed earlier. But others saw them as dangerous favoritism of particular religious traditions, especially Christianity, and thus a denial of the ever-increasing diversity and pluralism within American religious life. In essence, all these debates betrayed a cultural uncertainty as to just how much pluralism American society could embrace, and still maintain a sense of common identity and cohesion.

Pluralism's impact on spirituality and worship

The expanding pluralism of the later twentieth century influenced every sector of religious life, but perhaps none more obviously than the ways in which Christian worship became transformed and in which personal spirituality developed. In one sense, the Second Vatican Council propelled an interest in rethinking the character of worship when it permitted and seemed to encourage celebration of the mass in the vernacular. Once the church jettisoned Latin as the language for ritual activity, experimentation became the order of the day. Before the end of the 1960s, many spoke of a time of liturgical renewal. The process involved, though, was anything but new. In many cases, particularly among Protestant and Roman Catholic Christians, renewal meant absorbing elements of popular culture and refitting them for religious purposes. From using folk music in the 1960s to contemporary rock music at the beginning of the twenty-first century, those who crafted worship collapsed the separation between the sacred and secular worlds in much the way that Protestant reformers of the sixteenth century had done. Also, many newer hymn texts reflected the post-World War II interest in feminine images of the divine, for example, and the increasing ethnic diversity among the people in the pews. Many congregations began offering worship services in different styles; many abandoned the traditional "eleven o'clock Sunday morning" as the only time for formal worship.

> **The impact of the Sixties on personal spirituality**
> A journalist, Don Lattin, identified six characteristics of contemporary spirituality that had their roots in the religious culture of the 1960s:
> - Spirituality was supposed to be liberating, although sometimes it was divisive.
> - Personal spirituality was experiential, with little interest in doctrine or tradition.
> - Customized spirituality distrusted traditional religious authority of all kinds, although it sometimes accepted ideas of authoritarian leaders from other religious cultures and traditions (such as Asian gurus).
> - Eclecticism or mixing ideas and practices from a variety of religious traditions shapes spirituality.
> - The goal of this idiosyncratic spirituality is to unify body, mind, and spirit.
> - Being spiritual has a therapeutic effect; it is more concerned with reducing stress and bringing happiness than with something like eternal salvation.
>
> (Don Lattin, *Following Our Bliss: How the Spiritual Ideals of the Sixties Shape Our Lives Today* (San Francisco: HarperSanFrancisco, 2003), 238–39)

Part of the rationale was to keep pace with the increasingly complex lives Americans led as society became more thoroughly urbanized. Part was to appeal to those who found earlier ways no longer relevant to their lives. Part was also to assure that organized religion reflected the scientific and technological advances shaping the larger society. Analysts who specialized in assisting congregations to grow urged churches to find out what people wanted and then build their ministry around those concerns. By the 1980s, it was fashionable in some American Protestant circles to talk about "seeker services." These represented programs designed to attract those not nurtured in religious faith and also those who had dropped out of organized religion. Their advocates believed that these people—the non-religious or the formerly religious—were still looking for some meaning in life or seeking for something to give order and purpose to their existence. Congregations that did market research and then crafted a style of ministry reflecting its results showed astonishing growth in many communities, giving birth to what was called the "megachurch" or a congregation that might have in excess of 10,000 attending services in the course of a week.

Informing much of this experimentation was an increasing awareness that Americans were pursuing individual spiritual quests that might or might not tap into any organized religion. By the mid-1980s, polls suggested that more and more Americans considered themselves "spiritual, but not religious," meaning that they engaged in spiritual practices and held religious beliefs, but might or might not be part of any organized religious group. Second-wave feminism spurred some of this interest in personal spirituality, as women began to look for ways of being religious that reflected the experiences unique to women, from childbirth to menopause, while men probed expressions of spirituality that drew on popular notions of masculinity. Increasing awareness of ideas and practices associated with Asian religions, especially meditation techniques, meant that often individuals developed eclectic, idiosyncratic ways of pursuing their spiritual journeys, blending practices and ideas from one tradition with others from a different tradition into a package that brought some sort of direction to their lives.

This individualized spirituality was pluralism in the extreme, for it suggested that everyone could have a privatized set of beliefs and practices that might not have any direct connection with a particular religious group or tradition. Sociologists suggested that the push to privatized spirituality was a natural consequence of society's becoming increasingly urbanized and industrialized, and thus more complex. Others feared that personal spirituality lacked the commitment associated with earlier styles of being religious because individuals were free to change belief and practice as it suited their fancy, having little to transmit as a "religious tradition" or belief system to the next generation.

The explosion of spirituality affirmed, however, that a radical pluralism had taken root within American religious life, one that cut across lines of religious traditions or ethnic heritages. If the new immigration assured that more options were available from which Americans could draw in crafting their own ways of being religious, pluralism had come to denote that Americans individually could create their own religion, if you will, without having to conform to norms or standards of any sort set by a religious group.

Key points you need to know

- Many new religious movements took root on American soil in the 1960s and 1970s, several with an Asian background.
- Adherents found these groups attractive largely because they did not have the same cultural baggage as traditional religious groups.
- Critics talked about a "cult scare" and "brainwashing" because they felt these new groups to be so different from what they knew that they must be dangerous.
- Changes in immigration law in 1965 had significant consequences for religious life by expanding immigration from Asia, Africa, the Caribbean, Mexico, Central America, and South America.
- As a result of the new immigration, Islam, Hinduism and Buddhism began to grow rapidly in the U.S., challenging the dominance of religions associated with Judaism and Christianity.

- Within American Christianity, Hispanic immigration began to bring a more theologically conservative presence along with a more charismatic approach to worship.
- Expanding pluralism raised new questions about separation of church and state and freedom of religion.
- Some court cases challenged customs and practices thought to favor Christianity; others sought to guarantee the right for newer religions to express themselves and practice what they believed.
- Pluralism also began to change the way many religious groups approached worship.
- Especially significant was the impact of the new pluralism on notions of personal spirituality, which became ever more idiosyncratic and eclectic and more separated from participation in organized religion.

Discussion questions

1. What made new religions with Asian roots so appealing to Americans in the 1960s and 1970s?
2. Why did some Americans think these groups were dangerous?
3. How did the presence of these new religious movements expand the understanding of religious diversity and pluralism in American life?
4. What effect did changes in immigration law in 1965 have on religion in the U.S.?
5. How and why was the "new pluralism" different from the pluralism spurred by earlier waves of immigration?
6. What challenges did the new pluralism and increasing diversity bring to how the larger society understood the relationship between religion and the collective life of the American people?
7. How did the courts respond to the increasing pluralism?
8. In what ways did worship, especially among Christian groups, change in the later twentieth century?
9. How did personal spiritual practice reflect the new pluralism?
10. What impact did trends in spirituality have on traditional religion?

Further reading

Eck, Diana L. *A New Religious America: How a "Christian Country" Has Become the World's Most Religiously Diverse Nation.* San Francisco: HarperSanFrancisco, 2001.

Ellwood, Robert S., and Harry B. Partin. *Religious and Spiritual Groups in Modern America.* 2nd ed. Englewood Cliffs, NJ: Prentice-Hall, 1988.

Fuller, Robert C. *Spiritual but Not Religious: Understanding Unchurched America*. New York: Oxford University Press, 2001.

Lattin, Don. *Following Our Bliss: How the Spiritual Ideals of the Sixties Shape Our Lives Today*. San Francisco: HarperSanFrancisco, 2003.

Roof, Wade Clark. *Spiritual Marketplace: Baby Boomers and the Reawakening of American Religion*. Princeton, NJ: Princeton University Press, 1999.

Wuthnow, Robert. *America and the Challenge of Religious Diversity*. Princeton, NJ: Princeton University Press, 2005.

16 The many faces of pluralism in postmodern America

In this chapter

This chapter opens with a discussion of how what is called postmodernism has affected American religious culture. It then shows how one result of the interplay of postmodernism and religion developed in the surge of various forms of evangelicalism in the later twentieth and early twenty-first centuries, particularly the growing strength first of fundamentalism and then of Pentecostalism. Next comes consideration of how the mood of postmodernism has yielded diverse and sometimes contradictory responses when religious communities and individuals wrestle with a host of contemporary concerns that have ethical dimensions; the ongoing debates over abortion and homosexuality will illustrate this problem most forcefully. The final section reflects on the role of pluralism and diversity in American religious life and offers some observations about its continuing importance in the years to come.

Main topics covered

- Describing postmodernism
- The impact of postmodernism on religious institutions and denominations
- The erosion of mainline Protestantism in the U.S.
- Why evangelicalism gained ground from the 1970s on
- The resurgence of fundamentalism and the continuing growth of Pentecostalism
- How this evangelical escalation influenced popular culture
- Growing divisions among and within religious groups—and between individuals—when considering issues with deep moral dimensions, such as abortion, euthanasia, and especially homosexuality
- The many faces of pluralism throughout the course of American history
- What the future holds for the continuing importance of religious pluralism

Postmodernism brings other dimensions of pluralism

In literary and philosophical circles, pundits began talking seriously about postmodernism in the last half of the twentieth century. However, defining postmodernism precisely has proved as elusive as defining pluralism. Both terms have many dimensions. Whatever else postmodernism denotes, it almost always suggests an abandonment of absolute authority, particularly any authority outside personal experience. In this sense, postmodernism makes individuals and their own experience the locus of authority, or at most a group of individuals and their collective experience. In other words, no single truth or fixed standard exists; rather, what becomes accepted as true emerges from what a group experiences as true for itself, aware that another group might have different experiences and thus advance a different truth. Even within a group, postmodernism would not insist on uniformity. Rather, individuals appropriate for themselves what resonates as true for them from what the group affirms. This theoretical framework seems rather abstract. But however one struggles to define postmodernism, it has had concrete and specific impact on American religious life.

The ways that a personal spiritual quest has replaced religious institutions and traditions for many as the heart of religion reflect this postmodern ethos. So, too, the eclecticism or fusing together of diverse religious ideas and practices into a coherent personal worldview draws on the mood of postmodernism. For American religious groups long used to being organized as denominations, one result of postmodernism's ascendancy is a questioning of denominational authority and power, along with a parallel elevation of the authority and power of the local congregation for its members or even the personal sense of the individual member as to what to believe and do. For example, although the Roman Catholic Church still officially bans use of artificial means of contraception, American Catholics, as we have seen, use them in the same proportion as the rest of the population. In doing so, they illustrate one aspect of the postmodern style, the rejection of the absolute authority of a religious institution and the transferring of that authority to their personal experience of what is right.

Another example emerges in the presumed decline in membership of mainline Protestant denominations, which began in the 1960s, and the parallel rise in congregations that lack denominational affiliation or label. One reason often advanced for that decline is a resistance to the authority of denominational agencies and decision makers. An unaffiliated local congregation is free to develop programs and ministries that reflect the experience of its own immediate members without having to answer to denominational authorities. The postmodern style has impacted congregations and denominations in another way. Even congregations that remain affiliated with denominations are less inclined to offer financial support to the denomination and denomination-wide programs and agencies; they prefer to use their resources for local work or locally inspired ministries. In turn, using resources "at home" provides for greater accountability, and results are more immediately apparent. Many denominations have

Mainline Protestant growth and decline

Sociologists Penny Long Marler and Kirk Hadaway have examined the patterns of growth and decline in American mainline Protestantism in the years since the end of World War II. They observed:

> Interpretations of mainline growth and decline that emphasize values or theology confuse correlation and causation. Both mainline and conservative Protestant denominations grew in the 1950s, not because the mainline became more conservative, but because both groups capitalized on the baby boom and because the mainline attracted new adult members ... Because they failed to retain so many of the children born during the baby boom, the mainline effectively lost the children of the boomers. The net result was ever-increasing average age and ever-decreasing numbers of children to pass on the tradition.
>
> (C. Kirk Hadaway and Penny Long Marler, "Growth and Decline in the Mainline," in *Faith in America: Changes, Challenges, New Directions*, 3 vols., edited by Charles H. Lippy (Westport, CT: Praeger, 2006), 1: 19–20)

had to curtail programs and cut staff, as have ecumenical groups such as the National Council of Churches, as more and more congregations were drawn into the postmodern orbit of local control and authority.

When numerical decline began among American mainline Protestants in the later 1960s, pundits also attributed the loss to the engagement of mainline leaders in the social and political movements of the day, from the civil rights movement to second-wave feminism. The result was a widening gap between church leaders and people in the pews, with ordinary people apparently regarding denominational and pastoral leaders as liberal activists more focused on social change than on the salvation of souls. Of course, those drawn to alternative religions still saw the old-line groups as wedded to the status quo. Independent congregations experiencing growth and denominations whose numbers did not plummet seemed to be those more inclined to avoid such controversy, stick to traditional belief and practice, and resist social action beyond local areas. Conventional wisdom thus held that conservative churches and religious bodies would flourish, while liberal churches and groups would founder.

In retrospect, however, the dynamics were not that simple. For example, sociologists have demonstrated that the introduction of new methods of birth control, particularly oral contraceptives or "the pill," had ramifications for religious life. As with the population at large, the birth rate among mainline groups skyrocketed in the baby boom years after World War II; much of the post-war "revival" of religion reflected the rising birth rate more than it did recruiting adherents from among the "unchurched." As the birth rate began to drop naturally within post-war families, it dropped more dramatically with the introduction of the pill. Religious groups that did not oppose contraception on moral or theological grounds experienced a parallel drop in the numbers of children and youth in their ranks, those who would in time become adult members and leaders of their respective congregations. Groups experiencing growth tended to show a lower rate of use of artificial means of birth control. As smaller numbers were nurtured in the faith and some baby boomers dropped out of organized religion or experimented with alternative religions, decline in membership became inevitable.

Regardless, the reconfiguration that began in the later 1960s continued into the early twenty-first century. The United Methodist Church, for example, reported a membership of around 11 million in the U.S. in 1966, but fewer than 8 million forty years later, while the Episcopal Church dropped from almost 3.5 million to just over 2 million in the same period. Other mainline Protestant denominations—such as the Presbyterian Church in the USA, the United Church of Christ, the Evangelical Lutheran Church in America, the Disciples of Christ—experienced the same kind of loss. But even more conservative groups that experienced growth, such as the Southern Baptist Convention, saw their rate of growth drop below that of the general population. At the same time, public opinion polls indicated that roughly the same proportion of the population continued to identify themselves as belonging to a religious group as had done so for several decades. Even the surge among Muslims, Buddhists, Hindus, and others who were part of the new immigration accounted for only part of the reconfiguration. So the transformation in the style of American religion that echoed the mood of postmodernism reflected the confluence of many forces operating in tandem.

A resurgent evangelicalism brings more diversity

Those who pointed to conservative growth were still unprepared, however, for the extent of the evangelical resurgence within Protestant Christianity in the U.S. evident by the mid-1970s, particularly when that evangelicalism seemed closer to earlier fundamentalism than it did to the broad evangelicalism of much American Protestantism in the nineteenth century. In 1976, Jimmy Carter, then affiliated with the Southern Baptist Convention, successfully campaigned for the U.S. presidency, trumpeting his own evangelical religion with frequent references to his having been "born again." That phrase denoted an intense personal religious experience of conversion, often with emotional overtones, that evangelicals saw as the basis for a life of faith. Carter's political campaign reflected a trend that others observed; mass-circulation news magazines, for example, also trumpeted 1976 as the "year of the evangelical" for it seemed that Protestant congregations and denominations that were flourishing were those that emphasized this sort of affective experience as the foundation for religion.

In one sense, a strident evangelicalism was another manifestation of the postmodern ethos, but in a paradoxical way. Because it placed importance on individual experience, the new evangelicalism rejected traditional structures and authority. What a person felt, not what a denomination or tradition taught, was what mattered. At the same time, those who stressed such personal experience were not relativistic, a criticism often levied against those who advocate postmodern approaches. Inner experience was self-confirming and yielded a conviction that one's own beliefs were legitimate. Although the social turmoil of the Sixties generated much moral ambiguity, the evangelical experience presumed a correspondence between what one felt within and a divine truth that offered guidelines for how life ought to be lived. So the new evangelicalism moved away from a postmodern rejection of all absolutes, finding instead that absolute truth became affirmed in inner experience. What was absolute, however, was not the teaching of human institutions, even churches, but a transcendent truth known within. Thus, for example, nondenominational congregations that trumpeted postmodern approaches to worship could still hold to an ethical and social orientation that was by no means relativistic, but certain in its application of inner truth to moral quandaries.

In another way, though, the new evangelicalism of the later twentieth century, like some of the fascination with alternative religions, revealed a mounting dissatisfaction with a worldview rooted in reason and science. The optimism that industrial expansion, scientific advance, and technological innovation held the keys to transforming society into heaven on earth wilted when communications media, especially television, brought the horrors of war into American living rooms during the Vietnam War era. The napalm bombs that disfigured and destroyed in Southeast Asia became symbols of where unrestrained science led, as did the arms race between East and West. If scores of baby boomers had found traditional religions bankrupt because of their involvement with racism and sexism, evangelicals found traditional religions captive to a bankrupt scientism that replaced the depth of inner life with a stale and stark rationalism.

Reawakened evangelicalism, from a different vantage point, had waited for an opportune moment to reassert its enduring strength in American religious life. Those who had readily dismissed the fundamentalism of the 1920s as anachronistic failed to note that these more extreme evangelicals had developed internal networks that left them poised for new influence—publishing houses, schools and colleges, mission societies, and a host of other agencies that often lacked denominational affiliation and therefore denominational support and control. As well, the new evangelicalism was no longer content to exist on the margins of public life, abandoning the political sphere and common weal to others. For example, in 1979 Jerry Falwell (1933–2007), an independent Baptist pastor who later had ties to the Southern Baptist Convention, helped organize the Moral Majority, a non-denominational political action group dedicated to increasing conservative evangelical influence in the political sector by supporting candidates whose positions on issues such as abortion and gay rights reflected its own stance.

Soon fellow evangelical and television personality Pat (Marion G.) Robertson (1930–) entered the fray, seeking the Republican nomination for the presidency in 1988 and then forming the Christian Coalition to continue his political endeavors after he withdrew from the campaign. Falwell claimed that the Moral Majority was instrumental in the election of Ronald Reagan as president of the U.S. in 1980, although Reagan, like the "born again" Carter, generally did not aggressively attempt to promote the political platform of the new Christian Right, as it was called, even if he expressed sympathy for it. Falwell disbanded the Moral Majority in the late 1980s, and Robertson later withdrew from active leadership in the Christian Coalition. But their efforts led to an ongoing evangelical-fundamentalist engagement in the political process, often associated with support for candidates identified with the Republican Party.

Within evangelicalism, less paradoxical responses to the ethos identified with postmodernism are also apparent. Among the better known is the "seeker" movement initially spurred by the Willow Creek Community Church in suburban Chicago. Founded in 1975 by Bill Hybels (1952–), a onetime Chicago youth pastor, Willow Creek used research techniques to determine what adults unaffiliated with any religion were looking for in their lives and what they found unappealing about traditional religions. Hybels and his associates then organized a congregation designed to avoid what was unappealing while offering ministries that would provide whatever it was that people were seeking. Consequently, that approach and the kind of ministry that resulted became known as a "seeker" church. This designation suggests the postmodern reluctance to insist on a single truth and the idea that the religious quest is an ongoing journey rather than a set of fixed beliefs and practices. Willow Creek advocated the use of multimedia ventures in worship, erected a campus devoid of obvious religious symbols, offered services on days other than Sunday, welcomed people in casual attire, and urged the thousands who came to become part of small group ministries where they could have a sense of belonging. Although Hybels and the Willow Creek church had a denominational affiliation, there was little mention of it because market research had determined that those the congregation hoped to attract were put off by such labels. The resounding success of the seeker approach—nearly 20,000 now attend weekly services—led Willow Creek to offer training in its techniques to other religious leaders and congregations, many of whom became part of the Willow Creek Association. The use of market research and the development of a style of ministry in response to that research mark the seeker understanding as a postmodern expression of evangelicalism.

Yet other currents within the larger circle of evangelicalism were also experiencing growth as the twentieth century gave way to the twenty-first. In the late 1950s, liberal Protestant theologian and ecumenist Henry Pitney Van Dusen (1897–1975) forecast the rise of a "third force" within Christianity that would soon overtake the Catholic/Orthodox and Protestant impulses that he saw as the first two forces. That force was Pentecostalism and a corresponding charismatic thrust within all wings of

Christianity. In the United States, Pentecostal expression first came to the fore with the Azusa Street revival of 1906, but had become associated primarily with a cluster of relatively small denominations that had remained on the margins of American religious life. The term "charismatic" refers to many of the phenomena associated with Pentecostalism, not just speaking in tongues and divine healing, but highlights the expression of a range of spiritual gifts and the experience of spiritual power among persons within religious bodies and denominations other than those with links to the Pentecostal surge at the beginning of the twentieth century.

Undergirding the sense that a more diverse Pentecostalism was about to exert major influence in American religious life was an interest in divine healing that became an important current in some of the religious revivals in the years just after World War II. Evangelists like Kathryn Kuhlman (1907–1976) and especially Oral Roberts (1918–) led large rallies at which they prayed for individuals seeking healing of all sorts of physical ailments. Critics believed most of the healings contrived, but reports of successful healing spurred a wider interest in divine healing and other spiritual gifts as the nation sought to regroup after the end of the war. Many of the healing evangelists had ties to Pentecostal denominations. But soon there were charismatic stirrings that were by no means confined to traditional Pentecostal groups.

In 1960, for example, an Episcopal priest in California reported to his congregation that he had experienced the gift of tongues. By 1967, charismatic expressions were appearing within the Roman Catholic Church in the U.S., centered around an interest in recovering Pentecostal power at Duquesne University in Pittsburgh and at the University of Notre Dame. American Protestants and Catholics came together in 1977 at a conference in Kansas City, Missouri celebrating charismatic renewal in American Christianity that drew some 45,000 participants. This neo-Pentecostal revival or "third wave" of Pentecostalism gave birth to many independent congregations and groups, such as the Full Gospel Business Men's Fellowship International (founded in 1951), that drew people from many different religious backgrounds. The "third wave" label highlights the broad appeal of all sorts of supernatural gifts and experiences among the faithful, not just the gifts of tongues and divine healing.

Some of these associations decades later began to take on the trappings of emerging denominations. Both the Calvary Chapel movement started in California by Chuck (Charles W.) Smith (1927–) and the Association of Vineyard Churches that looks to John Wimber (1934–1997) and the Vineyard Christian Fellowship have linked like-minded congregations together in a broad appropriation of spiritual gifts and power, what Wimber called the "signs and wonders" that accompany the presence of the Holy Spirit. Among the largest of the neo-charismatic congregations is the independent Lakewood Church in Houston, founded by John Osteen (1925–1999) in 1959. A onetime Southern Baptist who had a profound charismatic experience, Osteen started his own congregation in part because Southern Baptists were apprehensive about claims to possession of spiritual gifts. After Osteen's death, his son Joel

(1963–) became the congregation's senior pastor. Within a decade of his ministry, Lakewood counted some 40,000 members and had transformed a former sports arena in Houston into the setting for its services.

Fascination with the supernatural, whether in terms of signs or the expectation of impending divine intervention in history, spread into popular culture. Such a preoccupation informed the series of sixteen popular novels that began to appear in 1995 when Tim LaHaye (1926–) and Jerry B. Jenkins (1949–) published *Left Behind*. The series focused on one idea peripheral to much Christian thought, but central to the new fundamentalism, namely the notion of the Rapture. This idea looked to a miraculous removal of believers from the earth to the heavenly sphere prior to the divine events that included the Second Coming of Christ and the final confrontation between the forces of good and evil that would usher in the end of time. On a more subtle level, the novels urged those uncertain of their eternal destiny to be "born again" and intimated that those "left behind" would have a chance for such a

> ## Accessing supernatural power
>
> Joel Osteen, pastor of Houston's Lakewood Church, believes the "word of faith" allows believers to tap into a realm of Pentecostal supernatural power. Before he preaches, the congregation in unison declares:
>
> - This is my Bible.
> - I am what it says I am.
> - I have what it says I have.
> - I can do what it says I can do.
> - Today I will be taught the Word of God.
> - I boldly confess.
> - My mind is alert.
> - My heart is receptive.
> - I will never be the same.
> - I am about to receive the incorruptible, indestructible, ever-living seed of the Word of God.
> - I will never be the same.
> - Never, never, never.
> - I'll never be the same.
> - In Jesus' name.
>
> (From David G. Roebuck, "Fundamentalism and Pentecostalism: The Changing Face of Evangelicalism in America," in *Faith in America: Changes, Challenges, New Directions*, 3 vols., edited by Charles H. Lippy (Westport, CT: Praeger, 2006), 1: 99)

conversion even though believers had already been whisked away from the earth. The more than 65 million copies of the series sold to readers from a variety of religious and denominational backgrounds reinforces the claim that, as the new millennium dawned, Americans found strength in a strong belief in the supernatural.

This new evangelical revival, with its fundamentalist, Pentecostal, and charismatic dimensions, added much to American religion as a whole. Because it looked to a wider range of spiritual gifts than earlier Pentecostalism, it made this style of Christianity more expansive. It came to existing denominations and congregations, as those who found charismatic power remained within non-Pentecostal churches operating as a kind of internal renewal movement. Regardless, the stunning growth of neo-charismatic groups and the new Pentecostalism of the later twentieth century suggest that its emphasis on accessing a realm of supernatural power resonated with millions. More dramatically than the reawakening of fundamentalism, it highlights the failure of science and technology to transform society into an actual utopia and the continuing belief that what one feels—in this case the power of the Holy Spirit—is as real and important to life as what one knows. Its strength received a boost with the striking increase of Latino/a immigration, since many of those coming from western hemisphere lands south of the U.S. brought with them a more Pentecostally inclined style of Christianity.

Public issues reveal moral differences

One long-term consequence of the evangelical move into the public arena through groups like the Moral Majority and Christian Coalition was an increasing awareness that scores of issues and policies confronting the American people had a decided moral dimension. As well, non-evangelical religious leaders became less hesitant to indicate which positions on matters of public debate were consonant with their own beliefs to influence both those making public policy and those within their own religious communities. Some, but not all, of those issues began to take shape as early as the 1960s, although their full force was not felt until later. Many also shook religious groups and denominations because of the diverse and sometimes blatantly opposing views held by members. Such diversity was yet another reflection of the impact of a postmodern style on American culture, in that it showed that asserting that any one position represented absolute right or truth lacked power. Juggling diverse views or a pluralism of responses to issues with ethical dimensions became routine by the opening decade of the twenty-first century.

Debates over abortion and homosexuality became the two most prominent, although there were many others—euthanasia and physician-assisted suicide, U.S. military engagement in Iraq and Afghanistan, ecology and the use of natural resources, global warming, stem cell research, to name a few. The ongoing national conversation concerning abortion raised questions of significant religious import, such as when human life actually begins (conception?), when a fetus is medically viable (birth?).

Those opposed to abortion under most circumstances ranged from staunch Roman Catholics to Southern Baptists, allowing some religious communities historically at odds with one another to forge alliances in order to increase their impact on government officials. Claiming the label of "pro-life," this voice equated abortion in most cases with murder. Some Roman Catholic bishops went so far as to declare that priests should not offer the church's sacraments to legislators who were Catholic but who did not actively support restricting or eliminating abortion. Those called "pro-choice" were not necessarily for "abortion on demand," as their polar opposites insisted, but argued that religious reflection on issues ranging from gender roles, genetic deformities, and even the origins of life were so delicately nuanced as to admit of no single response that would fit every set of circumstances. The range of views, however, suggested how deeply an ethical pluralism had become fixed in American religious life.

More distressing internally for religious communities were the disputes over homosexuality. The gay rights movement following on second-wave feminism and civil rights activities of the 1960s had led to the birth of the Universal Fellowship of Metropolitan Community Churches (UFMCC). In turn, that denomination's presence set the stage for wider debate when Eastern Orthodox Christian groups threatened to withdraw from membership in the National Council of Churches if UFMCC were allowed to join. Then, too, by the early 1970s, virtually every religious body in the nation—from Mormons to Conservative Jews, Roman Catholics to United Methodists, Presbyterians to Seventh-Day Adventists—felt the effects of the national conversation about homosexuality. Within many groups and denominations, homosexual, bisexual, and transgender persons formed their own organizations calling for full participation in the life of their respective group. Among the earliest were Dignity, a Roman Catholic group with roots in San Diego that became a national organization in 1973, and Integrity, its Episcopal counterpart, founded in 1974.

In many cases, such groups also called for the affirmation of gay, lesbian, bisexual, and transgender clergy, since most religious communities were reluctant to ordain other than heterosexuals, and often stripped gay and lesbian clergy of their ordination credentials if they were public about their sexual identity. Among the nation's larger religious communions, the United Church of Christ was among the first Christian bodies to accept homosexuals into the ranks of professional clergy, although individual congregations were not obligated to call them as pastors; Conservative Judaism, the largest cluster of Jews in the U.S., first allowed homosexual rabbis in 2006.

The most potent symbol of the depth of diversity actually came in 2003, when the Episcopal diocese of New Hampshire elected a gay priest as bishop. Since then, some Episcopal congregations and even dioceses have sought to withdraw from the denomination or affiliate with Anglican churches in other nations in protest; others applaud the vision in recognizing the range of forms in which human sexuality expresses itself. In Roman Catholic circles, a growing number of accusations claiming that priests lured adolescent boys into illicit sexual activity over decades only exacerbated the

Postmodern spirituality and American homosexuals

The postmodern push energizing quests for personal spirituality also encouraged gay, lesbian, bisexual, and transgender persons to become more aggressive in linking their sexuality with their religiosity. Sociologist Melissa M. Wilcox writes:

> For LGBT people, often ejected from their communities of "dwelling," the rise of religious individualism meant increased opportunities to be religious without having to be simultaneously closeted. LGBT people could "shop" for synagogues, churches, denominations, and religions that not only suited their own spiritual inclinations but also accepted or even welcomed them without demanding that they change or simply silence their gender identity or sexual orientation.
>
> (Melissa M. Wilcox, "Queering the Mainstream, Mainstreaming the Queer: LGBT People and Religion in the United States," in *Faith in America: Changes, Challenges, New Directions*, 3 vols., edited by Charles H. Lippy (Westport, CT: Praeger, 2006), 3: 113)

ways matters of sexuality complicated religious culture. The church paid millions to settle lawsuits brought by those claiming sexual abuse by priests, while it took steps to prohibit admitting those thought to have homosexual tendencies from entering the priesthood even if they remained celibate. Ongoing debates over homosexuality, the ordination of gays and lesbians to professional ministry, and issues such as same-gender marriage revealed anew that difference and diversity can breed discord.

Another issue much contested is the movement to recognize committed relationships between persons of the same gender. Because individual states determine the laws that govern marriage, these debates had political as well as religious dimensions. Once again, the depth of difference quickly became evident. Many states sought to guard against what religious critics called an assault on the traditional family by adding provisions to state constitutions proclaiming that marriage could consist only of a relationship between a man and a woman. Other states sought to placate religious voices opposed to gay marriage but honor committed relationships by sanctioning civil unions, relationships that carried virtually all the legal status of marriage, but avoided use of that term. After a state court ruled prohibition of same-sex marriage illegal in Massachusetts in 2003, that state became the first to allow gay marriage, beginning in May 2004. California courts in 2008 likewise struck down state laws restricting marriage to persons of opposite genders, though later that year voters approved measures to allow the state to recognize only marriages between a woman and a man.

The religious debate that accompanied the flurry of political activity as states tried to ban gay marriage, allow gay civil unions, or affirm gay marriage was most cantankerous in religious groups and congregations that saw marriage as a religious sacrament or religious rite, even if it was also a civil act. Those who saw gender difference and marriage between a male and a female as part of the order of creation, a way of organizing human life set up by divine decree, were those most stridently opposed to any action that recognized same-sex relationships, regardless of the terminology used. Those who regarded human sexuality as itself admitting of multiple expressions and those who saw marriage as a human institution that developed slowly over centuries were less inclined to condemn religious or political efforts to affirm the love between two persons, regardless of their genders.

What remained clear, however, was that religious Americans spoke with many voices when it came to issues with obvious moral dimensions facing the whole of the nation. In keeping with the postmodern ethos, there was no one religious response to abortion or same-gender unions acceptable to or accepted by all. Rather, pluralism had embedded itself in the public square as firmly as in the religious sector.

The many, changing faces of religious pluralism

Different analysts identify different characteristics that seem helpful in understanding the dynamics of American religious life across the centuries. Some of those reflect the times in which the person doing the analyzing lives and works. In the twenty-first century, with much discussion in every corner about globalization, stunning increases in immigration, and growing awareness of the multiplicity of world religious traditions within American life, pluralism and the diversity that it suggests provide useful lenses through which to look back on American religious life and track its development into the present.

Pluralism has pointed to many different features of American religion over the centuries. Prior to the arrival of European conquerors and settlers, pluralism describes the variety of Native American cultures, each with its own religious ethos, that flourished in the lands that later became the United States. During the time of European settlement, pluralism reflects as well some of the ethnic and religious differences among various groups, from French and Spanish Catholics to English Protestants. Even among English Protestants, and then a host of others from other European lands, there was a kind of pluralism in the numerous expressions of Protestantism that flourished in the New World, though some regarded others as promoting beliefs and practices that were dangerous.

Recognition of that pluralism came to the fore in the early republic when framers of the U.S. Constitution declined to have a religious establishment and in the First Amendment not only prohibited a national religious establishment, but also guaranteed the free exercise of religion. As religion became a matter of the marketplace, scores of new religions began to appear, older traditions such as Judaism became more firmly planted, and immigration assured that a variety of ethnic versions of Roman

Catholicism would make their way into American life. The ties of religion to ethnicity point to another facet of pluralism, one especially evident in the ways religious impulses expressed themselves among African Americans brought as slaves, and then in African American religious groups identified with Christianity.

Region also compounded and enriched the ways pluralism became central to American religious culture. Most distinctive perhaps are the ways evangelical strains of Protestantism became intertwined with the South and a distinctive style emerged in the Appalachian region. But other regions and other religious approaches also left their mark. One thinks, for example, of the interplay between religion and region in areas dominated by the Church of Jesus Christ of Latter-day Saints.

By the mid-twentieth century, political considerations nudged religious people to affirm a broad Protestant–Catholic–Jewish triad as the basis for an American religious culture, but a triad itself suggests pluralism. And, as previous discussion noted, that triad was also incomplete, for it omitted not only the ethnic and regional dimensions, but also traditions such as Eastern Orthodox Christianity. But this triad reflects considerable movement away from seeing pluralism as a convenient way to talk about the hundreds of different Protestant denominations that had a place in the U.S., the ethnic styles of Catholicism, or the Orthodox–Reform–Conservative dimensions within American Judaism.

Pluralism had more subtle ramifications, further complicating efforts to define the term in only one sense. Worship patterns evidenced considerable diversity and variety. By the twenty-first century, pluralism exploded as individual spirituality seemed to stretch religious possibilities almost to infinity and a new immigration triggered rapid growth of religions once on the margins and far removed from the old Protestant–Catholic–Jewish cluster. Buddhism, Hinduism, and Islam—along with Latino influence within both Catholic and Protestant communities—pushed pluralism in new

> **Moving beyond tolerance**
>
> Historian William Hutchison believes the concept of pluralism evolved in American religious life, by the dawn of the twenty-first century denoting both tolerance and inclusivity but moving even beyond that:
>
> > [C]ommitments to pluralism as tolerance and pluralism as inclusivity have by now after long struggles, become intrinsic to the social covenant; there can be no turning back. Beyond that ... the logical arguments in favor of a pluralism that goes beyond inclusivity, that is mutually respectful and nonpatronizing, are compelling ...
>
> (William R. Hutchison, *Religious Pluralism in America: The Contentious History of a Founding Ideal* (New Haven, CT: Yale University Press, 2003), 234–35)

directions. So, too, did public debates over issues affecting the common weal, but issues that had moral roots and revealed the deep differences among Americans. Many of those had to do with race, gender, and sexuality, and seem destined to shape much of the course of American religion in the decades ahead.

At the same time, though, moves towards increasing pluralism have brought conflict and revealed that religious prejudice has not vanished from American life. The association of the terrorist attacks of September 11, 2001 with Muslims rekindled old religious fears, sometimes directed against those who "looked" Muslim. Popular perception too often equated Islam with violence, though few understood Muslim teachings and practice. It was as if the anti-Catholic and anti-Semitic outbursts of an earlier era had returned, with a different religious "other" as the presumed enemy. As diverse, then, as the nation had become, resentment and conflict had not disappeared.

Pluralism, however defined, has become what historian William Hutchison called a symphony in which many instruments play different parts to create a single whole. In the twenty-first century, it is clear that pluralism provides nothing less than a full orchestra from which scores of diverse sounds echo across all of American religious life. Sometimes the result is full of discord, but the hope of harmony endures.

Key points you need to know

- Postmodernism added to the atmosphere promoting pluralism by questioning all fixed authority and absolute beliefs.
- Declining birth rates and dissatisfaction with the social engagement of religious groups both contributed to a loss of membership in mainline Protestant denominations.
- A new evangelicalism, with both fundamentalist and Pentecostal dimensions, swept through Protestant religious life in the later twentieth century.
- Some Americans found these evangelical approaches appealing because they were dissatisfied with what science and reason offered and instead emphasized feeling and personal experience.
- The new evangelicalism was more politically involved than earlier expressions of fundamentalism and Pentecostalism; it also left an imprint on popular culture.
- New forms of religious structures, such as seeker churches, emerged in response to postmodernism and revitalized evangelicalism.
- Diverse views in the public squares over issues such as abortion and homosexuality carried over into American religious life.
- Different, diverse responses to these issues reveal yet another face of pluralism.

- In retrospect, pluralism and diversity have had many different meanings over the centuries.
- Regardless, pluralism remains a vital key to understanding the dynamics of American religious history and life.

Discussion questions

1. How would you characterize postmodernism?
2. Why did mainline Protestant denominations begin to decline in membership in the later twentieth century?
3. What led to the resurgence of evangelicalism?
4. How did a revitalized fundamentalism differ from the fundamentalism of the early twentieth century? How was it similar?
5. How was the new Pentecostal-charismatic thrust different from the Pentecostalism associated with Azusa Street and similar phenomena? How was it similar?
6. What impact did the new evangelicalism have on popular culture?
7. What new public issues had strong ethical dimensions? How did those issues reveal the depths of pluralism?
8. What consequences did public debates over abortion and homosexuality have for religious life?
9. What different meanings has pluralism had in American religious culture over the centuries?
10. Why will pluralism continue to characterize American religious culture?

Further reading

Blumhofer, Edith L., Russell P. Spittler, and Grant A. Wacker. *Pentecostal Currents in American Protestantism*. Urbana: University of Illinois Press, 1999.

Burns, Gene. *The Moral Veto: Framing Contraception, Abortion, and Cultural Pluralism in the United States*. Cambridge, Eng.: Cambridge University Press, 2005.

Carpenter, Joel A. *Revive Us Again: The Reawakening of American Fundamentalism*. New York: Oxford University Press, 1997.

Frykholm, Amy Johnson. *Rapture Culture: Left Behind in Evangelical America*. New York: Oxford University Press, 2004.

Hutchison, William R. *Religious Pluralism in America: The Contentious History of a Founding Ideal*. New Haven, CT: Yale University Press, 2003.

Lippy, Charles H., ed. *Faith in America: Changes, Challenges, New Directions*. 3 vols. Westport, CT: Praeger, 2006.

Moon, Dawne. *God, Sex, and Politics: Homosexuality and Everyday Theologies*. Chicago: University of Chicago Press, 2004.

Glossary

adventism refers to the Christian belief in the Second Coming or Second Advent of Christ

Amana a German pietistic communitarian group that settled in Iowa

Americanist controversy related to debates within the Catholic Church over whether and to what extent immigrants from non-Anglo cultures should conform to American Catholic practice or organize as separate, ethnic churches

Anabaptists persons associated with the "left wing" of the sixteenth-century European Reformation who believed in rebaptizing followers who had been baptized as infants

Antinomian Controversy a debate in seventeenth-century Massachusetts challenging religious authority and claiming direct revelation for believers; authorities feared that would produce chaos

anti-Semitism hostile attitudes towards Jews, often leading to violence

anxious bench a "new measure" adopted by Charles Finney in his revivals where those undergoing conversion or anxious about their souls were called to sit in a special location

Arminianism the belief that persons of their own free will choose whether or not to accept God's offer of salvation

Ashkenazi Jews Jews with ancestral roots in Germany; source of Yiddish language

baptism a Christian rite for infants or believers recognizing one's identity as a Christian

Baptists Protestant denomination with roots in English Puritanism that holds to believer's baptism and liberty of conscience in matters of faith

benevolent empire the antebellum voluntary societies interested in social reform and promoting religious activity that crossed denominational lines

blue laws laws that regulated business and other activity on Sunday

B'nai B'rith Jewish fraternal organization

born again the designation given to a personal experience of conversion by evangelical Protestants

brainwashing denotes the belief that those who join non-traditional new religious movements do so because of psychological manipulation

camp meeting a religious gathering originating on the southern frontier that usually lasted for two or more weeks each year

charismatics persons who are part of Christian groups but who believe they have been given special gifts, such as healing or speaking in tongues, by the Holy Spirit

Christian realism a movement in twentieth-century American Protestant theology that recognized the limits of human possibility; a reaction to optimism associated with liberal theology

Christian Science a religious group founded by Mary Baker Eddy that viewed illness as a form of wrong thinking to be overcome by mental power

Church of England the established church of Britain and many of the English colonies; parent of the Episcopal church

circuit riders travelling preachers usually associated with early Methodism

civil religion beliefs and practices associated with national identity and patriotism that help promote social cohesion

Common Sense Realism a philosophy originating in Scotland that asserted that absolute truth, including the truth of the Bible, was self-evident and plain to everyone using common sense

communitarianism refers to groups and movements that live communally and usually share all resources in common

comparative religion a movement in the later nineteenth century to examine and compare beliefs and practices from many religious traditions, based on the assumption all were concerned with the same human issues

Congregationalists a religious group with roots in Puritanism that believes the local religious body or congregation holds the final authority within the church; in the later twentieth century, many became part of the United Church of Christ denomination

conjure a term associated with African and African American religious practice that assumes certain individuals possess supernatural powers to influence people or events or to conjure them

conquistadors Spanish explorers who sought to conquer people and lands in the Americas in the age of colonial empire

Conservative Judaism a movement or denomination emerging in the U.S. that tried to find a middle ground between strict adherence to Orthodox tradition and belief and Reform practice that readily jettisoned tradition

cult originally referred to the worship and devotional practice of any religious group; popularly came to refer to new religious movements regarded by some as dangerous

Darwinism views associated with Charles Darwin and his theory of the evolution of all species

Deism a form of Enlightenment rationalism that affirmed belief in a providential God but rejected miracle, revelation, and other supernatural phenomena

denomination a form of religious organization emerging in America that presumes membership is voluntary and that there is no established religion favored by the government

deprogramming efforts to convince adherents of new religious movements to withdraw from them on the grounds that they were psychologically manipulated and remained controlled by group leaders

dispensationalism a view that all history is divided into periods or dispensations leading up to the final confrontation between good and evil and the end of history

divination practices associated with tribal cultures designed to control the outcome of events or to access supernatural power to do so

divine healing a gift of the Holy Spirit in Christianity that allows persons to heal others of various conditions without medical involvement

eclectic idiosyncratic or a blending together of ideas and practices from many religious approaches

ecumenical movement efforts of religious groups to cooperate with each other or even to merge together into a single body

Edict of Nantes a French ruling in 1598 that allowed Protestants called Huguenots freedom under specified conditions in certain cities; revoked in 1685

election, doctrine of a belief associated with John Calvin that God alone chooses or elects some persons to salvation and some to eternal damnation

Enlightenment an epoch primarily in the seventeenth and eighteenth centuries in Europe that emphasized the use of reason and promoted liberty

Episcopalians name given to the denomination that emerged in the U.S. after the American Revolution that had been the Church of England; literally refers to a form of church government that relies on the authority of bishops

established church a term that refers to a single religious body recognized by the government of a nation and usually supported by taxation or other governmental means

establishment clause the phrase in the First Amendment to the U.S. Constitution that prohibits Congress from granting legal establishment to any religious group

ethnicity refers to the culture and heritage of a people from a particular place or region

evangelicalism a term with many dimensions, but most often referring to Protestant groups that place primary importance on personal religious experience; in the nineteenth century, included the Protestant denominations that exercised dominant influence in American culture

Five Pillars the summary of Muslim belief and practice: affirming belief in Allah, prayer five times daily facing Mecca, support for the poor and the mosque, fasting during the month of Ramadan, and making a pilgrimage to Mecca

fraternal orders organizations for fellowship and social service, usually gender specific, such as the Masons or Knights of Columbus

free exercise clause the part of the First Amendment to the U.S. Constitution that guarantees individuals the right to freedom of religion ("free exercise" of religion)

fundamentalism a movement first among American Protestants in the later nineteenth and early twentieth centuries that emphasized biblical authority, the divinity of Christ, the physical resurrection and anticipated Second Coming of Christ, and other orthodox beliefs in opposition to liberal or modernist thought

Ghost Dance revitalization movements with an apocalyptic character among Native American tribes in the Southwest that called for recovery of traditional practice and foretold the destruction of Euro-American power

glossolalia the charismatic gift of speaking in tongues or unknown languages

Great Awakening a series of evangelical revivals in the North American colonies flourishing around 1740–1760; an outburst of revivalism in the nineteenth century before the Civil War is sometimes called the Second Great Awakening

guru a spiritual teacher or guide; historically, one associated with an Asian tradition such as Hinduism

Holiness Movement a movement in nineteenth-century American Protestantism, especially Methodist circles, that emphasized personal holiness and a distinct religious experience after conversion when one had been made holy

Huguenots French Calvinist Protestants, many of whom came to North American English colonies following the revocation of the Edict of Nantes in 1685

humanism a philosophy and a religious worldview that emphasizes human potential and tends to downplay belief in a God that is supernatural

indigenous native to a region or area; Native Americans are also known, for example, as indigenous peoples

institutional church most narrowly, any organized Christian congregation, but also applied to urban congregations in the later nineteenth century that expanded programs to include social service and other activities besides religious ones

invisible institution the hybrid form of Christianity often associated with slaves and practiced in secret to avoid control by slave owners

Jehovah's Witnesses a religious movement originating in the later nineteenth century that has a distinct adventist quality and is known for aggressively seeking converts or witnessing to outsiders

Latter-day Saints the formal name for the religion founded by Joseph Smith in the 1830s, popularly called the Mormons

liminality literally meaning "in between" or in transition; often applied to a stage of a religious conversion experience

lost cause popular designation for the Confederacy during the U.S. Civil War and then for an expression of civil religion in Southern culture that sought to keep white Confederate ideals alive after the war ended

megachurch a large church attracting more than 5,000 to worship, usually oriented to "contemporary" or "praise" services and often not affiliated with a particular denomination

metaphysical religion includes numerous religious movements and groups that place emphasis on the power of the mind to control life

Methodists   religious group founded by John Wesley and originating in the evangelical revivals of the eighteenth century in England; helped spur the Holiness Movement in the nineteenth century; Arminian in theology

millennialism   refers to groups or movements emphasizing a 1,000-year period (millennium) that will lead to the end of history

modernism   a movement in religious thought in the later nineteenth and early twentieth centuries that emphasized the compatibility of science and religion, drew on liberal theological currents, and sought to make religion relevant to the industrial and urban world

monotheism   the belief in only one God or divine being

Moravians   a pietist group with origins in Germany that migrated primarily to areas in Pennsylvania and North Carolina

Mormons   the popular designation for the Church of Jesus Christ of Latter-day Saints, based on the teachings of Joseph Smith in the 1830s

mosque   name given to a house of prayer, worship, and study for adherents of Islam or the Muslim religious tradition

myth   a religious story that communicates a basic truth about human life that may or may not have basis in historical reality

nativism   a term applied primarily to movements in the nineteenth century that believed only native-born, white Protestants should have political power in the U.S.; often associated with anti-Catholic, anti-Semitic, and anti-immigrant outbursts

neo-orthodoxy   a school of religious thought that tempered the optimism of liberal theology with a return to classical doctrines, particularly ideas of sin and human weakness

New Christian Right   groups such as the Moral Majority that blend strictly conservative Protestant belief with equally conservative political views and that also promote social action

new measures   the techniques adapted from the frontier camp meetings in the early nineteenth century to promote religious revivals and conversion; associated primarily with Charles G. Finney

new religious movements   a designation given to sectarian groups and those started by charismatic individuals that often espouse ideas and practices different from those associated with mainline Christianity

Oneida community   a nineteenth-century utopian community that followed the ideas of Christian perfection advanced by John Humphrey Noyes; noted for its unusual approach to marriage and experiments with controlled sexual activity

Orthodox Judaism   a branch of the Hebrew tradition that stresses strict adherence to traditional belief and practice, such as adhering to a kosher diet

pacifism   encompasses belief that war and military activity are immoral; includes historic "peace churches" such as the Quakers

Penitentes   men, usually in the southwestern U.S., who engage in rigorous acts of religious devotion, especially during Lent, that echo earlier Spanish ideas and harsh discipline

Pentecostalism a movement and cluster of religious groups that believe the gifts of the Holy Spirit, such as speaking in tongues and divine healing, are available to believers today

perfectionism a range of movements and groups that believe individuals can achieve total holiness or perfection in this life

pietism a style of Protestant practice that emphasizes quiet devotion and simplicity

pluralism a term with many connotations that all in some way stress the multiplicity of religious choices and options in American life

postmodernism refers to movements in philosophy and religious thought in the later twentieth and early twenty-first centuries that downplay the idea of absolute authority apart from individual experience

pragmatism a school of philosophical and religious thought that claimed beliefs were legitimate if they had a practical (pragmatic) value in providing meaning in life

premillennialism the idea that Christ will return to earth in physical form to launch a 1,000 year period (millennium) that will lead up to the final confrontation between good and evil

Presbyterians a denomination with roots in the teachings of John Calvin; many early American Presbyterians had Scottish ancestry; placed governing authority in regional bodies known as presbyteries

Protestant Reformation a movement starting in sixteenth-century Germany with the teachings of Martin Luther that questioned some views and practices of medieval Catholicism

protracted meeting one of the "new measures" in nineteenth-century revivalism in which an evangelist would offer services daily over a period of several weeks; taken over from frontier camp meetings

Quakers a religious group that believes religious truth comes to individuals through an inner light; noted for their pacifism; central to the early religious life of Pennsylvania

Rapture an idea promoted primarily by later twentieth- and early twenty-first-century Protestant evangelicals that claims believers will miraculously rise through the heavens or be "raptured" when Christ returns

rationalism any movement that places primary emphasis on reason in matters of religious belief and practice; often associated with the Enlightenment and persons identified as Deists, Unitarians

Red Scare encompasses several episodes, especially in the 1920s and 1950s, when communists who were regarded as atheists were thought to have undue influence in American politics and religion

Reform Judaism a denomination within Judaism most open to updating traditional belief and practice to adjust to modern times; thought by some to be too willing to abandon essential beliefs and practices in order to accommodate to the larger culture

Reformed Church in America a Calvinist denomination with roots primarily in Dutch immigration in the colonial period

revitalization movement any religious expression that seeks to bring renewed life and vigor to belief and practice that appears to have lost its power; includes such phenomena as revivalism among Christians and the Ghost Dance among Native Americans

revivalism religious revitalization efforts primarily among Protestant Christians that seek both to gain new adherents and to rekindle the commitment of those who are already believers; examples include the Great Awakening, the frontier camp meeting, and the movement associated with Billy Graham in the twentieth century

ring shout a ritual among African Americans with roots in African tribal practice that usually included exuberant song and dance, with dancers forming a circle or ring

rite of passage any religious ceremony that involves a change of identity; examples include baptism, conversion, marriage

Roman Catholicism the branch of Christianity that acknowledges the pope as spiritual leader; the largest single body of Christians in the U.S. since the mid-nineteenth century

scientific modernism designation given to a school of religious thought primarily among American Protestants in the late nineteenth and early twentieth centuries that emphasized use of reason, sought to accommodate religious belief with scientific knowledge, and was often hesitant to base belief on supernatural revelation

Scots-Irish an ethnic community with origins in Scotland and a migration from Scotland to northern Ireland; the largest ethnic cluster of immigrants to the English colonies in the early eighteenth century; helped plant Presbyterianism in North America and bring evangelicalism to the South

sect a term that technically refers to any movement that separates or emerges from a larger group; often popularly used to designate a new religious movement, regardless of its origins; sometimes refers to groups within a denomination that seek to recover earlier forms of belief and practice associated with that denomination

Sephardic Jews refers to Jews whose roots lie in Spain and Portugal, many of whom migrated to the New World, coming first to South America and then to North America

Seventh-Day Adventists a religious movement founded in the U.S. that emphasizes the physical Second Coming of Christ, worship on the Sabbath (Saturday) rather than Sunday, and an interest in diet reform and health care

Shakers a communitarian, utopian religious group founded by Ann Lee that emphasized celibacy and strict separation of the sexes

shaman literally one who is a technician of religious ecstasy; often designates a tribal religious leader noted for the ability to access a realm of sacred or supernatural power, sometimes by going into a trance or engaging in other ritual activities

Social Darwinism an application of Darwin's theory of evolution to social structures; the idea that the fittest survive in society and rise to positions of economic and political power

Social Gospel a movement primarily in Christian circles that sought to apply the religious and ethical teachings of the Bible to the new social conditions that accompanied late nineteenth-century industrialization and urbanization; emphasized social reform as a way to make society conform to principles identified with the kingdom of God

spirituality ways in which one expresses religious identity and devotion; in the later twentieth century, came to denote personal religiosity as distinct from religious institutions

Stone-Campbell tradition a major wing of the Restorationist movement in American Christianity in the early nineteenth century that sought to recapture the essence of the New Testament church; gave birth to groups such as the Disciples of Christ and the Churches of Christ

Sulpicians a society of Catholic priests whose ministry was critical to establishing the French presence in colonial Canada; also pioneered Catholic seminary training in the U.S. and much mission work on the southern frontier

synagogue technically a place for Jewish men to study the Torah, the sacred text of the Jewish tradition; now used to designate places of prayer and worship as well as social community for Jews, whether Reform, Conservative, or Orthodox

synod an administrative body that takes in a geographic area; used by some, but not all Christian groups

toleration efforts to accept diverse religious perspectives and groups without necessarily agreeing with their positions

Transcendentalism a nineteenth-century literary, philosophical, and religious movement that had a kind of mystical quality, an interest in Eastern religious thought, and a commitment to forms of idealism

transubstantiation the Roman Catholic doctrine claiming that during the celebration of the mass, the bread and wine change substance and become the actual body and blood of Christ when consecrated by the priest

Unitarians a denomination emerging from a liberal wing of Puritanism that emphasized reason, questioned miracles, and tended to deny the notion of the Trinity in traditional Christianity, preferring to see the divine as a single unity

utopianism from the Greek meaning literally "no place" but popularly referring to endeavors to create the perfect or ideal society, often modeled by a particular communitarian body; examples include the Shakers, Oneida, Amana

Vedanta a body of writings originally in Sanskrit sacred to the Hindu tradition

Zionism efforts particularly after the end of World War I to form an independent Jewish state in Palestine that became realized when Israel became an independent nation-state in 1948

Resources

Use of additional resources will enrich the study of religion and religious diversity in American culture. Several encyclopedias and dictionaries amplify the discussion in this text. Among them are Charles H. Lippy and Peter W. Williams, eds., *Encyclopedia of the American Religious Experience*, 3 vols. (New York: Scribners, 1988), and the four-volume *Encyclopedia of Religion in America* (Washington: CQ Press, [forthcoming] 2010), also edited by Lippy and Williams. For information on particular religious groups, see J. Gordon Melton, *Encyclopedia of American Religions*, 3rd ed. (Detroit: Gale, 1989).

On particular traditions and movements, see Randall Balmer, *Encyclopedia of Evangelicalism* (Louisville, KY: Westminster John Knox, 2002); Stanley M. Burgess, ed., *International Dictionary of Pentecostal and Charismatic Movements*, rev. ed. (Grand Rapids, MI: Zondervan, 2002); Michael Glazier and Thomas J. Shelley, eds., *Encyclopedia of American Catholic History* (Collegeville, MN: Liturgical Press, 1997); Kerry M. Olitzky, ed. *Encyclopedia of American Synagogue Ritual* (Westport, CT: Greenwood, 2000); and Daniel G. Reid, Robert D. Linder, Bruce L. Shelley, and Harry S. Stout, eds., *Dictionary of Christianity in America* (Downers Grove, IL: InterVarsity Press, 1990).

Helpful maps are found in Bret E. Carroll, *The Routledge Historical Atlas of Religion in America* (New York: Routledge, 2000), and in Edwin S. Gaustad, Philip L. Barlow, and Richard W. Dishno, *New Historical Atlas of Religion in America*, 3rd ed. (New York: Oxford University Press, 2001). Samuel S. Hill and Charles H. Lippy, eds., *Encyclopedia of Religion in the South*, 2nd ed. (Macon, GA: Mercer University Press, 2005), looks at one region. On issues of region, the nine-volume "Religion by Region" series produced under the auspices of the Greenberg Center for the Study of Religion in Public Life (Trinity College, Hartford, CT) and published by AltaMira Press (2004–2006) offers much insight.

Rosemary Skinner Keller, Rosemary Radford Ruether, and Marie Cantion, eds., *Encyclopedia of Women and Religion in North America*, 3 vols. (Bloomington: Indiana University Press, 2006), is invaluable on the role of women.

Several resources offer biographical information. Especially helpful are Henry Warner Bowden, *Dictionary of American Religious Biography*, 2nd ed. (Westport, CT: Greenwood, 1993); John J. Delaney, *Dictionary of American Catholic Biography* (Garden City, NY: Doubleday, 1984); J. Gordon Melton, *Religious Leaders of America: A Biographical Guide to Founders and Leaders of Religious Bodies, Churches, and Spiritual Groups in North America* (Detroit: Gale Research, 1991); and Mark G. Toulouse and James O. Duke, eds., *Makers of Christian Theology in America* (Nashville, TN: Abingdon, 1999).

Valuable primary sources and theological writings are found in Edwin S. Gaustad and Mark A. Noll, eds., *A Documentary History of Religion in America*, 2 vols., 3rd ed. (Grand Rapids, MI: Eerdmans, 2003); Mark Massa and Catherine Osborne, eds., *American Catholic History: A Documentary Reader* (New York: New York University Press, 2008); and Mark G. Toulouse and James O. Duke, eds., *Sources of Christian Theology in America* (Nashville, TN: Abingdon, 1999).

Several websites are helpful in advancing the theme of this text. Most notable is that of the Pluralism Project at Harvard University, accessible at www.pluralism.org. Especially helpful on recent developments are the U.S. Religious Landscape Survey conducted by the Pew Forum on Religion and Public Life (http://religions.pewforum.org) and the Faith Communities Today study conducted by the Hartford Seminary Foundation (www.fact.hartsem.edu).

More specialized are http://northstar.vassar.edu that looks at African American religious life and culture, www.nd.edu/~cushwa that features Roman Catholic life and history, and www.ajhs.org, the website of the American Jewish Historical Society.

Index

abolitionism 87–8, 128
abortion 227–8, 237, 241
Act of Toleration (Maryland) 35–6
Adams, Abigail 52
Adams, John 52
adventism 95, 98–102
African Americans 47, 48, 50, 63–68, 145, 211–13; *see also* slavery
African Methodist Episcopal Church 71, 72
African Methodist Episcopal Zion Church 71, 72
Alaska 134
Albanese, Catherine 81
Alcoholics Anonymous 105–6
Alexander, Archibald 178
Algonquians 62
Allen, Richard 71, 72
Allitt, Patrick 223
alternative religions *see* new religious movements
Amana Society 97
American Anti-Saloon League 189
American Antislavery Society 87
American Bible Society 86
American Board of Commissioners for Foreign Missions 86
American Catholic Tract Society 114
American Jewish Congress 182
American Society for the Promotion of Temperance 87
American Sunday School Union 86, 88
American Temperance Society 87
American Tract Society 86, 88

American way of life, religion of the 206
Americanism, Roman Catholic 114
Americanist controversy 142
Amish 34
Anabaptists 34
anti-Catholicism 36, 109, 113–17, 142, 163, 190–3
Antinomian controversy 25–6
anti-Semitism 163, 182, 190–6
apocalypticism 156; *see also* millennialism
Appalachia 130–3
Arminianism 82
Asbury, Francis 49
Ashkenazi Jews 118
Assemblies of God 184
assimilation 119, 140
Association of Vineyard Churches 239
authority, challenges to 42; religious 57
Azusa Street revival 183

Backus, Isaac 48
Baird, Robert 88
Balfour Declaration 191
baptism 63; fire 183; of blood 129; second 183
Baptists 25, 34, 36, 39, 40, 46, 48, 49, 81, 82–3, 124, 126; *see also* Southern Baptist Convention
Barton, Bruce 198
Beecher, Lyman 83–4, 115–16
Bellah, Robert 214
benevolent empire 86–9
Ben-Hur 198
Besant, Annie Wood 159

Bhagavad Gita 218
Bill of Rights 53; *see also* First Amendment
birth control 235–6
bishops, controversy over 48
Black Muslims 212
Blake, Eugene Carson 208
Blavatsky, Helena Petrovna 159
blue laws 227
Book of Mormon 93, 94, 95
Booth, Evangeline 147, 148
Booth, William 147
Boston 24, 97
Brainerd, David 68
brainwashing 220
Brattle Street Church 47
Briggs, Charles A. 175–6
broadcasting, religious 197; *see also* radio
Brook Farm 97, 98
Brown v. Board of Education 211
Brownson, Orestes 98, 114, 115
Bryan, William Jennings 177, 179
Buddhism 135, 218, 221, 236; Mahayana 134; Tibetan 221
Buddhist Church of America 204–5
burned-over district 80, 93, 96, 99
Bushnell, Horace 128–9

Cajuns 58, 112
California 133
Calvary Chapel 239
Calvert, George 35
Calvin, John 9
Calvinism, erosion of 56; 81–5; key beliefs in 31
Camp Creek, NC 184
camp meetings 75–9, 80, 92, 124, 167
Campbell, Alexander 92
Campbell, Thomas 92
Canada 36, 48
Cane Ridge, KY 76, 92
Cannon, James 189
capitalism 180
Carnegie, Andrew 179
Carolina, colonial 36–7
Carroll John 49, 108–9, 110
Carroll, Michael 112
Carter, Jimmy 236

Cartier, Jacques 10
Cartwright, Peter 76–7
Catholic Prohibition League 190
Catholic Total Abstinence Union of America 190
Catholic University of America 141
Channing, William Ellery 114
charismatic movement 239–40, 241
Charleston, SC 117; religion in 37
Chauncy, Charles 42, 47
Chautauqua 168, 169
Cherokee 2, 3, 69–70
children, religious nurture of 88
Children of God 219
Chinese-Americans 134, 135
Christian and Missionary Alliance, 169
Christian Coalition 238, 241
Christian Methodist Episcopal Church 129
Christian realism 203
Christian Science 104–5
Christian Science Journal 105
Christian Science Monitor 105
church and state, separation of 54; *see also* establishment, First Amendment
Church of Christ, Scientist 104–5
Church of England 10, 21, 24, 27, 40, 46, 47, 48, 49, 52, 54, 62
Church of God (Cleveland, TN) 184
Church of God in Christ 184
Church of the Nazarene 85
Church of the New Jerusalem 102
church union 208
Churches of Christ 58, 93
Churches Uniting in Christ 208
city missions 146, 151
civil religion 50–52, 129, 214
civil rights movement 211–13
civil unions, 243–4
Civil War 123–30; as religious event 127–30
class meetings, Methodist 40
clergy, untrained 82–3
Clergy and Laity Concerned about Vietnam 213
colleges 129
colonies, French 19–21; Spanish 17–19
Colored Methodist Episcopal Church 129
Columbus, Christopher 5

Comanche 166
Common Sense Realism 57–8
communications media 186–98
communism 205–6
communitarianism 95–8
Community of True Inspiration 97
comparative religion 157, 173, 176–7
Congregation Beth Elohim 37
Congregationalists 40, 49, 53–3, 67–8, 83;
  see also Puritans, United Church of Christ
conjure 64, 73
Connecticut Missionary Society 86
conscientious objection 226–7
Conservative Jews 242
Constitution, U.S., 53–4; Article VI of, 53;
  First Amendment to, 53–5, 227
Consultation on Church Union, 208
convents 115, 116
conversion see experience, religious
Conwell, Russell 180
co-operation, inter-religious 86–7; see also
  ecumenical movement
Cotton, John 25
Coughlin, Charles 204
Creeks 3
Crusades 14

da Gama, Vasco 5
Dale's laws 21
Darby, John Nelson 168
Darrow, Clarence 179
Darwin, Charles 173, 174, 179
Darwinism, social 179, 182
Davies, Samuel 66
Dayton, TN 178
de Brébeuf, Jean 20
de Champlain, Samuel 19, 30
de Las Casas, Bartolomé 18
Deism 42
DeMille, Cecil B. 198
denominations: African American, 70–3;
  development of, 55–6; evangelical 83
depression: economic, 201–2; religious, 202
deprogramming 220
DeSmet, Jean Pierre 111
devotion, Catholic 112
Dewey, John 181

Diaz, Bartholomew 6
Dignity 242
Disciples of Christ 58, 93, 236
discrimination 120; see also anti-Catholicism,
  anti-Semitism, nativism, prejudice, racism
dispensationalism 168–9, 174, 176, 177, 180
dissent 26, 27, 53, 36–7
divination 64
Divine Light Mission 218
division, denmominational 125–6
Dixon, Thomas 194
domesticity, cult of 88–9
Dominicans 18
Dort, synod of 41
Dreamers, Native American 165
Drexel, Katherine 113
Duchesne, Rose Philipine 113
Dutch, 30–1
Dutch Reformed Church 31
Dwight, Timothy 79

Eastern Orthodox Christianity 8, 144–5, 150
Eastern Rite Catholics, 142
Ebenezer 97
ecumenical movement 207–8
Eddy, Mary Baker 103–5
Edict of Nantes 20–1, 37
Edwards, Jonathan 38–9, 68, 78
Eisenhower, Dwight D. 205
election see predestination
Eliot, John 62
Elizabeth I 10, 109
Emerson, Ralph Waldo 97
England, John 114
Enlightenment 40–2, 52, 78, 114
enthusiasm, religious 78
Episcopalians 49
establishment, religious 21, 41–2, 48, 53–4
ethnicity 120–1, 145, 150–1, 192–3, 223
evangelicalism 38–40, 42, 65–6, 124, 147;
  antebellum 75–89; resurgence of, 236–41
Evans, Hiram Wesley 195
Evans, Warren Felt 102–3
evolution 173, 179
experience: ecstatic, 76–77, 78, 165, 166;
  religious 39–40, 65, 84–5, 77–8, 81–2,
  182–3

Falwell, Jerry 237–8
Federal Council of Churches 150, 151, 207
feminism, second-wave 212–13
Fillmore, Charles 105
Fillmore, Myrtle 105
Finney, Charles Grandison 79–81, 83, 84, 85, 110, 124, 146
First Provincial Council 110
First Amendment 53–5, 227; *see also* free exercise, separation of church and state
Ford, Henry 192, 209
Fordham University 141
Fosdick, Harry Emerson, 177
Fourier, Charles 98
Fox, George 26
Franciscans 18, 20
Frank, Leo 191
Franklin, Benjamin 41
fraternal orders 163, 202
free exercise 55, 119
Free Religious Association 158
free thought 133
freedom, religious 24–5
Freemasonry 163; *see also* fraternal orders
Freud, Sigmund 181
Full Gospel Business Men's Fellowship International 239
Fuller, Charles E. 197
Fundamental Constitutions of Carolina 36–7
fundamentalism 176–79, 240; basic beliefs of 177

Gandhi, Mahatma 211
Garrison, William Lloyd 124–5
gay marriage 243–44
gay rights 237
gays 213; *see also* homosexuality
gender 145–6, 159–64; roles, 88–9
Georgetown University 109
Gere, Richard 221
German Reformed Church 34
ghetto 143
Ghost Dance 165–71; Cherokee, 69–70
Gibbons, James Cardinal 142, 158
Gladden, Washington 148–9
glossolalia 182, 239
Gnostic gospels 8

God, feminine images of 228
Goen, Clarence C. 126
Gospel Broadcasting Association 197
Gospel of Wealth 179
Graham, Billy 210–11
Gray, Asa 174
great migration, 145
Great Awakening 38–40, 78, 80; Second, 79, 81
Great Plains 133
green corn dance 3

Hadaway, C. Kirk 235
Hallelujah Lassies 151
Handsome Lake 69
Hare Krishna 218, 221
Hatch, Nathan 56
Hawthorne, Nathaniel, 98
healing, divine, 102, 103–4, 161, 239
Hebrew Union College 118
Hecker, Isaac 98
Henry VIII 9
Herberg, Will 206–7, 214
heresy 175
Higham, John 192
Himes, Joshua 99
Hinduism 158, 159, 218, 221–2, 236
historical-critical method 173, 175, 176–7
Hitler, Adolf 204, 209
Hodge, Charles 175, 176
holiness 131
Holiness movement 84–85, 167, 169
Holy Spirit Association for the Unification of World Christianity, 218–19
homosexuality 241–4; *see also* gay rights
homosexuals, ordination of 242
Hopedale 97
Hudson, Henry 30
Hughes, John 116–17
Huguenots 11, 20–1, 37
Hurons, 20
Hutchinson, Anne 25–6, 94
Hutchison, William R., 245
Hutterites 133
Hybels, Bill 238
hymns 146

identity, religious 205–6
immigrants, Americanization of 188
immigration 46, 56, 110–13, 138–46, 156;
  Asian 134; German 118; Hispanic 224–5;
  Irish 110–11; Japanese 134; new 220–6;
  restrictions on 190–1
indentured servants 63
Indian removal 69–70
individualism 42, 82, 230
industrialization 137–9
initiation rites 77
Inskip, John 168
inspiration, biblical 175, 178
institutional church 147–8
Integrity 242
International Society for Krishna
  Consciousness 218, 221, 226
invisible institution 66
Iroquois 20, 69
Islam 10, 14–15, 158, 212, 222–3, 236; five
  pillars of 222; see also Nation of Islam

Jackson, Andrew 69
James, William 180
Jamestown, VA 21–2
Japanese Americans 204
Jefferson, Thomas 41, 47, 50, 52–3, 54, 58
Jehovah's Witnesses 100–1
Jenkins, Jerry B. 241
Jesuits 20, 111
Jewish Theological Seminary 143, 144
Jews, 37, 47, 117–20, 143–4, 150; expulsion
  of 13; see also Judaism
John XXIII 208
Johnson, Lyndon 220
Jolliet, Louis, 20
Jones, Charles Colcock 124
Jones, James Warren (Jim) 219
Judaism 10, 13–14, 143–4; Conservative
  143–4; Orthodox 143; Reform 118–19
Judeo-Christian tradition 206

Kallen, Horace M. 182
Kennedy, John F. 209
King, Martin Luther, Jr. 211–12
King of Kings 198
Knights of Columbus 163

Know-Nothing party 116
Ku Klux Klan 191, 193–6
Kuhlman, Kathryn 239

LaHaye, Tim 240
laity, role of 21
Lakewood Church (Houston) 239–40
Lakota Sioux 3, 166
land, tribal sense of 46, 67, 69
language, inclusive 228
Latter-day Saints 93–95; 130–31, 132;
  Church of Jesus Christ of 58
Laymen's Missionary Movement 155
Le Jau, Francis 64
Lee, Ann 57
Lee, Jarena 72
Lee, Robert E. 128
Left Behind 240–1
lesbians 213; *see also* gay rights,
  homosexuality
liberal theology 174
Liberator 125
liminality 77–8
Lincoln, Abraham,127–8, 129
lodges 163; *see also* fraternal orders
Lord's Supper 78
Louisiana,58
Luther, Martin 9
Lutherans 32, 33, 49, 150, 208, 236

McGiveny, Michael J. 163
McGready, James 76, 92
Madison, James 53
Mahan, Asa 81
Maharaj ji, Guru 218
Malcolm X 212
male continence 96
Man Nobody Knows 198
Marler, Penny Long 235
Marquette, Jacques 20
marriage 223; complex 96; plural 93; same
  gender 243–4
Marshall, Daniel 124
Mary Tudor 10, 109
Mary Queen Scots 109
Maryland 35–6
Mason, Charles H. 184

Masons 163; *see also* fraternal orders, Freemasonry
Mathews, Shailer 176
Max Müller, Friedrich 157, 158
Mayhew, Jonathan 40–1, 42, 47
Mead, Sidney 125
medicine men, 5
membership, religious 40, 49–50, 55, 84, 111, 143, 164, 234–5, 236
men, spirituality of 162–4
Men and Religion Forward Movement 164
Mennonites 33, 133
Mesmer, Friedrich (Franz) 102, 103
metaphysical religion 102–6
Methodists 39, 46, 49, 81–3, 84, 125–6, 149, 208, 236
milleniarianism *see* millennialism
Millennial Harbinger 92
millennialism 95, 98–102, 165
Miller, William 99, 126–7
miracles 177
Miranda, Julian 141
missions: Anglo 65–8; French 19–20; global 155–6; Roman Catholic parish 141; Spanish 18–19, 58
modernism 174
modernity 172–86
Monk, Maria 115
Moody, Dwight L. 146, 147, 158, 168
Moody Bible Institute 168, 177, 180, 197
Moon, Sun Myung 218–19
Moonies 218–19
Moral Majority 237–38, 241
Moravians 37, 46–7, 68
Mormons *see* Latter-day Saints
Morse, Samuel F.B. 116
mosque 222
Mother Bethel African Methodist Episcopal Church 71, 72
Mott, John R. 155
Mount St. Mary's College 109
mountain religion 130–3
Muhammad 14
Muhammad, Elijah 212
muscular Christianity 164
music, folk 228
Muslims *see* Islam

myth 2, 93; of origins, 4–5, 6

Nation of Islam 212
National Camp Meeting Association for the Promotion of Holiness 85, 168
National Catholic War Council 193
national churches, Roman Catholic 140
National Conference of Christians and Jews 209
National Council for Community and Justice 210
National Council of Churches 207, 209
National Council of Jewish Women 162
Native American Church, 166
Native Americans 46, 51, 52, 61–62, 65–68, 164–7, 213; tribal religions of 1–5
nativism 113–17; *see also* discrimination, prejudice, racism
Nauvoo, IL 93
neo-charismatics 241
new measures 80, 83
new religious movements: criticism of 219–20; nineteenth century, 98–106, twentieth century 219–20, 236
New Deal 204
New England Tract Society 86
New Netherland 31–2
Newport, RI 117
Niebuhr, Reinhold, 202–4
non-violence, 211
Noyes, John Humphrey 96–97
nuns 20, 56, 113, 140–41, 151

Oberlin College 79, 81
Ocean Grove, NJ 85
Odd Fellows 163; *see also* fraternal orders
Olurun 6
Oneida community 96
orishas, 6
Osteen, Joel 239–40
Osteen, John 239
other, sense of 11
Our Lady of Guadaloupe 224
Ozman, Agnes 182–3

Pacific northwest, as region 133
pacifism 34

Palmer, Phoebe 84–5, 159
Parham, Charles Fox 182–3
parish system 22–3
Parker, Quannah 166
parochial schools 140
Paviotso 165
Peale, Norman Vincent 106
Peirce, Charles Sanders 180
Penitentes 19
Penn, William 32, 35
Pennsylvania, religion in colonial, 32–34
pentecostalism 182–4, 238–9
perfectionism 81, 96
periodicals, Roman Catholic 141
Perry, Troy 213
peyote 166
phalanx, Fourierist 98
Philadelphia Association of Baptists 34
philosophy, Asian 97
pietists, German 33
Pilgrim Holiness Church 85, 169
Pilgrims 24
Pledge of Allegiance, 206
pluralism: contemporary trends in, 244–6; new, 217–31
Plymouth Brethren 168
polytheism 11–12
positive thinking 106
possession, spirit 7
possibility thinking 106
post-millennialism 99
postmodernism 234–6
Prabhupada, A.C. Bhaktivedanta Swami 218
pragmatism 180, 181
praying towns 62
preaching 66
predestination 31, 78, 82
prejudice 36, 109, 113–17, 163, 190–6; see also anti-Catholicism, anti-Semitism, nativism, racism
premillennialism 99, 168–9, 173, 176, 177, 180
Presbyterians 37, 81, 83, 126, 155, 175–6, 208, 236
Prince Hall Masons, 163; *see also* fraternal orders
Princeton theology 175, 176

Progressivism 149
Prohibition 161, 188–90, 193, 195–6
Protestant Council of the City of New York 210
Protestantism, decline in 234–5
Protocols of the Elders of Zion 192, 194, 209
psychology 180–1
pueblos, 18
Puritans 10, 24–5, 32, 36

Quakers 10, 26–7, 32–4, 56, 57, 87
Quimby, Phineas T. 102–4
Quo Vadis 197

racism 129–30, 183–4, 193–6, 211–13; see also nativism, prejudice
radio 196; *see also* communications media
Ramakrishna 158
rapture 168, 240
rationalism 40–1, 52, 78
Rauschenbusch, Walter 148–9
Red scar, 101
Reformation, Protestant 9; left wing of 34
regionalism 130–5
restorationism 58, 91–5
reunion, denominational 129
revitalization movement 68–70, 85, 164–7, 214
revivalism 38–40, 79–81; Roman Catholic 141; urban 146–7, 176
Revolutionary War 48–52
Rhode Island 25
ring shout 63
Ripley, George 97–8
rites of passage 4, 7, 63–4, 77
rituals 4, 7, 12, 63
Riverside Church 177
Roberts, Oral, 239
Robertson, Marion G. (Pat) 238
Rochester, NY 79
Rockefeller, John D. 177
Roe v. Wade 227–8
Roman Catholics 8, 17–21, 34, 35–6, 47, 49, 56, 58, 98, 108–17, 139–42, 150, 224, 228, 239, 242; charismatic 239
Roosevelt, Franklin 204
Russell, Charles Taze 100–1
Russian Orthodox Church 134

Rutherford, Joseph 101
Ryan, John A. 149
sacrifice, 7
St. George's Methodist Episcopal Church 71
Salem witch trials, 27–8
salvation, preparation for 26
Salvation Army 147, 148, 150, 151, 193
Sankey, Ira D. 146
Santería, 225
Scandinavians 32
Schechter, Solomon 143
Schuller, Robert H. 106
science 174
Science and Health with Key to the Scriptures 105
scientific modernism 176, 181
Scofield, Cyrus I. 169
Scofield Reference Bible 169, 180
Scopes, John 178
Scopes trial 178–9
Scotland 39
Scots-Irish 34, 46, 111
Scottish Common Sense Realism 176
second blessing 84
Second Coming of Christ 99, 240; *see also* millennialism, post-millennialism, premillennialism, rapture
Second Vatican Council *see* Vatican II
seeker movement 238
self-help 106
Seneca 69
Seneca Falls, NY 160
separation of church and state 213; *see also* First Amendment, free exercise
Sephardic Jews 117, 118
September 11 223
serpent handling 131–2
Serra, Junípero 18
Seton, Elizabeth Ann 113
settlement houses 148, 151
Seven Years' War 36, 39, 45–6
Seventh-Day Adventists 99–100, 227
sex scandals, Roman Catholic 242–3
Seymour, William J. 183
Shakers 57
shamans 5, 73, 165
Silver Bluff Baptist Church 71

Simmons, William Joseph 194
Sisters of the Blessed Sacrament 113
Sixties 229
slave religion 66
slavery 32, 52, 63–5, 87–8, 123–7
Smith, Al 193
Smith, Chuck (Charles W.) 239
Smith, Joseph 93
Smohalla 165
social creeds 149
Social Darwinism 179, 182
social gospel 148–9, 174, 202–3
social reform 86–9, 148–9, 188–90, 241–4
socialism 203
Society for the Promotion of Christian Knowledge 67–8
Society for the Propagation of the Gospel 62
Society of the Sacred Heart 113
Southern Baptist Convention 126, 236, 239, 242
Southern Christian Leadership Conference 211
southwest, as region 133
space, sense of 125
speaking in tongues 182, 239
Spencer, Herbert, 179
spirituality: privatized 230; trends in 228–30
spirituals 70, 71
Stanton, Elizabeth Cady 160
state church *see* establishment, religious
Stearns, Shubal 124
Stone, Barton W. 92
Stone-Campbell movement 92–3
Stone Mountain, GA 194
Strong, Josiah 138, 142
Student Volunteer Movement 155
suffrage, woman 161
Sulpicians 20, 109
Sumner, William Graham 179
Sunday, Billy 146–7, 176, 189
Sunday schools 167, 168; Jewish 119
supernatural, sense of 4, 7, 28, 131
Supreme Court 211, 213
sweat lodge 4, 5
Swedenborg, Emmanuel 102, 103

Tavibo 165
temperance 147, 160–1; *see also* Prohibition
Temple University 180

temples, Asian religious 221
Theosophical Society 159
third force (in Christianity) 238–9
time, sense of 125
toleration 53
Tomlinson, Ambrose Jessup 184
Torrey, Reuben A. 177
Trail of tears 69
Transcendental Meditation 218–9
Transcendentalism 97–8, 114
transubstantiation 109
tribal cultures 62; Native American 2–5; African 6–8
tribal religions, misunderstanding of 11–3
Trine, Ralph Waldo 105
true woman 159
Truman, Harry 210
Tsali 69
Tucker, Frederick Booth 151
Turner, Nat 125

Union Theological Seminary 175–6, 293
Unitarian Universalist Association 208
Unitarians 42, 47, 114, 158
United Church of Christ 208, 236, 242
United Methodist Church 236; *see also* Methodists
United States Catholic Miscellany 114
Unity School of Christianity 105
Universal Fellowship of Metropolitan Community Churches 213, 242
Universalists 42, 114, 158; *see also* Unitarian Universalist Association
University of Chicago 176
University of Scranton 141
urbanization 137–9, 155
Ursulines 20, 115, 116
Utah 94
utopianism 95–8

Van Dusen, Henry Pitney 238
van Gennep, Arnold 77–8
Vatican II 208–9, 213
Vedanta Society 159
Vietnam War 213
Vincent, John 168
Vineyard Christian Fellowship 239

Virginia 21–3, 52–3
Virginia Act for Establishing Religious Freedom 53
Vivekananda, Swami 158, 159
voluntary societies 86–7, 124

Wallace, Lew 198
Wanapum 165
Warfield, Benjamin Breckinridge 175, 176, 178
Washington, Booker T. 130
Washington, George 41, 47, 49
Watch Tower Bible and Tract Society 100–1
Weld, Theodore Dwight 124
Wesley, Charles 39
Wesley, John 39, 40, 84
Wesleyan Church 85
Wesleyan Methodist Church 85
White, Ellen Gould Harmon 99–100
White, James S. 99
Whitefield, George 38–39, 78
Wilcox, Melissa M. 242
Willard, Frances 160–1, 188, 189
Williams, Roger 25, 27, 47, 94
Willow Creek: Association 238; Community Church 238
Wilson, Jack 165, 166
Wimber, John 239
Wise, Isaac Mayer 118–19
witchcraft 27
Wodziwub 165
Woman's Bible 160
women 27–28, 50, 52, 56, 84–5, 88–9, 145–6, 148, 151, 159–64, 212–13, 228, 230; African American 72–3; in Christian Science, 105; Jewish 119, 162; as missionaries 156; Native American 5; ordination of 161, 212; Roman Catholic 112; in Salvation Army, 151
women religious *see* nuns
Women's Christian Temperance Union 161, 188, 189
Woodworth-Etter, Maria 161, 162
World War II 201–2
World Council of Churches 207
World Trade Center 223
World's Parliament of Religions 134, 157–8, 162

worship 228–30
Wovoka 165, 166
Yale College 79
Yiddish 143
Yogi, Maharishi Mahesh 218–19
Yoruba 6
Young, Brigham 94, 95, 132

Young Men's Christian Association (YMCA) 146, 155
Young Women's Christian Association (YWCA) 155

Zionism 191, 209–10
Zwingli, Huldreich, 9

eBooks – at www.eBookstore.tandf.co.uk

A library at your fingertips!

eBooks are electronic versions of printed books. You can store them on your PC/laptop or browse them online.

They have advantages for anyone needing rapid access to a wide variety of published, copyright information.

eBooks can help your research by enabling you to bookmark chapters, annotate text and use instant searches to find specific words or phrases. Several eBook files would fit on even a small laptop or PDA.

NEW: Save money by eSubscribing: cheap, online access to any eBook for as long as you need it.

Annual subscription packages

We now offer special low-cost bulk subscriptions to packages of eBooks in certain subject areas. These are available to libraries or to individuals.

For more information please contact webmaster.ebooks@tandf.co.uk

We're continually developing the eBook concept, so keep up to date by visiting the website.

www.eBookstore.tandf.co.uk